Creating Fear

SOCIAL PROBLEMS AND SOCIAL ISSUES

An Aldine de Gruyter Series of Texts and Monographs

SERIES EDITOR

Joel Best, *University of Delaware*

Creating Fear
News and the Construction of Crisis

DAVID L. ALTHEIDE

ALDINE DE GRUYTER

New York

ABOUT THE AUTHOR

David L. Altheide is Regents' Professor in the School of Justice Studies at Arizona State University. A former president for the Society for the Study of Symbolic Interaction, he has focused much of his work on the role of mass media and information technology for social control. Among his previously published books are two from Aldine de Gruyter: *Media Worlds in the Postjournalism Era* (with Robert P. Snow, 1991), and *An Ecology of Communication* (1995).

ALDINE DE GRUYTER
A division of Walter de Gruyter, Inc.
200 Saw Mill River Road
Hawthorne, New York 10532

This publication is printed on acid free paper ∞

Library of Congress Cataloging-in-Publication Data

Altheide David L.
    Creating fear : news and the construction of crisis / David L. Altheide.
        p. cm – (Social problems and social issues)
    Includes bibliographical references and index.
    ISBN 0-202-30659-3 (cloth : alk. paper) – ISBN 0-202-30660-7 (pbk. : alk. paper)
    1. Mass media and public opinion – United States.   2. Fear – United States.
3. Mass media – Psychological aspects.   4. Public opinion – United States.   I. Title.
II. Series.

P96.P832 U62 2001
302.23'0973—dc21   2001045919

Manufactured in the United States of America

10 9 8 7 6 5 4 3 2 1

For Carla and our fearless children, Tasha and Tod

Contents

Preface

This book is about fear and its expanding place in our public life. I document the increase in the word *fear* and the rise of a "discourse of fear" in the mid 1990s: the pervasive communications, symbolic awareness, and expectation that danger and risk are all around us. I offer an explanation of how this occurred and suggest some social consequences that it has had.

Fear is a scary thing. This book has helped me understand it better, but it has not been easy. I "formally" began studying fear in the news media and popular culture about ten years ago, but I have experienced fear in other ways. I have seen firsthand what a massive dose of news media reports about crime and fear can do to people. My extraordinary ninety-year-old mother-in-law often speaks of being afraid and notes how many of her friends at the "senior center" discuss recent news reports about crime and mayhem, whether those reports originate in Tempe, Arizona, where she lives, or in New York City, or in Japan. This is ironic since this woman is one of the most courageous people I know and has dealt with many aspects of life and death that would "frighten" most people. By any accounts, she is a "rock of stability" and throughout her life has not been afraid of anything. Yet, she speaks as though the world has gone out of control. Likewise, my eighty-six-year-old father will often describe, in the same letter, how much better his life is, but then conclude with the observation that the world is "getting worse and worse." This, too, seems ironic given the courageous life that he has lived. While much of the preoccupation by these elderly people can be blamed on "being older," I think that more is involved. I suspect that one thing that contributes to a feeling of vulnerability by many elderly people is that their more limited mobility and opportunities to participate directly in social life leads them to rely more on the "indirect participation" through the mass media and especially news reports, both print and electronic. And the overwhelming message of these reports is fear.

This book was in the final stages of production when deadly attacks on New York and Washington, D.C. occurred on September 11, 2001. While no analysis of the massive news coverage is offered in this work, readers familiar with the news media coverage of these horrific events can find many parallels with key points that I make in the following chapters. The entertainment format, use of visuals, emerging icons of fear, slogans, and especially the emphasis on the fear frame and "evil" provide many examples of how these attacks contributed to the expansion of the discourse of fear into more attempts at social control.

I have been working on this book for more than a decade, but the overall project defines my academic life. This project concerns the nature and use of social power and social control. There is a simple thesis that joins this work with my previous modest efforts: The mass media play a significant role in shaping social definitions that govern social action. Relatedly, my methodological and theoretical foundation in classical social theory, existential-phenomenology, ethnomethodology, and symbolic interactionism leads me to view social power as the capacity to define situations for self and others. Most of my academic life has been focused on sorting out the ways that the mass media and popular culture help define social situations. Therefore, it is important to understand the nature, process, and organization of mass media operations, including news procedures, perspectives, and formats. It is also important to recognize the need to expand our methodological frameworks so that we can use new information technologies and information bases to "ask different questions" than we have in the past.

Different versions of several of the pieces of this book have appeared elsewhere.

Chapter 3, *The Sociological Quarterly,* 1997 (38): Courtesy of JAI Press.
Chapter 4, *The Sociological Quarterly,* 1999 (40): Courtesy of University of California Press.
Chapter 6, from Jaber F. Gubrium and James A. Holstein, eds., *Handbook of Interviewing.* Thousand Oaks, Calif.: Sage Publications. Forthcoming.

This project has been aided by many others, particularly my colleague (happily retired!) Robert P. Snow, who shared the effort to identify the nature and consequences of media logic and communications formats for constructing social definitions, social identities, and social order. Our work over two decades has stressed that it is the "form" of mass media and entertainment logic and formats that is the most significant for social life and not the "content," per se. We have attempted to elaborate this conceptual process and to demonstrate its use across social institutions.

Many other people have contributed to this project over the years, including John Johnson, the late Carl Couch, Richard V. Ericson and his students, and many others. I am particularly indebted to the creative work by graduate students who have taken our modest efforts and extended them to additional analyses and topics. I have been very fortunate to work with R. Sam Michalowski, who contributed materials and ideas (particularly in Chapter 4), as well as Barbara Sharp, Enrico Tufano, and Kristi Wimmer for their work with

"Tracking Discourse" on some very challenging projects from which I draw in Chapter 6. Students in several graduate seminars helped explore further the connection between fear and victims: Barbara Gray, Roy Janisch, Lindsey Korbin, Ray Maratea, Debra Neill, Joseph Reaves, and Felicia Van Deman. Their insights were helpful in recognizing how pernicious the "victim" status has become, how it is used by social control agencies, and how important it is for creative thinkers to move beyond "victimization" toward more creative and supportive frameworks for recognizing consequences of social power and providing meaningful ameliorative options. The editor of this series, Joel Best, has been very supportive and I appreciate his intellectual leadership in gaining a better understanding of the interplay of culture, media, and social control. Finally, I can't complete any project without thanking Carla for loving me and believing in my work. I am most fortunate.

1

Give the Devil His Due:
Fear in Its Place

Americans do not know fear.
—Pakistani journalist

Most Americans would not agree with the Pakistani journalist. Many Americans would identify with "Judy," a resident of upscale—low crime rate—Scottsdale, Arizona. An *Arizona Republic* article, March 17, 1996, reported:

> Tucked inside [Judy's] Gucci bag is a tiny .38-caliber revolver. It eases her mind. "Things are crazy out there," the Scottsdale woman says. "I just want to have options."
> Judy is one of the latest Arizonans to get a permit to carry a concealed weapon. And she is fairly typical: Affluent, white, suburban.
> Since the law went into effect in July 1994, more than 35,000 Arizonans have obtained concealed-weapons permits. . . . A computer analysis of permit holders . . . reveals that the highest rates are not in the parts of the Valley where the need for self-preservation appears greatest: neighborhoods filled with crack houses, gangs and violence.
> The highest rates are in such upscale low-crime neighborhoods as Sun City West, north Phoenix, Scottsdale, Ahwatukee and Mesa. (A1)

This book is about fear and its role in contemporary society. It is also a personal story about my modest attempts to understand how the mass media and popular culture are shaping our social world. My thesis it that the mass media and popular culture entertainment formats have contributed to changing social expectations and everyday life routines by promoting entertainment and fear. Journalists, social scientists, and others have made numerous observations that Americans seem to fear the "wrong things"(e.g., Furedi 1997; Glassner 1999; Margolis 1996), including crime (Garland 2000). While I draw on keen insights offered by others about fear in social life, my focus is on how fear has become part of a public discourse and a perspective for viewing social experience.

As noted throughout this work, the discourse of fear refers to the pervasive communication, symbolic awareness, and expectation that danger and risk are central features of the effective environment or the physical and symbolic environment as people define and experience it in everyday life (Pfuhl and Henry 1993). This conception is offered as a palliative to a conceptual vacuum linking mass media reports and popular culture emphases with audience perceptions. Others have noted the role of specific fears in public perceptions about crime and drugs (Ferraro 1995; Warr 1990). But what the news media contribute to public perceptions has been less clearly examined, particularly why certain fears persist. Drawing on a range of work by others, Barry Glassner's (1999) *The Culture of Fear: Why Americans Are Afraid of the Wrong Things* chronicles Americans' perceptions about risks regarding crime, child abductions, aircraft crashes, school violence, and other dangers widely reported by the news media. While the work reminds us how much fear is part of popular culture, the author essentially restates the conclusion of a classic study (Cantril et al. 1940) that Americans' fears reflect pervasive and often unfocused anxieties about their environment in a particular historical period. And while the mass media are given their due for contributing to the particular worries, the media are also given some credit for occasionally offering "perspective" pieces on why such fears may be foolish compared to, say, the risks from routine activities such as automobile crashes.

Frank Furedi's (1997) work offers a stronger assertion about the context of fear, particularly that the perceived lack of control over our lives has led to a preoccupation with safety and risk. The absence of "subjectivity," he argues, against mounting pressures that promote individuation, experts, objective conditions, risks, and so forth make us more vulnerable. His comments and citations about the connections between anxiety about everyday life and the efforts to control children resonate with some of the materials in my research:

> We have created a world for our children in which safety is promoted through fear. The message of campaigns such as "One false move and you're dead" is one of deference to the source of the danger. That such a world can be advertised without apparent embarrassment by those responsible for the safety of children, and without provoking public outrage, is a measure of how far the unacceptable has become accepted. (Hillman, Adams, and Whiteleg 1990, 111)

Still, Furedi (1997) doubts that the mass media play a significant role in fear and perceptions of risk. He argues:

> However, it is important to remember that the media amplify or attenuate but do not cause society's sense of risk. There exists a disposition towards the expectation of adverse outcomes, which is then engaged by the mass media. The result of this engagement is media which are continually warning of some danger. But the media's preoccupation with risk is a symptom of the problem and

not its cause. It is unlikely that an otherwise placid and content public is influenced into a permanent state of panic through media manipulation. (52)

Notwithstanding the heuristic claims by others that pervasive worrisome cultural undercurrents may contribute to fears, such speculation does not benefit from a rich body of literature about the role of the mass media and popular culture in setting agendas, defining situations for audiences. Nor does it speak to power and the question of who benefits from such fear. The emphasis of the discourse of fear is on the pervasive presentation of cultural meanings involving fear and dread in public discourse. Symbols occupy public spaces that, with the aid of expanding research capacities and innovative designs, can be identified and queried in order to comparatively examine cogent relationships over time. I suggest that there is a clear media presence and impact on cultural symbol systems from which societal members draw to make sense of routine and extraordinary events. Such perspectives or discourses are shaped over time, and these guide—but do not determine—perceptions and interpretations to provide meaningful assessments of both specific and general conditions.

Fear becomes a matter of discourse when it "expands" beyond a specific referent to use as a more general orientation (Ericson, Baranek, and Chan 1989; van Dijk 1988). As suggested in previous work (Altheide and Michalowski 1999), entertainment formats contribute to the emphasis on "fear" rather than, say, "danger," which is more specific and more easily incorporated into an everyday life perspective. When fear is repeatedly used with children and the spaces they occupy, for example, in schools, a meaningful association emerges. Over time, with repeated usage, nuances blend, connotations become denotations, fringes mix with kernels, and we have a different perspective on the world. This is why the distinctions between meaningful borders between children, school, and community are so important. I trace the development of a discourse of fear surrounding children over time in order to demonstrate how fear has come to be associated with certain topics and issues as part of a problem frame.

My basic argument is that fear has become a dominant public perspective. Fear begins with things we fear, but over time, with enough repetition and expanded use, it becomes a way of looking at life. Therefore, it is not "fear of crime," for instance, that is so interesting to me, but rather how fear has emerged as a framework for developing identities and for engaging in social life. Fear is one of the few perspectives that citizens share today; while liberals and conservatives may differ in their object of fear, all sides express many fears and point to "blameworthy" sources—often each other! The fear "market" has also spawned an extensive cottage industry that promotes new fears and an expanding array of "victims." An army of social scientists and other intellectuals—or "issue fans"—serve as claims makers, marketing their target issues and agendas in various forms and forums, such as self-help books, courses, research funds, and expertise (Best 1999, 2001). Much of the success of "problems" is related to expanding mass media outlets (e.g., cable, the Internet, small-circulation specialty newspapers).

> This transformation has changed the nature of social problems construction. It is increasingly possible to promote issues of concern to a particular segment of the population through the arenas offered by that segment's media . . . [and] fragmented media aimed at homogeneous audiences attract a less critical reception for prospective social problems claims. To the degree that a homogeneous audience shares moral assumptions, it is easier to devise rhetoric that portrays social problems in terms convincing to that audience. (Best 2001, 6)

The book focuses, then, on how fear as a perspective has developed in public discourse and how it has expanded throughout social life. I know something about fear. The devil is the first thing I feared. It is easy for me to say that now—having spent most of my life rejecting the religion that gave me that fear—but it wasn't as a child. I remember looking out our car window as we passed taverns and movie theaters and trying to see inside their doors. I was looking for flames, fire so hot it would melt sin as surely as it would destroy the buildings. These were the "devil's houses," I believed, and all who went there were playing with fire. I just expected to see the flames. I still think about fire and flames and sin and the devil. But I no longer fear them; at least, I try not to admit that I do!

I did not just learn about this fear; I lived it. It was part of my life growing up in a fundamentalist household, where my loving parents, steeped in versions of old-fashioned Pentecostal faith, tried to arrange their lives in order to keep us together, keep us safe, and give us a future in spite of having very little money. I heard countless stories about the devil and the power of evil, how one wrong move could damn me forever. Many stories were told about unfortunate sinners who had gambled with Satan and lost. There were Bible stories, and old ladies in our church told "real life" stories about poor lost souls. Indeed, one of my brothers, who tended to be rebellious as a youth, resisted the urging of a small-town evangelist to repent and be saved. A few moments later, the controlling minister told my mother that my brother was bound for hell, at which point my other brother and I joined our mother in desperate prayer to save his soul.

I would not encounter another such self-righteous and cruel person until I learned about a local Phoenix sheriff, Joe Arpaio, who publicly degraded and humiliated county jail inmates by placing them in tents in the 110-degree Phoenix heat. He continued in office despite sophisticated evaluation studies that showed his tactics were ineffective in reducing recidivism. Nothing could touch him politically, not even when his deputies killed an inmate—an accident resulting from a "procedure" that cost me and my fellow citizens millions of dollars in legal fees and damage awards. To the contrary, he continued to be more popular than ever. What in the world was going on? Why would rational adults sanction such conduct? A female student majoring in justice studies admitted that she liked "Sheriff Joe" because he is "trying to get people to straighten up." She went on to describe how her uncle, who used drugs, never seemed to be punished as harshly as he should have been. Over the years, I have had many people tell me they supported Sheriff Joe, who is well known for his flippant "hard line" replies to national media outlets and for his Web page "Jailcam," where you can see live shots of his lockup. They tell me that they "agree with him" and that "we've got to do something." Sheriff Joe represents something to audiences who accept the basic message that something is wrong and needs to be fixed.

What do these people have in common: the minister, a man of God—scaring a young boy and his mother—and a sheriff, representing "the law" and flaunting power with such bravado that he becomes a folk hero and, of course, a TV personality? My answer is fear, or, more precisely, mass-mediated fear.

When I was younger, I knew the "fear of God." I owe a lot to my parents for the life they gave me, because, even though they had very little, they gave me everything they had. Their faith was part of it, but the control was another part. This involved fear of retribution, Satan, and the awful vengeance of a just God, who knew all and always got the last word. The last act. Justice. And this meant pain. It also meant that I was cautious and worried about doing things and thinking thoughts, and then more worried about possibly thinking the wrong things. It was the ultimate control. It was emotional, before reason, before reflection, and it was fundamental. So I understand fear as it is lived and experienced.

But I want to understand how fear is developed and passed along to others. How are we to explain why so many people, who, by most measures, are quite safe and secure, have fear? How is it that "everyone knows" about fear, and how does this come about? Margolis (1996), who has investigated disagreements between experts and "laypeople" over environmental issues, states:

> Somehow—exactly how lies at the frontier of work in social psychology, sociology, and political science—it comes about that certain ideas take hold as things "everyone knows." Or more exactly, "everyone" in the reference group for a particular individual. Defining what becomes a person's reference group (which can even vary for the same person contingent on the issue) is itself a challenge. But roughly, it is how "people like me" see things. By and large, however, what "everyone knows" sometimes is what it would be advantageous for that individual to believe. And yet some of the things we come to know are open to grave doubt (even some of the things that are nevertheless advantageous to the individual to believe). So what "everyone knows" sometimes eventually comes to be what "everyone knows" is wrong. But that social knowledge nevertheless accounts for a large fraction of what we (think we) know, is clear. (121)

I argue that the mass media and popular culture are the most important contributors to fear. The pervasive use of fear in public documents and discourse has helped create a perspective or frame for viewing the world in an entertaining way that is shared by many members of our society. We live in a secular society, so the mass media do not include many references to the "fear of God"; they do refer a lot to "fear of crime."

Another major contributor to the discourse of fear is that we simply live longer today, so we spend more time worrying about being threatened and dying. Longevity in the fourteenth century was about thirty years; in the early twentieth century people lived until about forty years of age; while in the year 2000, average lifespan was around seventy-five years, extending to eighty years in Japan. There is a major paradox of our time: The same citizens—older and more affluent—who are living longer, with more secure and comfortable lifestyles than at any other time in history, are also the ones who express the most fear and uncertainty about life. Indeed, sociologists note that contemporary life is so predictable and routine, so "boring," that many people take risks in "adventures" (e.g., skydiving, white-water rafting, mountain climbing). This paradox is a key source of social upheaval in many countries today, and it is driving political agendas that promote cruelty and even inhumane treatment of citizens, especially youth (Chapter 7) in the name of security and safety. So, in Arizona, we have Sheriff Joe, but most large counties in the United States have another version of him: mass media.

What I learned as a child was important for me in so many ways, but it did not directly affect many other people. It was "our life"—my family's—and a view of the world, heaven, and hell subscribed to by others who shared our faith. It was sacred, parochial, and not secular; it was more private and not public. Others, who were not rooted firmly in our faith, did not know much about it, and it surely did not stop them from "sinning" or visiting the taverns and the movie theaters we expected to see engulfed in flames. My fear as a small boy, then, did not involve rejection, abuse, hunger, or abandonment. I was lucky. But I knew fear, and now I want to understand how a society can "fear" and what difference this can make.

We fear what we learn through countless stories and "morality tales" told by parents, relatives, friends, and, increasingly, the mass media. These stories or narratives provide the foundation for what we like, dislike, embrace, avoid, fear, and take for granted. These narratives provide our "knowledge." My research indicates that more of these stories involve fear. Fear appeared in more headlines and news reports in the mid-1990s than the 1980s. The same is true of a related term, *victim,* which is discussed in a later chapter. I refer to this expanded use of fear as a "fear thematic," that when used in numerous stories and everyday conversation becomes a discourse of fear or the pervasive communication, symbolic awareness, and expectation that danger and risk are central features of everyday life. In short, as a child I learned my identity in terms of how "people like us" saw the world. I learned through stories, or narratives. These days, for the majority of people, the mass media shape identities and narratives.

THE MASS MEDIA AND IDENTITY

Fear as a perspective is expanding in social life as it plays a larger role in our public discourse and language. Shared social identities that incorporate fear as part of a view of everyday life are emerging (Altheide 2000). Social change involves communication technology, processes, uses, and styles. Both classicists and symbolic interactionists suggest that ultimately new habits and routines appear (Berger and Luckmann 1967; Cooley 1922; Mead and Morris 1962; Schutz 1967).

Three things happen when identities and products are marketed interchangeably and synergistically: (1) We experience them in the same time, place, and manner; (2) the product and process are reflexive—the product is the identity—and identity appears explicitly and implicitly in numerous advertisements; (3) media images "loop" (Manning 1998) through various media types and messages, moving, from initial claim to established fact, to background information. Product labels as key membership categories are a triumph for popular culture and mass mediation. Even merchandise promotes label identity as personal identity and membership. For example, the labels of Nike and Guess become important symbols independently of the product (e.g., shoes or shirts). To display the label is to be identified as a certain kind of person. And the freedom to purchase and "become" a member—and participant—reflects the actor's individual freedom and decision-making power. Social interaction with peers begins to reflect and turn on such familiarity with products.

Popular culture and communication formats contribute to the changing face of identity. First, there is the massive involvement of audiences with media and the gamut of popular culture in the United States and many Western countries. Whether measured in terms of hours of television viewed, movie attendance, music and compact disc purchases, or the popularity of clothing brands, the popular culture experience, while far from uniform in our pluralistic society, is enormous (Comstock 1980). Second, popular culture affords individuals a plethora of styles, personas, and potential role models. Third, popular culture audiences are also participants, albeit in varying degrees. Fourth, the physical and symbolic environment reflects media culture as theme parks, theme cities, shopping malls, and even wars adopt media forms. Fifth, the criteria and frameworks for authenticity, credibility, competence, and acceptability can be widely shared and, indeed, taken for granted as audiences interact in this media context. Fear is part of these processes.

The mass media and popular culture contribute to the definition of situations in social life. This process informs the generalized other for some actors, as well as demonstrates that the media perspectives inform certain situations and subsequent definitions. We can describe the process even if the precise moment of individual impact cannot be established for millions of people. The experiential foundations of the identity process have always included communication opportunities, styles, and competence. Numerous works now document how pervasive information technology alters "social space" by providing access to a myriad of content rich in potential meaning, as well as communication formats for the selection, organization, and presentation of information (Altheide 1985; Beniger 1986; Cerulo et al. 1992; Meyrowitz 1985). Social stability and change are recognized, explained, and resisted through symbolic communication. Blumer's (Blumer 1962, 184) statement locates this position within the work of Mead:

> Fundamentally, group action takes the form of a fitting together of individual lines of action. Each individual aligns his action to the actions of others by ascertaining what they are doing or what they intend to do—that is, by getting the meaning of their acts. For Mead, this is done by the individual taking the role of others—either the role of a specific person or the role of a group (Mead's "generalized other"). In taking such roles the individual seeks to ascertain the intention or direction of the acts of others. He forms and aligns his own action on the basis of such interpretations of the acts of others. This is the fundamental way in which group action takes place in human society.

Much of our theory asserts that we exist as social beings in the midst of process. We don't "have" or own an "identity," but rather, identity emerges and is acknowledged in situations; we live in the identity process.

> Almost all writers using the term imply that identity establishes what and where the person is in social terms. It is not a substitute word for "self." Instead, when one has identity, he is situated—that is, cast in the shape of a social object by the acknowledgement of his participation or membership in social relations. One's identity is established when others place him as a social object by assigning the same words of identity that he appropriates for himself or announces. It is in the coincidence of placements and announcements that identity becomes a meaning of the self. (Stone 1992, 93)

I concur with Scott and Lyman (1968) that "media communities" are part of speech communities that emerge, which define appropriate identities, roles, language, and styles for their members (Scott 1968). They are reflexive of previous role performances, yet directive of future identity affirmations. When age-graded audiences pass cultural rites of passage, the media community persists albeit in recycled forms, which in turn direct future preferences and performances that look, sound, and feel right. Like the Eagles fabled song "Hotel California," one can check out of one community, but never leave.

The significant contribution of fear in the context of these mass-mediated communities is that it provides both an identity and definition of the situation. Waller (1961) puts it this way:

> Many persons living together in a common group life for many overlapping generations have mapped out clearly the limitations of behavior inherent in the social situations most common in their culture. From their experience has arisen a consensus concerning what is and what is not thinkable in those situations. From these situations as they have been defined have been generalized certain group products which have in turn become important conditions of life in that group. We may refer to these group products as definitions of situations. (162)

The entertainment format contributes to social definitions and provides a common ground that the advertising industry essentially owns and operates. As suggested by Snow's (1983) analysis of "media culture," the entertainment format emphasizes, first, an absence of the ordinary; second, the openness of an adventure outside the boundaries of routine behavior; and third, a suspension of disbelief by the audience member. In addition, while the exact outcome may be in doubt, there is a clear and unambiguous point at which it will be resolved. Packaging such emphases within dramatic formats (visual, brief, and action-oriented) produces an exciting and familiar tempo for audiences. Moreover, as audiences are exposed more to these formats, the logic of advertising, entertainment, and popular culture becomes taken for granted as a "normal" form of communication.

News and popular culture are laced with fear. Both play significant roles in shaping audience members' expectations and their criteria for self-presentation. Evocative rather than referential forms of communication now dominate the meaning landscape (Couch 1995). The referential forms fall before the electrified rolling formats that change everyday life with the look and swagger of persona, entertainment, and action.

When both actor and audience have at least one foot in popular culture, they hold shared meanings for validating the actor's performance. The key conceptual tie for identity and the definition of the situation are the generalized other, but the media provide numerous others. Actors still want to present a self, but the time, place, and manner in which they do it has been fundamentally altered by new awareness contexts stressing more evocative and "present" orientations rather than consequential and future ones.

Identity is contextualized and produced in a symbolic environment shared by other actors. The rise of popular culture, and particularly of mediated communicated formats that infuse everyday life, including architecture, entertainment, prayer, play, and work, adds a dimension to the effective environment—

the physical and symbolic environment we experience and share on an everyday basis (Grodin and Lindlof 1996). This dimension exists more temporally than spatially; it resides in increasingly portable, fast, and, above all, chic, valued, stylish mediated interaction (Meyrowitz 1985). Identity as a feature of mass media and popular culture increasingly is presented as a product and resource to be used and marketed as a noun and an adjective, such as "identity politics." Advertising pushes products, not processes; identity has been gradually transformed from being an esoteric social science *process* to a mass-mediated and readily available *product* (Zurcher 1977).

The mass media promote identity to satisfy individually oriented needs and interests to "be whomever you want." Popular culture's emphasis on entertainment and commodification of the self provides an important linkage to fear-related identity "talk." Grossberg, Wartella, and Whitney (1998) agree with numerous researchers who have documented the impact of media logic on everyday life: "Ultimately the media's ability to produce people's social identities, in terms of both a sense of unity and difference, may be their most powerful and important effect"(206).

A key element in the expanding use of fear for viewing social life is a perspective that connects the present with the future. In the temporal order of popular culture, the present can be projected into future belonging and acceptance via the market, and especially cultural styles. Popular culture is lived through participation. One symbolic way of participating is to agree about "fear" and to explicitly and implicitly "share" and "behave" in accordance with fear guidelines. Identity is an accomplishment of interaction with the broader market/context, rather than merely with one's peers, which is likely to promote the diverse range of popular culture trends and guidelines to capture the largest possible market. The impetus for change and identity formation rests on acting, presentation of self, and conduct consistent with products widely shared by fellow consumers, comprising the legitimating audience for one's performance. This may involve purchase and use of "cell phones" for convenience and "safety," as well as obtaining car alarms and other auto-theft protection devices, such as The Club.

Fear promotes shared markets and identities for these products. With the merchandising of products there emerges the skillfully crass connection of marketing identities-as-products, but also identities-for-products. Self-promotion through proclamation and purchase has been around for a long time. Participating in social life and seeing "people like us" in commercials creates a vicarious sense of community—and great commercials!

> Implicit in the very notion of the audience as consumers operating in a market is the need to continually make people think of themselves as consumers . . . to help construct a consumer society by encouraging people to locate their identity in their leisure tastes and consumer practices rather than in other roles such as jobs and churches. The ideological message is that what we buy says more

about who we are than other facts, including where we get the money. Media programs and advertising are all about this redefinition of self-identity. (Grossberg et al. 1998, 212)

NARRATIVES OF IDENTITY AND CRISIS

Social narratives reflect social order and communication processes (Burke 1966; Carey 1989; Crane 1992; Ericson et al. 1991). Prior to the mass media's routine acceptance in everyday life, narratives reflected other cultural experiences and meanings. Although they may not have been "accurate" or "objectively true," they were a pretty good indication of the experiences and perspectives of the people telling the stories. Things are different today. Now narratives reflect mass media accounts. Stories told to us by friends and relatives often originate from the mass media, news reports, "60 Minutes," Sally Jesse Raphael, Oprah, and Jerry Springer. The "teller" knows that audiences find certain narratives to be interesting, so they are adapted, both in terms of content (e.g., crime and fear) and in terms of entertainment value or format (which is discussed more in Chapter 3). Many of these narratives about crime and fear are believable because they "sound and look right," but they are really false, simply incorrect, often created and distorted by news sources (e.g., police departments, the Pentagon, and numerous "reform" and "social movement" groups).

Cerulo's (1998) investigation of how narratives are sequenced illustrates the implications of the discourse of fear. In her study of how the structure of news reports can convey whether a violent act was deviant or normal, Cerulo provides an important methodological foray into the structure of communication formats: "In processing information, the organization or structure of a message is equal in importance to its content" (Cerulo 1998, 22) Her work demonstrates that the sequence of narrative action matters for audience perceptions and whether we condemn, condone, or simply bemoan violent acts (e.g., whether the emphasis is on the victim—the most common "criminal" accounts; on the performer—a police officer shooting someone; or whether the crime is more contextual or double-casting—as in physician-assisted suicide). She found, for example, that most news scripts of violence and crime are supportive of the fear thematic:

> When it comes to violence, media stories may unintentionally form public images of right and wrong . . . story-tellers must consider the very real possibility that the routine formatting of violent accounts may be constructing social opinion rather than reflecting it. Thus, the role of story sequencing in violent accounts must enter discussions of media responsibility. (Cerulo 1998)

Fear is more widely used today because news organizations and news sources benefit from it. The narrative structure of news reports reflects information technology, commercialism, and entertainment values, as well as official news sources that provide the majority of information (Altheide and Snow 1991). Print and electronic news media use entertaining news formats that make their work more predictable and manageable while also delivering entertaining information that news consumers have come to expect. News sources, and especially social control agencies (e.g., police departments), have adjusted their messages to comply with the media logic and entertainment format criteria of news organizations. Consequently, news reports and social control work have become joined through mass communication organizations (Best 1995; Ericson et al. 1987, 1989; Fishman and Cavender 1998).

A great political scientist, Murray Edelman, argued that "crises" are simply certain events that are defined in a certain way and promoted to serve the political interests of leaders—and, we could add, other interest groups—who will benefit from these definitions. He observes that "crisis" is oriented to a decisionmaker's audience and to convince the audience to allow the leader to take decisive action (Edelman 1971, 1985). Fear is used increasingly to define crises and to bump along those claims so that leaders can take political action, against "external enemies" or "internal enemies."

> The media-induced public conviction during the early to mid-1980s that violent crime throughout America was rising at epidemic proportions (despite statistics to the contrary, also reported in the media) enabled Ronald Reagan to expand police powers beyond anything Richard Nixon could have dreamed of. (Massumi 1993, 26)

Often these acts are decisive, even brutal, as when populations are targeted for murder, albeit under different names, such as "tactical strikes" or "defensive action." One looks in vain at news accounts to find an instance in which a leader states, in effect, "Yes, sure, we decided to go in there and slaughter men, women, and children because we thought it would be in our best interests to do so." Inevitably, these targets are selected because they are threatening and engendering fear among us. Such acts are consistent with definitions of *terrorism,* defined as the purposeful act or threat of violence to create fear and/or compliant behavior in a victim and/or an audience (Lopez and Stohl 1984). These acts, however, are nearly always preceded by numerous reports showing the culpability, viciousness, and untrustworthy nature of the potential target. The mass media, and especially the news media, are the main source and tool used to "soften up" the audience, to prepare them to accept the justificatory account of the coming action. Fear in a democratic society requires the mass media. If these media are perpetuating claims about the "other"—the likely targets of future state action—then this fear-generating endeavor becomes an act of mass media terrorism on the "public body," if not individuals who subsequently suffer from state actions. This is why narratives are important and why mass media emphases, formats, and operating procedures in the construction of fear are critical to understand in a free society.

It is our "knowledge" of things that is the problem: I knew about the devil and hell from stories I was told. So do most people, but their stories might not be about the devil. They might be about communists, atomic weapons, or terrorists. Or they might be about crime, drugs, child molesters, or gangs. All of these have played a large role in what people have feared since World War II. I did not know about crime until I was much older. Crime was not a dominant theme in the stories I learned, told by parents and other adults who shared my parents' views of the world. Most of the "popular" stories today are told in newspapers, television programs (news and entertainment), movies, and popular music.

Radio was the first entertainment medium I can remember. My brothers and I listened to thrillers, mysteries, and westerns. They were exciting, chilling, and scary, but they were not fearful. We knew it was make-believe, although we would "believe" enough to enter the plots and the minds of the characters. We played games incorporating some of these characters, and we even imitated certain actions. We also listened to religious broadcasts on the radio. One religious radio personality, "Brother Ralph," implored us to repent and be saved. Indeed, when we were sick, he told us to put our hands on the radio and we would be in touch with God. A few years later, TV evangelist Orel Roberts asked us to place our hands on the TV set for the same effect. The first time I saw television was in the late 1940s. It was in the palatial home of some rich people who lived about a quarter mile from my family. These people were well heeled, with a swimming pool and a tennis court. Television was for wealthier people in those days. But this changed very quickly; by the mid-1950s, half of the people in the United States had TVs. Today, nearly 98 percent of the population owns at least one television set.

So, even though my early childhood included radio and television, I knew more about the world from the stories I heard about good, evil, and the devil. Part of what I learned was how social reality was organized: My childhood view was very simple—right and wrong, good and evil. I also learned a lot about control and who has the right to issue commandments. After years of research, I came to understand that what we fear is greatly influenced by how we learn about the fear, as well as who can benefit from that fear. It was as though the story form used by my parents and others, the messages about the devil, and the obligations to perform a certain way were all related. After all, only a few adults told the stories; children listened. Adults were the main communicators, although, ironically, they were concerned that some of the radio programs (e.g., "The Shadow") might frighten us.

SOCIAL CONTROL

Fear is part of social control. There are many definitions of *social control,* but a basic one is *the process by which people behave in ways that meet the expectations of others.* More simply, when we do what others expect us to do, social control is evident. Conversely, when others do what we expect them to do, we have asserted social control. Numerous scholars agree that social control and "getting along" involve an individual and an audience in a situation and context (Blumer 1969; Mead and Morris 1962). Social control involves an interaction or expectation between two or more individuals. The trick, of course, is to get people to do what we expect of them, and conversely, to generally refrain from doing what we don't expect of them. Most of the time we aren't even conscious of social control because our expectations are realized. For example, only rarely does the approaching driver cross the center line and move into our lane. Only rarely does the approaching stranger pull out a gun and demand our money or, worse yet, shoot us. And only rarely do our checks (or credit cards) "crash" or get rejected by the clerk. Things work out most of the time. But, we do remember those times when social control does not work; these are usually the times we say "something went wrong." This makes news.

Fear plays a large part in social control. There are several reasons for this. First, let's examine the process that makes social control work. The things we fear are related to how we communicate and learn about everyday life. I wasn't the first person to base his fears on what he was told. Stories (oral communication) have been the dominant communication medium until the last few hundred years. Social life in the United States and most industrial societies has moved toward a "risk society," organized around communication oriented to policing, control, and prevention of risks (Ericson and Haggerty 1997; Staples 1997).

> The moment a population is identified as a risk, everything within it tends to become—necessarily becomes—just that. Risk has an allusive, insidious potential existence that renders it simultaneously present and absent, doubtful and suspicious. Assumed to be everywhere, it founds a politics of prevention. (Ewald 1993, 221)

On the one hand, societies that rely on the use of storytelling—an "oral tradition"—tend to hold more parochial and "sacred" views of social order. The rise of the mass media and widespread popular culture, on the other hand, tend to promote fears that are more secular (e.g., crime rather than, say, "personal salvation"). Each brings with it a different sense of control. I return to this point several times in the following chapters, but here I focus on how fear and social control are related. One way to examine this is to look at how we recognize fear.

THE ICONOGRAPHY OF FEAR

Every era promotes fear. The nature of fear and the methods of its promotion simply differ. The promotion of fear and attendant "solutions" have been a staple of social control efforts throughout history. Just as my parents sought to scare the "bejesus" out of my brothers and I in order to save our souls and keep us out of trouble, politicians and heads of state have been concerned with keeping the population in check. For my parents, the fear of God was to be our salvation. Many people today use fear similarly, but there is a difference: My parents were really trying to help me; most politicians are trying to help themselves. However, whether we call it "spiritual development," "upbringing," "education," or just plain "propaganda," the process is the same: Convince people that one way of thinking is best and make this a process that they want to follow. We see in the following sections that this process became more of a "science" with the arrival of the mass media and advertising.

Numerous analyses of propaganda have connected the process of fear construction with various political and economic interests (Altheide and Johnson 1980; Ellenius and European Science Foundation 1998; Jackall 1994; Jackall and Hirota 1999; Powell 1999). Fear defines a cultural space that is shaped with experiences, interpretations, and narratives by storytellers like my parents, journalists, and others who uncannily connect something new(s) with something old. In time, as astute students of propaganda have suggested, what was new becomes commonplace; today's idiosyncrasy is tomorrow's orthodoxy, especially when embraced by common cultural trappings (Jackall 1994). I argue in the following chapters that entertainment and profits are a major impetus for the propaganda that engulfs us. Novelist Michael Crichton's (1999) character, Robert Doniger, puts it this way:

> Ask yourself . . . What is the dominant mode of experience at the end of the twentieth century? How do people see things, and how do they expect to see things? The answer is simple. In every field, from business to politics to marketing to education, the dominant mode has become entertainment. . . . Today, everybody expects to be entertained, and they expect to be entertained all the time. Business meetings must be snappy, with bullet lists and animated graphics, so executives aren't bored. Malls and stores must be engaging, so they amuse as well as sell us. Politicians must have pleasing video personalities and tell us only what we want to hear. Schools must be careful not to bore young minds that expect the speed and complexity of television. Students must be amused— everyone must be amused, or they will switch: switch brands, switch channels, switch parties, switch loyalties. This is the intellectual reality of Western society at the end of the century. . . . In other centuries, human beings wanted to be saved, or improved, or freed, or educated. But in our century, they want to be entertained. The great fear is not of disease or death, but of boredom. A sense of time on our hands, a sense of nothing to do. A sense that we are not amused. (442–443)

Notwithstanding Crichton's tremendous success selling fiction, I suggest that the connection is a bit more complex. People do want to be "saved" and "freed," but they want to be saved and freed from fear, and this is what makes the messages of fear so compelling and important for public policy and the fabric of our social life.

There are clear political implications of this process that affect our culture and public order. The complex relationship between stories about fear and social order also depends on a certain form of communication. My childhood mainly consisted of oral communication: Conversation, "tales from the pulpit," and numerous "Bible stories" showed me the path. But these also had a "visible" or "visual" aspect. The words without the images or symbols would not have been as effective. Visual guidelines are very important. This is where icons come into the picture.

Icons are symbols that represent complex ideas. The Christian cross is an example. It stands for many things, including, from my own experience, fear. In advertising, Coca-Cola and Nike represent not just products, but lifestyles, social status, and cultural preferences. The same can be said for guns and the law. Consider this chapter's opening example about "Judy," who lives in a low-crime area. Why a woman in one of the safest cities in the United States would be packing a gun is part of the puzzle we hope to unravel in the rest of this book. We want to know why people who are quite safe perceive themselves to be in danger?

A good place to start is to locate how icons such as guns, and other objects of fear, have evolved. This requires a brief look at iconography from a historical view. The study of icons and how they evolve is called *iconography*. (There are several other academic subfields that study the development and consequences of key symbols, including semiotics). Throughout history, fear has been depicted in certain ways. The study of this is called the *iconography of fear*. The iconography of fear continues to evolve with political contexts and information technology. As Carl Couch (1984) notes, the information technology of the day interacts with political context in important ways to influence the shape of information and to what purposes it will be put. We can think of Judy (first page of this chapter), who lives in Scottsdale but reads about crime and violence in her newspapers, watches it depicted in TV newscasts and "real TV" shows and probably sees it played out in movies she rents, hears her neighbors discuss "safety," and is "represented" by local, state, and national politicians who call for tougher laws against crime. Can you blame Judy for arming herself? It is this context that led Carl Couch (1995) to argue quite forcibly:

> [I]t is incumbent on social scientists to undertake sustained systematic studies of the intertwining of social relationships and information technologies. This can best be accomplished not by focusing our analytic power on neither social relationships or information technologies but rather on the social acts that create and perfect information technologies and the social acts that put in place, affirm, modify and destroy social relationships. (241)

Judy is a product of our information age that promotes entertainment through fear. What we fear is related to our everyday life experience and what sense is being made of this by superiors and leaders in society. Just as children defer to parents, so do "citizens"—especially less-powerful peasants—defer to those who wield power. However, the way the power is wielded is influenced by how we communicate.

Directing fear in a society is tantamount to controlling that society. Every age has its fears, every ruler has his/her enemies, every sovereign places blame, and every citizen learns about these as propaganda. The key is to recognize the process and not get captivated with the "boogey man" of choice in any particular time—our time! Icons of fear have changed as we have moved from the predominantly oral tradition of the fourteenth century to the electronic media of today, in which literacy and visual information prevails. A key part of the process involves authorities that provide information to the news media. Whether viewed from the standpoint of "what is feared" or its structural connection to "the target of fear," the role of authorities in promoting and sustaining a certain focus of attention remains to be questioned. Thus, the frameworks of fear, its architecture, targets, and icons remain significant. Children play a dual role in terms of innocence and brutality, protection and control. We can justify excess in protecting children, and, increasingly, we can excuse excess in punishing them, particularly—and paradoxically—if extreme sanctions will protect the innocence of children.

Fear has long been a concern for individuals but the focus and context of fear has shifted drastically throughout history. The notion of risk is central to modern attempts at social control.

> The notion of risk appeared at the end of the Middle Ages with maritime insurance, when it was used to designate the perils that could compromise a successful voyage. At that time, risk designated the possibility of an objective danger, an act of God, a force majeure, a tempest or other peril of the sea that could not be imputed to wrongful conduct.
>
> In the nineteenth century, the notion of risk underwent an extraordinary extension: risk was no longer exclusively in nature. It was also in human beings, in their conduct, in their liberty, in the relations between them, in the fact of their association, in society. This extension was due in part to the singular appearance of the problem of the accident, a kind of mix between nature and will. . . .
>
> Beginning at the end of the nineteenth century, risk designated the collective mode of being of human beings in society: it had become social. Similarly, evil was no longer the opposite of good, but resided in the relation between goods; risk was no longer inscribed in the relation between humanity and simultaneously benevolent and hostile nature, but in the relation between human beings, in their common quest for good. (Ewald 1993, 226–227)

Naphy and Robert's (1997) work on fear in history provides a heuristic framework as well as a context for getting a relatively long-term perspective on fear by comparing it with anxiety and panic and the role of public officials in focusing resources and symbolic emphasis on certain topics. This study of fear in early modern (fourteenth- and sixteenth-century) cities in Europe stresses that fear is focused but less immediate, while anxiety is more pervasive and less immediate. Their thesis is that fears are connected to the social contexts of the time, but how they are acted upon is key, and the role of authorities in promoting fears or preventing them from becoming panic is important.

> Indeed, the ability of the authorities to contain or manage fear may have proved crucial in preventing an anxious situation from turning into one of panic. In this sense, fear can be seen as a sort of institutional health reflecting the efficacy of local and central government in curbing the negative effects of fear. (Naphy and Roberts 1997, 6)

The major concerns of citizens five centuries ago were salvation, disease, especially plague, and fire. The church was the dominant institution in the fifteenth and sixteenth centuries. Focus on these issues is found in the language used in the texts of the day; the fledgling printing industry was controlled by religious power. Arson was considered equivalent to the most heinous crimes of sodomy, witchcraft, and heresy. Plague spreading could get you executed. Plague conspirators were thought to benefit by being "plague workers," who, once the plague was spread, would be called upon to clean up as fumigators and linen-washers; their good wages suggest that they cleaned up in several ways. Plague spreading and witchcraft were linked, although records suggest that men were more likely to be charged with arson while witchcraft was more the province of women (Naphy and Roberts 1997).

RATS AND GUNS

History has its rats and Judy has her gun. We can help locate Judy's fear of crime and her purchase of a weapon by putting her decisions in the context of history, including mass communication and popular culture. The mass media and popular culture also use narratives; they tell stories in different formats than were used in the sixteenth century, but there remains an underlying order. I examine this in a later chapter. However, in order to put these concerns in perspective, we can look at how certain problems were viewed in the sixteenth century. The blameworthy aspects of the sixteenth-century cosmology draw out the peculiar relationship between agents of social control, especially the aristocracy, and the emergence of taken-for-granted notions of public order, including who defines the situation and with what impact. In the sixteenth century, rats were not part of the iconography of disease as they are today. The animals associated with plague were dogs and cats, and they were killed in large numbers. But their extermination also depended on what they symbolized, according to some historians, since not all dogs were killed, least of all those owned by the aristocracy. Commenting on a pamphlet to "suffer no dogs nor cats to come into your houses," it was noted:

> The slaughter of dogs was thus more than an extension of the policy of household isolation that played so important a part in the response to plague. Dogs in streets were not simply breaking sanitary regulations. They were quite literally masterless. In London in 1563 and 1584–86 they were allowed out so long as they were on a leash and thus visibly and physically fixed within a particular social relationship. Their slaughter was a symbolic warning to the rest of the population. . . . It is to this overall context of the coercive exercise of authority and of social differentiation that we should look when we try to understand these dog massacres. They were not based upon simple ignorance, nor were they the febrile panic reactions of a terrified generation unable to control their environment. Rather, they articulated a variety of fears about human relationships with each other, with the bestial aspects of humankind and with the wider world. (Naphy and Roberts 1997, 56)

Evil and the plague occupied the thoughts of Europeans several hundred years ago. The situation has changed, largely, as we shall see, due to historical changes in people's everyday lives, including the massive growth and infusion of popular culture and the mass media, especially news reports. As mentioned earlier, longevity in the fourteenth century was about thirty years; in the year 2000, it was approximately eighty years. The plague is not a major threat today. In most countries of the world, life is more secure, more predictable, and definitely more comfortable than it was five centuries ago. This is particularly true for most citizens of the United States and Western Europe. Nevertheless, U.S. citizens are currently exposed to more news and entertainment programs that use the word *fear* and promote it, and audiences apparently believe that fear describes the state of affairs.

Opinion polls and survey data suggest that Americans are more fearful and less trustworthy. While there is scant data on fear per se among public opinion polls, most measures of fear in recent years are associated with crime. Numerous public opinion polls show that fear of crime and for personal safety reign above most other concerns. Indeed, many Americans feel that their lives are unsafe and more subject to harm than at previous times. While there are many things for which Americans express fear, the most revealing data are for crime. At least one-third of citizens regard crime as a serious problem (70 percent of older people), resulting in massive behavioral changes in terms of how people dress (23 percent in 1988), where they go (50 percent in 1991), how they travel, whether they purchase a weapon for self-protection (18 percent in 1991; 25 percent of homes contained a handgun in 1994), and with whom they talk. Indeed, 4 of 10 Americans claimed to avoid talking with any strangers because of fear (Roper Center 1995).

Fear and mistrust are related, but they are not identical (Margolis 1996). For example, many opinion polls indicate that Americans do not trust government officials, but this would have less to do with fear than with public information available about the dishonesty and insincerity of politicians. As Shaw (1996) argues:

> But for all their protesting and clamoring for positive news, surveys—and TV ratings—also show that people seem more interested in negative news, sensational news, news about crime and violence and corruption than in what we customarily think of as "positive" news. To remain in business, the news media must—to some extent—give people what they want. The better, more responsible news media are also supposed to give people what they need—and while few people say they want or need more cynicism, it continues to mount. (Shaw 1996 [1994])

Perhaps the support for "tough legislation" about crime is related to perceptions that officials are not trustworthy. Margolis (1996) suggests that the public may be

> getting what it wants, even if experts are distressed at what they see as the extravagant irrelevance or perversity of some of the things the public wants (such as "three strikes and you're out" provision in crime bills). For a segment of the electorate too large for a political figure to risk offending, "three strikes" has become a litmus test for whether a person is serious about crime. On the other hand, there is also a good deal of evident mistrust of government from a sense that the government wastes taxpayers' money on programs that do not work. So it makes some sense to consider that things might work better if the process could be reformed in some way that makes it less likely that there will be politically irresistible public support for things that in fact will not work. (194)

Mistrust of officials is not unrelated to mistrust of fellow citizens, especially in the context of crime and danger. In 1972, according to the General Social Survey, 46.3 percent of respondents felt they could trust others. This percentage has steadily declined to 34.4 percent in 1994 (National Opinion Research Center 1996). Despite a gradual decline in news media usage over the last few years, Americans have been voracious news participants over the last decade and a half, with some 60 percent claiming to read articles about violent crime in the newspapers and 71 percent viewing violent TV news reports daily. Poll data are consistent with Graber's (1984) panel study of Chicago-area news readers, who demonstrated a high recall of crime-related news reports. Indeed, people who watch TV news daily—particularly women—are less likely to trust others (General Social Survey 1994).

Numerous news reports about fear pertain to children. Children are part of the iconography of fear in our age (see Chapter 7). The news media's emphasis on fear with children is consistent with work by Warr (1992) and others on the significance of "third-person" or "altruistic fear"—the concern for those whom you love or are responsible. Specifically, Warr (1992) found that children are the most common object of fear in households. Much of this concern is generated around crime and drugs. For example, in the mid-1990s, crime and violence were regarded by 27 percent of the public as the most important problem facing the country today (Gallup Poll 1995). Except for a brief appearance by "immorality, crime, and juvenile delinquency" in 1965, crime did not reappear among the top public concerns until around 1990, when drug abuse was cited by 18 percent as the second most significant problem. One important contributor was the way politicians emphasized crime and drug problems (Roberts and Doob 1990).

Kenneth F. Ferraro's (1995) important work on the fear of crime suggests the concept of "perceptual criminology," or the notion that "many of the problems associated with crime, including fear, are independent of actual victimization . . . because it may lead to decreased social integration, out-migration, restriction of activities, added security costs, and avoidance behaviors" (Ferraro 1995, 3). While he did not investigate the role of the mass media in public perception of crime and its impact on lives, Ferraro (1995) acknowledges that such a study should be conducted: "Beyond the crime rates considered in this research, it would be intriguing for future research to also integrate other ecological variables which may influence fear of crime." (Ferraro 1995, 121). Moreover, he wrote, "Added attention to media effects may also be a propitious avenue of research . . . it may be useful to give added attention to media effects. Specifically, how do media portrayals and media exposure affect the risk interpretation process? These questions appear worthy of further investigation" (Ferraro 1995, 124).

Work by Chiricos and others (Chiricos, Eschholz, and Gertz. 1997; Chiricos, Padgett, and Gertz 2000) makes it clear that the mass media, and especially TV news, do affect perceptions about crime. Indeed, in recent years, journalism has begun to take a look at the impact on American life of such distorted coverage of crime and fear. Two journalists (Westfeldt and Wicker 1998) very critical of the news coverage of crime observe, "In 1997, even as the prison population was going up and the crime rate was falling the public rated 'crime/gangs/justice system' as 'the most important problem facing the country today'—and by a large margin." As they chronicled the preoccupation with crime by local newspapers and TV broadcasters in promoting a fear of crime agenda, the authors observed the culpability of national and prestigious news outlets in pushing the same views, including TV network news:

> The Center for Media and Public Affairs reported in April 1998 that the national murder rate has fallen by 20 percent since 1990—but the number of murder stories on network newscasts rose in the same years by about 600 percent . . . not including the many broadcasts of or about the O. J. Simpson trial. (Westfeldt and Wicker 1998, 2)

These views are consistent with other research on the impact of news (Chiricos et al. 1997) and other programming on public perceptions of crime and its causes (Sasson 1995).

A PREOCCUPATION WITH FEAR

We are a secular society so we are less concerned with the fear of God. But we are concerned about fear of crime, along with many other issues. It is clear that a lot of attention has been given to crime for several decades, but why? Part of the answer does not involve crime: It involves popular culture and entertainment. Crime is a convenient example that combines several important elements of a morality tale, or a classic relationship between symbols of good and evil. Indeed, one researcher argues that crime news and entertainment programs promote scenarios in which the innocent "sheep" (the public) are being protected from "wolves" (criminals) by "sheepdogs" (police and the "state").

> The social dynamic underlying the image of crime forwarded by the media— an image that has not changed much over the hundred-year history of the mass entertainment media—is one of a trisected society composed of wolves, sheep, and sheepdogs. In the mass entertainment media vision of society, evil and cunning predator criminal wolves create general mayhem and prey on weak, defenseless—and often stupid—victim sheep (women, the elderly, the general public), while good crime-fighting hero sheepdogs (middle-class, white, and male) intervene and protect the sheep in the name of retributive justice. Over the course of this century the character of this portrait has darkened. Media criminals have become more animalistic, irrational, and predatory—as have media crime fighters—and media victims have become more innocent. . . . In a subtle shift, the earlier predatory but rational criminal wolves have become unpredictable, irrational mad dogs, while over the years the noble sheepdogs have become wolflike vigilantes for whom the law is an impediment to stopping crime. . . .
>
> By depicting a predatory social dynamic the entertainment media project messages to the audience, both criminal and law-abiding, concerning whom to trust, whom to victimize, and how victims and criminals should act. (Surette 1998, 49)

However, part of the answer also involves salvation in a secular age that is very affluent and mobile, yet disconnected from community, or a shared sense of identity, purpose, and concern. Fear is related to cultural values and social structure. Americans rely on fear to save them. The uncertainty of many changes, failed social policies, unfulfilled expectations of a trouble-free life is explained away by fear. Popular culture and entertainment values promote and celebrate our market-oriented and commodified social order with fear (Massumi 1993). The dominant popular culture promotes identities, visions, and futures that reflect social affluence in a market economy. This means that things, people, dreams, and hopes are bought and sold as "commodities." Technical, chemical, and psychological information are combined to produce a commodified social order that is valued more for its symbolic meanings than the utility of the products. The electronic media, particularly the visual "magic" of television, movies, and advertisements, set the spectator pace and define the significant cultural space. The advertisement is the message of the age; problems are uniformly "solved" through application of technology and products; people are believed to "lack" objects, information, and style that bring success and happiness. Audiences are all important and are everywhere. Peer groups still matter, but increasingly it is the mass-mediated styles and standards that rule the day, pervade the hour, and help us make time by adjusting to visual rhythms that increasingly define our days, years, careers, and decades.

Visual culture is expectant; what you see need not be imagined so much as sought and grasped. But the anticipated salvation that accompanies the commodified machinery is not realized. The success of my parents' efforts to "raise me" would come through salvation; I would be saved from the "lake of fire," and that expectation was enough for them (but, of course, it was not enough for me). Salvation in a secular society is more troublesome, far more demanding, and less predictable because the timetable is not "eternity" but rather the here and now, or at least in "this lifetime." As more students have the opportunity for an education, we have also increased expectations of each other; no longer can one's background be "held up" as the reason for more sharply defined benchmarks of acceptability, accomplishments, and success. Now, success is more personal. The responsibility is the individual's. Recipes for repose and action are offered through drugs, including alcohol, "preparation for another future" (e.g., escapism), and above all, ownership, play, and mastery of a multitude of technological innovations that enable us to "communicate" more consistently with each other but, in particular, to participate in the highly visible communicative order. Members of this social order have little in common except for their ability to market themselves, consume, and participate in the ubiquitous popular culture that drives it all. Part of the success of this popular culture industry is that models for success are held high as well as explanations and accounts of the lack of personal well-being and contentment. This social palliative is fear. "It is nothing as sharp as panic. . . . It is low-level fear. A kind of background radiation saturating existence. . . . It may be expressed as 'panic' or 'hysteria' or 'phobia' or 'anxiety'" (Massumi 1993, 24).

Fear is a social product and not an individual failing. Fear is a manufactured response that has been produced by a mass-mediated symbol machine. (My undergraduate students report that their major "fear" is failure.) Without fear, citizens may come to question the nature of a particular thing or issue. Fear provides explanations and solutions that often involve formal agents of social

control (FASC), involving police, control, and surveillance. They are already
part of American business and educational practice.

The mass media and popular culture influence social life in different ways.
Much of the research has focused on media content (cf. Comstock 1980). Students of the mass media and popular culture agree on two basic social facts: (1)
that popular culture includes a relatively large amount of information and images pertaining to fear, including crime and violence; and (2) audience members perceive social life to be very dangerous. It is the relationship between
these two "social facts" that remains unclear.

The mass media and public perceptions of issues and problems are inexorably linked, although researchers disagree about the nature of this connection and direction of this influence. For example, several decades of work have
yet to resolve definitively whether television and newspaper reports about
crime and fear are a "cause" or an "effect" of public concerns about crime and
fear (cf. Gerbner and Gross 1976; Hirsch 1980; Skogan and Maxfield 1981;
Ericson 1995; Gunter 1987; Sparks 1992; Katz 1987; Schlesinger, Murdock,
and Elliott 1991; Zillman and Wakshlag 1987). From the standpoint of media content as "cause," the question is asked whether news reports can "cause"
or "lead" people to focus on and fear crime, including to what extent relevant
values and perspectives may be "cultivated" (cf. Gerbner et al. 1978). From
this perspective, the mass media play a large role in shaping public agendas
by influencing *what* people think about (Shaw and McCombs 1977). Studies
of media violence have suggested that violent content can lead viewers to perceive life as dangerous and fearful (cf. Gerbner and Gross 1976; Gerbner 1988).
For researchers focused on media content as a result of their other experiences,
the query becomes whether people's experiences of crime in their everyday lives
lead them to be more interested and attentive to crime programs, including
news reports, as well as provide an impetus for journalists to cover crime.

Several projects have argued that the media do contribute to political agendas as well as people's perceptions and interests in everyday life (cf. MacKuen
and Coombs 1981). Iyengar and Kinder (1987) employed an experimental design to demonstrate "that television news shapes the relative importance
Americans attach to various national problems" (113). Focusing on energy, in-
flation, and unemployment, they argued that TV is most powerful at "priming" or providing accessible bits of information that viewers may draw on to
help interpret other events. Making it clear that ultimately it is the viewers'
perceptions and everyday life experiences that help interpret social life, nevertheless, TV contributes: "By priming certain aspects of national life while ignoring others, television news sets the terms by which political judgments are
rendered and political choices made" (Iyengar and Kinder 1987, 4). In another
work, Iyengar (1991) suggests that priming and framing of reports as either
"episodic"—focusing on individual circumstances and responsibility—or
thematic—contextual and societal responsibility—has a bearing on what
viewers take from TV news reports (cf. Ericson 1993).

Notwithstanding varied research agendas and approaches used in addressing the "causal connection" of media and public perceptions, in the context of the positivistic paradigm, Gunter's (1987) conclusion seems to capture the paradox:

> Probably nearest to the truth though may be a notion of circularity in the relationship. Greater fear of potential danger in the social environment may encourage people to stay indoors, where they watch more television, and are exposed to programmes which tell them things which in turn reinforce their anxieties. (270)

This circularity contributes to a conceptual path that led numerous researchers to a process and production model of the mass media's role in social life. A major assumption is that the communication process and content are inexorably joined, with one always having implications for the other. In this sense, "new knowledge" and information is always connected to a stock of knowledge and symbolic interpretation.

FEAR IN THE COMMUNICATION ENVIRONMENT

The mass media and popular culture are part of our environment. The remainder of this chapter offers a perspective for understanding how some aspects of our culture are constructed. It suggests that media materials contribute to public perceptions, albeit in less-than-precise ways, whether as "priming" (Iyengar and Kinder 1987), agenda setting, or, as the following suggests, shaping of public discourse through news formats. It is all part of our culture and the task is to attempt to continue to map conceptually the myriad symbolic connections we are able to make between our everyday lives, popular culture, information technology, and news of the day.

> The mass media work to short-circuit the event. They blur the event's specific content into an endless series of "like" events. . . . "Like" events rush past. No sooner does one happen that it is a has-been. The who, what, when, and where become a what not ("anything can happen") and a what's next . . . retrospective analysis is replaced by a shudder and a shrug, memory quickly elided by expectation. Broadcast is a technology of collective forgetting. It is not that the event is lost. On the contrary, it is accessible for immediate recall: instant replay. (Massumi 1993, 25)

Numerous studies suggest that public perceptions of problems and issues (the texts they construct from experience) incorporate definitions, scenarios, and language from news reports (cf. Snow 1983; Altheide and Snow 1991; Comstock 1980; Bennett 1988; DeFleur and Ball-Rokeach 1982, 244*ff.*; Ericson 1995). Gerbner (1988) and others (Gerbner and Gross 1976) have noted that fear is pervasive in our symbolic and effective environment. It is perceived as real to a few of us, and virtually real to most of us.

A columnist writing a postmortem on the 1996 presidential election noted the irony of how our materially strong nation is "dying from within":

> Fear stalks this nation every day. Fear of making a wrong turn in a neighborhood in Los Angeles, riding the subway or jogging in Central Park in New York, fear symbolized by locks, guns and alarms to protect ourselves. Fear of talking to those who don't look like us. Fear of growing old in a country that does not have the resources to care for us. Fear of the government and civil war. (Devji 1996, H3)

Despite clear evidence showing that Americans today have a comparative advantage in terms of disease, accidents, nutrition, medical care, and life expectancy, they perceive themselves to be at great risk and express specific fears about this. According to numerous public opinion polls, American society is a very fearful society, some believe "the most anxious, frightened society in history." (Shaw 1994) Indeed, an article in the *Los Angeles Times,* September 11, 1994, reported that 78 percent of Americans think they are subjected to more risk today than their parents were twenty years ago, and a large source of this perception is crime news coverage.

> Why did many Americans suddenly decide last fall, for the first time, to tell national pollsters that crime is "the most important problem facing the country"? Could it have been because last year, for the first time, ABC, CBS and NBC nightly news programs devoted more time to crime than to any other topic? Several media critics think so; as a *Los Angeles Times* Poll showed early this year, people say their "feelings about crime" are based 65 percent on what they read and see in the media and 21 percent on experience. (Shaw 1994)

The most critical shifts in fear involve the growth of audiences who share and participate in popular culture as part of their everyday affairs. U.S. audiences take fear for granted. On the one hand, we do not worry as much about it, but on the other hand, it is more pervasive, more central to everything we do. Fear is part of our language. Fear has shifted from concerns with the physical world and the spiritual realm of salvation during the last four hundred years to the social realm of everyday life. It is other people but not just immigrants—the historical "other" that have troubled previous immigrants-now-solid-citizens; it is the "other," that category of trouble that can unseat solid expectations and hopes for a future that is never to be realized in what is perceived to be a constantly changing and out-of-control world. Fear rests on the border between expectations and realizations, between hope and reality. This includes the foundation of identity in consumption rather than work, in play rather than prayer, and in the here and now rather than the hereafter. Fear has been transformed from natural events, catastrophes, and "uncontrollable phenomena" that characterized life in the Middle Ages to social life. It is neither the plague, typhoid, tuberculosis, nor polio that troubles most Americans; it is crime, gangs, drugs and youth, and terrorism. The following chapters discuss how this has happened and what social processes propel it, including how I investigate this topic (Chapter 2); the entertainment logic that has produced this emphasis (Chapter 3); the extent that fear pervades news and public information (Chapter 4); how the journalistic interview has changed to help produce this more entertaining "slant" on events (Chapter 5); the role of news sources in promoting this perspective (Chapter 6); the most recent focus of fear on children (Chapter 7); and the final chapter (Chapter 8) examines the relevance of the "lens of fear" for understanding social crises and offers suggestions for what can be done about it.

2

Tracking Discourse

The aim of this chapter is to set forth the relevance of mass communication formats and content for analysis of the intersection between culture and cognition and for suggesting a few bridges across some conceptual and methodological divides in mass communication research. I offer a conceptual and methodological approach—tracking discourse—to the study of mass media. This approach looks for key words and follows them across time and various topics in order to see how they emerge as powerful symbols that in turn guide individuals as audience members to extend these symbols across arenas of experience in the quest for meaning.

Tracking discourse is one way to gain a perspective on our present by exploring the past, as represented in news reports and many aspects of popular culture. The ability "to see" differently can provide insights. For example, NASA space explorations to Mars and other planets have provided visual images of the earth and the moon together from a third point (the satellite position) in space. Advanced radio telescopes have extended our gaze into the "past" and have, essentially, provided a kind of time travel in the sense that we can see where the solar system has been and ultimately from where we came. Tracking discourse permits us to use technology to look back and conduct comparative analyses that, essentially, would not be possible without advanced information bases and computer technology which permit electronic storage of reports, searches of these information bases, and retrieval of data. Additional information technology and software permit more sophisticated searching, manipulation, and analysis.

There are numerous approaches to the study of discourse. Indeed, several journals, crossing various disciplines—from the humanities to the social sciences—are devoted to discourse analysis (cf. Wuthnow 1992; Perinbanayagam 1991; Grimshaw and Burke 1994; Weiler and Pearce 1992; van Dijk 1988; Zhondang and Kosicki 1993). While there are many differences in the approaches, all share an assumption that symbolic representations are enmeshed in a context of other assumptions that are not stated as such. My approach draws on many of these assumptions, but blends interpretive, ethnographic, and ethnomethodological approaches with media logic, particularly studies of news organizational culture, information technology, and communication formats.

New information technology when combined with a theoretical and methodological approach to qualitative document analysis can extend our capacity to study and understand public discourse. Previous work on news formats and "news codes" (Altheide 1985, 102*ff.*) directs our attention away from the intention of the journalist who speaks about an event to "what does the news message look like?" or "what words and powerful cultural symbols are used in discussing the event?"

How we think and how we act are connected in several paradoxical ways. One social science perspective on this process, set forth in the work of George Herbert Mead (Mead and Morris 1962) and a legion of symbolic interactionists (Blumer 1969; Hall 1997), is that mind, self, and society are intricately connected. The general emphasis is on the communication and interpretation processes that play out in social interaction between two or more individuals. For Mead, brains and minds are not synonymous, and indeed, mind is not something that is entirely owned and operated by the individual: It is something posited and affirmed as a kind of beacon of meaning and orientation. While Mead was not overly concerned with the physiology and electronics of constructs such as synapses and the like, he was aware that all are social constructions (Brissett and Edgley 1990), that our actions provide a context of meaning for audiences to affirm whether we are thinking at all, whether there is a mind behind the face, and above all, whether things make sense. Several generations of sociologists and psychologists have studied how social reality is presented, affirmed, discussed, and negated in hundreds of social arenas and social institutions (Goffman 1959). This work, then, with the help of many others, is the essential foundation for the notion that reality is socially constructed (Burke 1966, 1969; Schutz 1967; Berger and Luckmann 1967). Indeed, Schutz's (1967) notion about the significance of the "natural attitude" in everyday life hinges on his thoughtful elucidation of a process through which societal members engage in intersubjective understanding. Schutz's analysis of interpretive procedures contributes to ethnomethodology's agenda of investigating commonsense understanding as a feature of situated language use (Cicourel 1974; Douglas 1970) and provided an early approach to a "cognitive sociology." This general perspective and, particularly, the notion that cultural actors acquire and use communication logics in interpreting reality in social situations inform the comments that follow.

The thinking process is connected at some point to the world of experience and what people take for granted. Both take place in contexts of meaning. And both are connected to audiences with whom individuals communicate. As

Zerubavel (1997) argues, how we perceive, attend, classify, assign meaning, and reckon with time is subject to cultural variation. Culture gives us broad as well as specific contexts of meaning and *scripts,* or plausible statements and courses of action that are accepted by others familiar with situations we share (Carey 1989). Complex rules of communication involve the interaction between minds, seldom seen but always presumed, selves, and social situations. The critical point is that what we think about and talk about is reflexively joined with how we communicate.

One social science concept that draws together these parts is known by various terms such as the "definition of the situation," or the sense of "what we have here," "what we're doing," and "we know what it means." Questions involving the nature, process, and consequences for defining the situation cut across most social science theory and research. I argue that the process involving the definition of the situation is a significant act of power.

My main interest is in the role of the mass media and popular culture in shaping such definitions, including what we think about and discuss, the language we use in doing so, and the interpretive frameworks we bring to bear on events. Over the last several years, more researchers have focused on the role of the mass media and popular culture in influencing members' definitions and perspectives of social reality, including the shaping of culture, communication formats, and the formulation of mundane as well as policy issues and practical matters in high places and in everyday life (for example, (Altheide 1985, 1994; Best 1995; Cerulo 1998; Couch 1984; Crane 1992; Ericson, Baranek, and Chan 1991; Ferraro 1995; Ferrell and Sanders. 1995; Gerbner and Gross 1976; Glassner 1999; Meyrowitz 1985; Snow 1983). Zerubavel's (1997) provocative discussion of collective memory seems pertinent for a broader understanding of the contributions of a culturally informed approach to an emerging cognitive sociology:

> A *mnemonic tradition* includes not only what we come to remember as members of a particular thought community but also *how* we remember it. . . .
> Needless to say, the schematic mental structures on which mnemonic traditions typically rest are neither "logical" nor natural. Most of them are either culture-specific or subculture-specific, and therefore something we acquire as part of our mnemonic socialization. (87–89)

My argument is that the mass media provide a lot of material about our "mnemonic socialization" in content as well as in a logic of perception and expectation about the appearance, shape, form, and rhythm of credible information about experience. Tracking discourse is an approach to investigate the prevalence and impact on public communication about social issues. A few general comments about content pertaining to crime and fear is followed by an overview of mass media formats and the logic they carry.

The mass media provide the bulk of cultural experiences for citizens about crime and fear. And while some researchers have examined the place of fear in some cultural venues of American life (Glassner 1999), most accounts do not significantly expand our understandings beyond those set forth by Hadley Cantril and his colleagues (Cantril et al. 1940) nearly sixty years ago. I contend that the mass media are central players in socializing audiences in what and how to experience culture, and that the language and imagery associated with popular culture are integrated into everyday life routines and inform perceptions beyond the specific programming parameters. Fear is one example.

While fear is commonly associated with crime, I suggest that fear provides a discursive framework of expectation and meaning within which crime and related "problems" are expressed. Media practices and major news sources (e.g., law enforcement agencies) have cooperatively produced an organizational "machine," fueled by entertainment and selective use of news sources, that simultaneously connects people to their effective environments even as it generates entertainment-oriented profits (Altheide 1997). As one law enforcement official stated about Arizona's televised crime stoppers dramatizations, "If you can have a little entertainment and get your man, too, that's great." This discourse resonates through public information and is becoming a part of what mass society holds in common: We increasingly share understandings about what to fear and how to avoid it.

I noted in Chapter 1 that fear is a key element of creating "the risk society," organized around communication oriented to policing, control, and prevention of risks (Ericson and Haggerty 1997; Staples 1997). A constitutive feature of this emerging order is a blanket reminder of fear. "Fear ends up proving itself, as new risk communication and management systems proliferate" (Ericson and Haggerty 1997, 6). More is involved in media socialization than content and images of certain characters and story scenarios. It is the way popular culture is organized and presented, including its underlying logic and formats, that shapes audience expectations, preferences, and ability to recognize one type of program rather than another, one type of action as "credible" rather than another. Because popular culture is so pervasive and the entertainment orientation infuses virtually all forms of public communication, it is important to be aware of underlying organizational principles.

These questions are consistent with my familiarity with the nature and process of TV news work, including all aspects of the production process, such as the important role of news sources providing items that can fit with the news workers schedule and preference for zippy visual reports (Altheide 1976; Epstein 1973; Tuchman 1978).

The problem to be investigated helps clarify the unit or level of analysis. For example, as noted previously, in TV news reports, one could use the entire newscast, individual news reports, or parts of reports. If one is studying newspapers, the unit of analysis could be a particular page such as the front page, individual articles, or perhaps even paragraphs. In most cases the unit of analysis is the individual news report. In studies of television violence, the unit of analysis could be a week, an evening, a program such as certain cartoon shows, or the number of individual violent acts presented in a program.

The capacity to define the situation for self and others is a key dimension of social power. One reason to study mass media documents is to understand the nature and process by which a key defining aspect of our effective environment operates and to attempt to gauge the consequences. The media are consequential in social life. Numerous studies strongly suggest that public perceptions of problems and issues (the texts they construct from experience) incorporate definitions, scenarios, and language from news reports (cf. Snow 1983; Altheide and Snow 1991; Comstock 1980; Bennett 1988; DeFleur and Ball-Rokeach 1982, 244*ff.*). What we call things, the themes and discourse we employ, and how we frame and allude to experience are crucial for what we take for granted and assume to be true. Simultaneously, we have experience, reflect on those experiences, and direct future experiences. When language changes and new or revised frameworks of meaning become part of the public domain and are routinely used, then social life has been changed, even in a small way. This is why the topic of discourse, or the kinds of framing, inclusion, and exclusion of certain points of view, is important.

News agencies have creatively adjusted news work and news production to fit with entertainment formats (Altheide 1997, 28). The packaging of information is done in organizational contexts that are dedicated to generating profits through entertaining programs and content. The news business does this with formats, themes, frames, and promotion of evocative discourses that are recognized and routinely used by audiences.

Formats pertain to the underlying organization and assumptions of time (temporal flow, rhythm), space (place and visual editing), and manner (style) of experience (Snow 1983). Formats, basically, are what make our familiar experiences familiar and recognizable as one thing rather than another; that is, we can quickly tell the difference between, say, a TV newscast, a sitcom, a talk show. The entertainment emphasis contains elements of action noted by Goffman (1959) and others, but clarified by Snow (1983) in his work on the rise of "media culture." First, there is an absence of the ordinary; second, there is the openness of an adventure, outside the boundaries of routine behavior; and third, the audience member is willing to suspend disbelief. In addition, while the exact outcome may be in doubt, there is a clear and unambiguous point at which it is resolved (Berg 1989; Zhondang and Kosicki 1993).

Frames are like the borders around pictures that separate them from the wall, and from other possibilities. An example is treating illegal drug use as a "public health issue" as opposed to a "criminal justice issue." These are two different frames that entail a way of discussing the problem and the kind of discourse that will follow. Frames focus on what will be discussed, how it will be discussed, and, above all, how it will not be discussed (Altheide 1976; Epstein 1973; Fishman 1980). Themes are more basically tied to the format used by journalists who have a short time to "tell a story" that the audience can "recognize," "that they have probably heard before," and, moreover, to get specific information from sources that can be tied to this (Iyengar 1991). These "message dimensions" are critical for the development of the problem frame, a key component of the entertainment logic used in all news, but especially TV news. The problem frame is discussed in Chapter 3. What is relevant for the remainder of this chapter is to emphasize that entertainment is a significant context for the rise of the discourse of fear.

The focus on media forms and logic of communication underlies an expanding agenda for understanding how the mass media can influence culture in terms of content, messages, and agenda, as well as the prevailing media logic(s) that pervade the popular culture shared by many segments of society, albeit unevenly. I draw on this general perspective to offer an approach that is helpful in following continuity and change over time in public documents.

FROM CONTENT TO DISCOURSE

There have been numerous creative studies of the content of popular culture, in general, and news media, in particular. However, students of culture are aware that what also matters is not only the repetition of, say, certain words and actions, for example, violence (Gerbner and Gross 1976), but whether and to what extent a view of the social world is actually adopted and applied to everyday life situations. While research clearly suggests that public opinion is closely in line with news media accounts of issues ranging from politics (Zhondang and Kosicki 1993) to crime as a problem (Warr 1983; Taschler Pollacek 1990; Surette 1998; Fishman 1980), how such issues change over time in terms of media language and application is less apparent. I refer not only to crime beats, using institutionalized "crime" news sources, such as the police, but extend the coverage as a matter of discourse. When something becomes a matter of discourse, it is not mere words that matter, but rather more of an orientation and perspective on the world. This perspective may be more directive and adapted by audience members with repetition.

One way to approach these questions is by tracking discourse, or following certain issues, words, themes, and frames over a period of time, across different issues and across different news media. Tracking discourse involves locating changes in usage, particularly with different topics and issues, over time. The focus is on the term *fear,* but we are interested in where it appears, with what meaning, and what kinds of themes derive from it. Fear is salient when we apply it to a situation as a relevant meaning. It involves an interaction between an individual and a situation, but it can drastically alter how we deal with that situation and ultimately the nature of the situation itself. Indeed, fear may be most important when it is implied as part of a general framework through which events are cast. When fear is used in this way, it becomes a matter of discourse (van Dijk 1988). As an institutional construction of knowledge that is reflexive of "territories, material objects, people, rules, formats, and technologies," the discourse stands for its own foundation and interpretive framework (Ericson and Haggerty 1997, 84). This is accomplished through the use of media logic, formats, and frames that shape mass media content (cf. McLuhan 1960; Couch 1984; Altheide and Snow 1991).

While noting frequencies in various categories over time, tracking discourse is a qualitative document analysis technique that applies an ethnographic approach to content analysis to new information bases that are accessible through computer technology, such as Nexis (Altheide 1996; cf. Wuthnow 1992; Grimshaw and Burke 1994; van Dijk, 1988). This method relies on analysis of numerous documents in order to become familiar with formats and emphases, while suggesting topics and themes. The initial manifest coding of fear and related topics then incorporates emergent coding and theoretical sampling in order to monitor changes in coverage and emphasis over time and across topics.

Involving twelve steps, tracking discourse entails initial familiarity with a sample of relevant documents before drafting a protocol, which is then checked for reliability and validity against additional documents. However, materials may also be enumerated and charted. For example, in studying fear, a protocol was constructed to obtain data about date, location, author, format, topic, sources, theme, emphasis, and grammatical use of *fear* (as noun, verb, adverb) in a sample of news media documents. Once collected, the materials were placed in an information base and analyzed qualitatively using Microsoft Word 97and NUD*IST, a qualitative data analysis program, as well as quantitatively with the spreadsheet program Excel. This approach was also used in a very ambitious extension of the project, a graduate seminar, in which students examined several uses of the words *fear* and *victim* in national as well as international news media (Altheide et al. 2001).

The approach blends interpretive, ethnographic, and ethnomethodological approaches with media logic, particularly studies of news organizational culture, information technology, and communication formats. In sum, several elements are involved:

- A comprehensive information base that is readily accessible
- A rationale for comparative searching over time
- Enumerating shifts and trends
- Examining denotative and connotative shifts
- Combining words into meaningful patterns and themes
- Expanding patterns into other mass media and popular culture

Informed by conceptual and theoretical insights about the organization of news work and especially the role of entertainment formats and the use of themes, tracking discourse moves from specific words (or groups of words) to themes and linkages of specific issues and topics over time. Through the use of Boolean searches (e.g., *"fear"* within 10 words of *crime"*) documents can be found and analyzed, search terms adjusted, and additional searches made of either random or "theoretical samples" (e.g., *"fear"* within 10 words of *schools* before the shootings at Columbine High School in 1998"). The capacity to examine numerous documents with specific conceptually informed search terms and logic provides a way of "exploring" documents, applying natural experimental research designs to the materials, as well as retrieving and analyzing individual documents qualitatively. Moreover, because the technology permits immediate access to an enormous amount of material, comparative exploration, conceptual refinement, data collection, and analysis can cover a longer time period than other technologies afforded.

I used this general approach to study fear and prepare the material for this book. On the one hand, this approach makes it possible to answer such questions as "is fear associated with different topics over time?" On the other hand, the latent and emergent approach is very conducive to problem frame analysis as well as systematic comparison of thematic emphases, which are discussed in Chapter 3. The general point to keep in mind is that over time an orientation to fear develops such that it becomes part of a broader framework.

My aim is to understand the themes and discourse that surround fear and make it salient for the presentation and discussion of certain issues to audiences. These queries hinge on issues about change, but systematic study of news content and themes over time can benefit from the recent development of information bases. Notwithstanding the Vanderbilt University Television News Index and Archive, systematic study of TV news of the kind described in the following will be very difficult until visual information bases become as accessible.

Most materials were obtained from the online information base LexisNexis (LN), the most comprehensive source for legal, news, government document, and public information available. Comparative data on the use of the word *fear* in headlines and bodies of news reports were obtained from a dozen major U.S. dailies: *Arizona Republic, Atlanta Journal, Boston Globe, Chicago Tribune, Dallas News, Kansas City Star, Los Angeles Times, New York Times, Seattle Times, St. Petersburg Post,* and the *Washington Post.* A drawback with LexisNexis is that newspaper holdings vary, so all papers were not comprehensively represented for the period of this study. For this reason, more materials were collected from the *Arizona Republic (AR), Los Angeles Times (LAT),* and *New York Times (NYT).* Issues of the *AR* were available in LN dating from 1993. During the project, more transcript materials from ABC News became available and were incorporated, as appropriate. This was particularly helpful in the latter stages of analysis about reports featuring *fear* and *victim.*

LN is an interactive information base that permits searching for key words, delimited in numerous ways, such as by segments (sections of the newspaper), date, or other criteria. Issues of the *AR* prior to 1993 were obtained from the CD-ROM information bases ARIZONA REPUBLIC and NEWSBANK. These sources provided some comparative materials that were adequate for tracking some changes over time, although the majority of the qualitative analysis focused on reports from 1994 to 1996.

The search process is made possible by sophisticated information bases, but they are not comparable in all respects, and some newspapers involve multiple counts. Three major search decisions were made. One was to search for *fear* in the segment body, rather than through the entire text. This means that articles having *fear* in the headline might have been excluded. However, these were picked up in subsequent searches for "headlines." Second, searches for *fear* within a certain number of words or topics were conducted in all text (and not just the segment body) in order to include all relevant materials. Third, articles were sought across sections on a dozen topics that have been useful in earlier analyses of media formats and emphases (e.g., violence, crime, community, neighborhood, schools, drugs, gangs, retribution, children, terrorism, environment, and immigrants). In addition to the preceding points, a theoretical sample of nearly two hundred articles from the *Arizona Republic* was analyzed, along with samples from several other media including the *Los Angeles Times, New York Times,* and *ABC News.*

I wanted to trace the "career" of fears, noting their origins and consequences. An initial overview of some of the material to follow can illustrate the results of this process and point to the questions that I try to answer in the rest of this book, the most important of which are these: why has fear increased so much in news coverage? and what relevance does this have to social life? Table 2.1 presents data on the frequency of fear in news reports. Data were obtained for the *Los Angeles Times* (*LAT*) and *ABC World News Tonight* (*ABC*) for 1985 and 1994 from the LexisNexis information base. The entire newspaper and newscast were included.

Two things stand out and can best be illustrated by referring to the *LAT* coverage. First, *fear* was used in more news reports in 1994 than in 1985. This is probably an understatement when one considers the dozens of talk shows on radio and TV that are devoted to fear and related problems in everyday life. There was a 64 percent increase in the use of the word *fear* in the *LAT.* (ABC's regular evening news programs—with an increase of 173 percent—were consistent with this shift.) Second, there was an even larger increase in use of the word *fear* in headlines—161 percent. These percentage increases suggest that a qualitative shift occurred in the meaning and use of the word *fear* in news reporting, particularly in headlines. But more information is needed to see how "thick" and "widespread" the shift in discourse may have been. In order to check on this, similar searches were conducted for other newspapers that had been on LexisNexis for several years (this is a drawback for long looks "back"

Table 2.1.   Fear in Los Angeles Times and ABC News Reports

	Fear in Text (N)			*Fear* in Headline (N)		
	1985	1994	Percent change	1985	1994	Percent change
LAT	4,519	7,415	+64%	271	707	+161%
	1990	1994	Percent change			
ABC	142	387	+173%			

Note: The *ABC* data are from the regular evening newscasts. However, between August 1989 and January 1, 1995, more than 2,700 references to *fear* appeared in all ABC news shows, which include special reports, *20/20, Nightline,* and other similar programs.

in time) as well as *ABC News* transcripts. Most important is the disproportionate way in which *fear* has moved into the headlines of newspapers and the leads of network news, at least at ABC. In most of the major newspapers examined, there was a larger increase in the appearance of the word *fear* in headlines than in regular reports.

Tracking discourse can be very helpful in documenting changes in frequency and use of important symbols; more details about this expanding use is presented in later chapters. However, it is the association of such symbols with other meanings that helps us understand cultural change and especially the way we talk about our lives. The major emphasis of qualitative document analysis is to capture the meanings, emphases, and themes of messages and to understand the organization and process of how they are presented (cf. Glaser and Strauss 1967). This requires that we include the widest range of relevant messages in our sample. However, it is difficult to know what this range is at the start of the research. It must emerge as the researcher inspects and reflects on some initial materials. A researcher would be advised to have an ideal about the kinds of materials to be included in the study. With this in mind, a reality check can then be made against practical limitations such as time, access, availability, and research funds. For example, a researcher might want to investigate the decision-making process of presidents and their advisors. Ideally, this might entail having direct access or even being a participant in behind-the-scenes conversations about certain issues discussed at the White House. However, this is not likely to be possible, so a mental search for alternative sources might ensue.

The general model is rather straightforward: When a word is repeated frequently and becomes associated routinely with certain other terms and images, a symbolic linkage is formed. For example, fear is a pervasive meaning and symbol in American culture. Frequently associated with crime, fear is more expansive, and our research shows that it covers a much wider symbolic territory than crime. Tracking discourse permits gauging how closely together similar words appear as part of thematic emphasis and discursive practices. Indeed, after repeated usage together, the initial meaning of a word, for instance *gang,* can incorporate *fear* as a connotation.

The rationale for this approach is that the meanings of two words are suggested by their proximity, their association. Indeed, over time, terms merge in public discourse. Consider the example of *violence* and *crime* in the following three sentences:

1. "An act of violence that might be regarded as a crime occurred Saturday night."
2. "A violent crime occurred Saturday night."
3. "A [crime (violence)] occurred Saturday night."

Both words are used as nouns in the first sentence, separate, but perhaps related. In the second sentence, *violent* is an adjective for *crime,* part of its description and meaning. But the third sentence shows what happens when terms are continually used together, often merging. This sentence suggests that crime has incorporated violence into its meaning, and the word *violent* need not be used. As the audience becomes more familiar with the meaning of the term and the context of its use, it becomes redundant to state "violent crime" since the mass-mediated experience suggests that "crime is violent" (despite research to the contrary, that is, most crimes are property crimes). Surette's (1998) lucid description of the "social ecology of crime" in entertainment media illustrates this point. Other work in cultural studies, deconstruction, and semiotics also demonstrates how this happens (Manning and Cullum-Swan 1994). Not only is the event distorted by this word coupling, but the audience's capacity to deal with it in different ways may be compromised. A similar coupling occurs when TV reports about crime and violence show individuals of certain racial and ethnic groups. Thus, TV visual formats can contribute to social definitions. Conversely, coupling may not occur between words and topics if they have traditionally been viewed as quite separate. This may be why it is difficult to convince people that domestic violence is real violence and also a crime. Until fairly recently, the notions of family, crime, and violence have seldom appeared within close proximity in routine news reports.

CONCLUSION

Tracking discourse is one approach to investigate the organization, structure, denotations, and connotations of mass media reports over time. It can be a helpful tool for understanding how cultural meanings have changed about fear and, more importantly, how fear has become a general perspective in public discussion and views of social life. Tracking discourse is a perspective as

much as a method that has been inspired by questions posed by cultural sociologists about changing social definitions. As such, it can be helpful to use in
systematically observing changes in public language and monitoring how social control terminology and perspectives (e.g., fear) are ordered and integrated
across various social issues.

Not only is our past newsworthy, but our futures can also be shaped by images of the past that are reified and acted upon. As more of our social reality
is informed by mass-mediated images shaped by entertainment formats, we
must understand the processes through which multiple realities are set forth,
a few supported, and others put aside as irrelevant. In the following chapters
I argue that a discourse of fear is one key area that has been cultivated for
decades by the entertainment media and formal agents of social control alike.
The latter are often the "sources" or "experts" for the former, but the routine
display of numerous statements, images, and anticipations of fear provides a
cultural and cognitive baseline of experience for more and more society members. A discourse of fear offers a conceptual elaboration for a process through
which numerous messages resonating with themes of fear can be circulated,
recast, and institutionally promoted through public policies, media reports,
popular culture, and cognitive frameworks. What happens to other discourses,
for example, those of trust, community, and fellowship, in the face of the discourse of fear is not my topic, but it is surely worthy of investigation.

3

The Problem Frame and the Production of Fear

Not since the Dark Ages has there been so much concern about organized forces of evil.

—Frank Furedi, *Culture of Fear*

This chapter addresses how the "problem frame" emerged and now exists as a "fear machine" in news production. Another aim is to clarify the learning process involving media logic and the role this plays in linking private and public perceptions and fears. The problem frame promotes *a discourse of fear that may be defined as the pervasive communication, symbolic awareness, and expectation that danger and risk are a central feature of the effective environment.* This is examined in more detail in Chapter 4.

Fear is pervasive in American society and has been produced through the interaction of commercial media, entertainment formats and programming, and the rise of the problem frame. Scholars have noted that this condition is also true of countries in Europe, particularly the United Kingdom (Furedi 1997). The mass media, in general, and especially the electronic news media, are part of a "problem-generating machine" geared to entertainment, voyeurism, and the "quick fix." Problems are routinely constructed through an ecology of communication, or emerging relationship between information technology, communication formats, and social activities (Altheide 1994; 1995). As noted earlier, victims are seemingly everywhere, laying claim to catalogs of abuse and social exploitation. But I argue that victims are part of the problem frame that promotes fear. Victimization (or victimhood) as a status relies on pervasive fear because this is what makes victimization meaningful and plausible to audiences. Chapter 4 examines how a discourse of fear gets promoted as a result of the problem frame and entertainment formats. A major theme transcending the specific issues produced by the postjournalism media is fear (Altheide and Snow 1991).

Fear did not just happen or emerge from the lack of community or uncertainty of life in the United States. Nor is it a mere outgrowth of a sense of lack of control over our lives. I believe that these considerations contribute to the support and credibility of fear for audiences, but far more is involved than this. I contend that the entertainment formats of mass media and popular culture, along with several generations' familiarity and assumptions about media use in everyday life, have contributed to this development.

C. Wright Mills (1959) was concerned that sociologists were blinded by limited theoretical perspectives that prevented them from seeing major social shifts, particularly the much heralded distinction he drew between personal "troubles" and "issues." For Mills, there was not enough attention paid to issues. He called for social scientists to cultivate a sociological imagination that "consists of the capacity to shift from one perspective to another, and in the process to build up an adequate view of a total society and its components" (Mills 1959). Such an imagination is essential if we are to understand the major paradox of our time: The "objective" reality of most citizens is that they are safer, healthier, living longer, and more secure in their environments than virtually any population in history, yet there is widespread public perception that risk and danger are everywhere, that we are not safe, and that the future is bleak. I contend that these perceptions are very much influenced by the mass media and popular culture in two senses: (1) the massive amount of negative and problem-oriented news reports that promote a sense of numerous crises and impending danger, if not doom, from many sources, including our physical environment (e.g., air, food, and water), our neighbors, children, major social institutions, disease, crime, and stress. There are numerous reports and scenarios about these problems presented to citizens on a daily basis. Often cast as "problems," these issues are produced by entertainment-oriented media machinery. (2) A second significant factor in the way the mass media and popular culture contribute to anxiety and public pessimism is through "media logic," or the assumptions, patterns, and format of the way that the various media operate. In general, this means that the "logic of media," particularly through electronic and visual technology, has infiltrated the rest of social life and has changed it (Altheide and Snow 1991). The most significant effect is that more of our everyday lives seem to mimic popular culture and television. A key element of this adopted format and underlying foundation of much of our daily experience is entertainment.

Following an overview of the relevance of media content and forms for perceptions of fear, an analysis of the "fear production" formats of news is presented. The impact of this format on the production of fear is illustrated with an analysis of how various topics have been treated as fear over a period of time.

FEAR IN THE COMMUNICATION ENVIRONMENT

The mass media and popular culture influence social life in different ways. Much of the media research has focused on media content (Comstock 1980).

Students of the mass media and popular culture agree on two basic social facts: (1) Popular culture includes a relatively large amount of information and images pertaining to fear, including crime and violence, and (2) audience members perceive social life as very dangerous. It is the relationship between these two social facts that remains unclear.

Publishers and editors love drama, evil, and suffering. They disapprove of its occurrence while celebrating its aftermath. For example, the cover of *Newsweek* magazine (May 21, 2001) featured the single word *Evil* in bright red, over a background of a muted figure with "devilish" eyes. The subtitle: "What Makes People Go Wrong?" This image appears in seemingly countless mass media reports featuring Satanism, the occult, demonology, extraterrestrial abductions, ritualistic mutilations of animals, visuals of individual crimes (e.g., "Columbine High School"), and international tragedies (e.g., Rwanda, Bosnia). It is not just the events that are covered, but rather the promotion of their commonality, "another one," "another tragedy tonight," dread, danger, and catastrophe. Indeed, as many have argued (Best 2001, 1995), the growth in cable TV, the Internet, and numerous "specialty publications" provides airtime that must be filled, ranging from TV news magazine shows to reality TV with real cops to Oprah Winfrey, Jerry Springer, and others. News shows employ formats that permit celebration of tragedies— always with an eye to "informing the public"—but with the emphasis on generating advertising revenue.

> The result is less a marketplace of competing ideas than a shopping mall of ideological boutiques, each willing to cater to walk-ins, but each still counting on the business of committed, repeat customers from its homogenous target market. (Best 2001, 7)

A major assumption is that the communication process and content are inexorably joined, with one always having implications for the other. In this sense, "new knowledge" and information is always connected to a stock of knowledge and symbolic interpretation. I suggest that many news reports are produced through a process that reflects entertainment considerations and formats, which, in turn, have promoted the problem frame, which then helps frame fear as a dominant discourse in news reports.

Formats, Frames, and Fear

Formats and frames shape mass media content (Altheide 1995; Altheide and Snow 1991; Couch 1984; McLuhan 1960). Communication and media formats enable us to recognize various frames giving a general definition of what is before us. Studies of media forms and formats have complemented findings from studies of media content while also giving them a conceptual foundation in the practices of media agents. Seeking to clarify the process by which media messages of violence and fear are presented, this approach essentially asks *how* events and issues are packaged and presented to audience members who may interpret the messages in a variety of ways.

The focus on the processes, practices, and perspectives of news workers has clarified how an organized production process shapes news reports, as well as other entertainment-oriented programs (Altheide 1976; Fishman 1980; Gitlin 1980; Graber 1984; Tuchman 1978). A key part of this process is the development and use of *formats,* or the way in which selecting, organizing, and presenting information shapes audience assumptions and preferences (Altheide 1985; Altheide and Snow 1991; Ericson, Baranek, and Chan 1989; Meyrowitz 1985; Schlesinger, Murdock, and Elliott 1983). The relevance for audiences and social activities turns on the way such formats come to be learned, taken for granted, and expected. For example, when people interact with certain formats over a long period of time, they expect and assume that events and issues will have a certain look, a "proper media look" (Altheide and Snow 1991).

Additional work has shown that the media logic underlying the use of formats has been acquired and widely adapted by various organizations and state agencies that serve as major news sources for the news media. I noted in Chapter 2 that as news organizations and the parties they cover share similar views and approaches to what is newsworthy, the line between the journalist and the event essentially disappears. In this way, private and public concerns have been joined through information technology (IT) and mass media formats. This collapsing of symbolic boundaries has produced a hybrid array of messages and views of social reality that has been delineated as a postjournalism news media. As McDonald (1994) provocatively notes:

> Formats are complex and multidimensional. They include a constellation of people, activities, and the implements important to them, as well as the kinds of discourses and relations that result. . . . The formats of technology and power are intimately connected because formats structure social fields of behavior—the possibilities for human perception and relationships. These techno-formats blur and redefine the boundaries between public and private self in the learning process. (538)

This is especially true when it comes to news. Certain news forms have been developed as packages, or frames, for transforming some experience into reports that will be recognized and accepted by the audience as news (Ericson et al. 1989). Tracing the emergence of new forms illuminates how social perspectives and definitions are reflexively joined to news practices.

My use of *framing* incorporates several dimensions (Altheide 1996, 28*ff.*). Frame, theme, and discourse are also related to *communication formats,* which, in the case of mass media, refer to the selection, organization, and presentation of information. Formats pertain to the underlying organization and assumptions of time (temporal flow, rhythm), space (place and visual editing), and manner (style) of experience (Snow 1983). Formats basically are what make our familiar experiences familiar and recognizable; that is, we can quickly tell the difference between, say, a TV newscast, a sitcom, and a talk show.

Frames are the focus, a parameter or boundary, for discussing a particular event. Frames focus on what will be discussed, how it will be discussed, and, above all, how it will not be discussed. It is helpful to think about frames as very broad thematic emphases or definitions of a report, like the border around a picture that separates it from the wall and from other possibilities (Altheide 1976; Berg 1989; Epstein 1973; Fishman 1980; Zhondang and Kosiki 1993). An example is treating illegal drug use as a public health issue as opposed to a criminal justice issue. These are two different frames that entail a way of discussing the problem, or the kind of discourse that will follow. Themes are more basically tied to the format used by journalists who have a short time to "tell a story" that the audience can "recognize," "that they have probably heard before," and moreover, to get specific information from sources that can be tied to this. That's where sources of information get linked to news media—they not only have the information, but they have learned to put it together in ways that are compatible with the different media formats. The kinds of reports identified by Iyengar (1991) as "episodic"—or focusing on individual circumstances—are conceptually part of themes if we view such reports as angles to illustrate well-established thematic messages.

Our lives are mediated increasingly in postindustrial societies where work and play involve symbols and symbolic manipulations. Mass audiences are connected via information technology (especially TV) to common issues and problems. We learn about these in rather brief periods of time, usually during several weeks. Issues and problems that we learn about are constantly changing with an effective life (agenda) span of two weeks to six months. As Iyengar and Kinder (1987) note, "Our studies show specifically that television news powerfully influences which problems viewers regard as the nation's most serious" (4). More of our daily activities are symbolic, often involving access to some electronic media or working to comply with "document requirements" that will be processed electronically (Altheide and Snow 1991; Carey 1989; Couch 1984; Meyrowitz 1985). What we call things, the themes and discourse we employ, and how we frame and allude to experience is crucial for what we take for granted and assume to be true. I suggest that fear has become a more pervasive component of American life because of the problem frame that dominates many media messages. This frame is tied to the entertainment format that now dominates news production.

THE ENTERTAINMENT PERSPECTIVE

Changes in information technology and communication formats have influenced the way we think about social problems and issues. The entertainment format of news is key to the rise of the problem frame. The entertainment

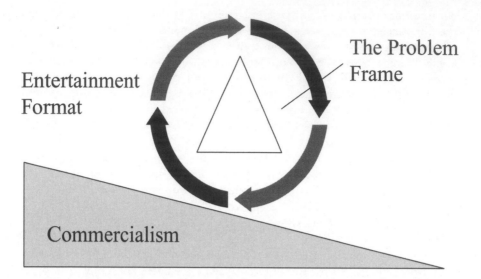

Figure 3.1   The Problem Frame in Context.

emphasis contains elements of action noted by Erving Goffman and others but clarified by Robert P. Snow (1983) in his work on the rise of "media culture." First, there is an absence of the ordinary; second is the openness of an adventure, outside the boundaries of routine behavior; third, the audience member is willing to suspend disbelief. In addition, while the exact outcome may be in doubt, there is a clear and unambiguous point at which it will be resolved. Packaging such emphases within formats that are visual, brief, action-oriented, and dramatic produces an exciting and familiar tempo to news audiences.

The news media's use of formats treating complex events as problems is quite consistent with entertainment. Figure 3.1 illustrates how the driving force of commercialism promotes the entertainment format, through which the problem frame has emerged. The point is that the distinction between news and nonnews has been bridged by entertainment criteria that characterize the postjournalism era (Altheide and Snow 1991).

Previous work suggests that entertainment programs are becoming more like news programs as standard formats mold programming for a culture geared to a media logic that subtly folds TV criteria, discourse, and perspectives into everyday life (Altheide 1995). Indeed, reality TV celebrates the stereotypes and images of news reports about crime and fear (Fishman and Cavender 1998). Not surprisingly, a majority of American viewers thought that an entertainment program, *America's Most Wanted,* featuring dramatic reenactments of brutal crimes, was a news show. Another example is the way in which news coverage foreshadows future TV movies. In this way, TV news becomes a kind of preview or advertisement for coming attractions. News as a form of knowledge is transformed through news as entertainment into news as advertising. The Waco debacle that ended in April 1993 is a good illustration of news as advertising, in which a movie was in production before the events unfolded. Thus, the time period between the "real" event and its prime-time airing as a TV movie has been reduced to matter of weeks, or, in some cases, days.

The Problem Frame as Entertainment

The problem frame is an important innovation that satisfies the entertainment dimension of news. The problem frame promotes fear on a routine basis, and this in turn promotes victimization as a widely viewed and read status. The problem frame is an organizational solution to a practical problem: How can we make real problems seem interesting? Or, how can we produce reports compatible with entertainment formats?

The major impact has been on the way organizations produce news as a commodity to sell. The mass media and especially the news business have contributed to the emergence of a highly rationalized problem frame that in turn generates reports about fear. The relationship between everyday life events, the problem frame, and a mass-mediated accumulation of fear experienced by audience members is illustrated in Figure 3.2. A key strategy to develop audience identification and interaction with the message is to provide new information. For example, "here's what's happening now," within a familiar context of meaning (e.g., "another killing in the valley today").

The problem frame is a secular alternative to the morality play. I examine this in more detail later. Its characteristics include the following:

- Narrative structure
- Universal moral meanings
- Specific time and place
- Unambiguous content
- Focus on disorder
- Cultural resonance

Built on a narrative structure that adds story-like coherence, with a beginning, middle, and end, the problem frame is both universal and specific, abstract and real. For entertainment and audience identification purposes, the closer the reader/listener/viewer is to the actual event, the more salient the report. Local news reports stress the problem frame, particularly crime reports, far more than national or network news. Of course, following many local re-

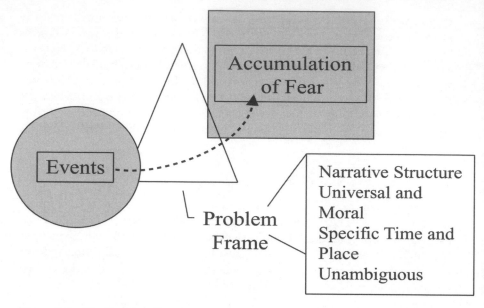

Figure 3.2   The Problem Frame.

ports constructed on the problem frame, national and network news need only refer to one or two examples in making general points about fear and danger.

The problem frame combines the universal and nonsituational logic and moral meanings of a morality play (Unsworth 1995) with the temporal and spatial parameters of a news report—something happened involving an actual person in an actual location (e.g., street address). Unlike a morality play, in which the characters are abstractions facing death and damnation, news reports focus on actual people and events, packaging the entire narrative as realistic. Complex and often ambiguous events and concerns are symbolically mined for moral truths and understandings presumed to be held by the audience, while the repeated presentations of similar scenarios "teaches" the audience about the nature and causes of disorder (Ericson et al. 1989). It is immaterial whether the audience has other experiences with crime or related problems; the result-ing messages both reinforce certain experiences and perceptions and provide a meaning about the pervasiveness of fear. This component of media logic per-vades the industrial world as part of the entertainment format. Furedi (1997) observes that the Queen of England commissioned a memorial to the "suffer-ing of the unknown victim":

> This gesture towards the spirit of the unknown victim by the British royal family is very much in keeping with the promotion of the culture of victimhood

on both sides of the Atlantic. In today's world, it is evident that victimhood and suffering represent a moral claim on society. [Princess Diana's BBC interview established that] [h]er claim was that her suffering made her a better person— entitling her to act as an ambassador on behalf of the British people. (173)

Mass-mediated problems are oriented to be everyone's problems, whether as direct or potential experience or as sympathetic audience members. The prevailing media logic is to establish a relationship between the viewer and the format and the story form. Increasingly, viewers are even asked to vote on an issue or to contribute funds to a cause, a tragic illness, to defer funeral expenses, and so forth. More typically, the viewer is invited to tune in later, read more about it, or even consult a Web page for more information. These expanding intra- and intermedia connections share commercial interest in getting viewers involved.

The majority of topics, problems, and issues presented as news involves those framed as problems. Suffering, misfortune, distress, and inconvenience are the stuff of contemporary news, but they are not "the problem." The problem characteristics are part of a format organized around a narrative that begins with a general conclusion that something is wrong, and the media know what it is. Those aspects of a complex situation that are presumably familiar and uncontested (e.g., the seven deadly sins, "evil causes evil," "corrupt officials") are selected for illustration of the underlying truth containing the correction. While historians suggest that medieval morality plays viewed solutions in terms of divine redemption (e.g., mercy, justice, temperance, and truth), the kicker to most reports framed as problems involves the state/government. Unlike morality plays in which the audience is reminded of eternal threats and truths, the problem frame features everyday life filled with problem-generating fear.

In sum, the problem frame is reflexive of media formats, especially TV, but is easily adjusted to oral and linear media as well. The problem frame incorporates a particular temporal/spatial relationship (here or close by and now) to make it relevant to the audience. A story about fear is produced and packaged in a process that formulates social complexities as simplistic problems. The cumulative effect is to produce a discourse of fear that then becomes a resource on which the audience may draw when interpreting subsequent reports. The problem frame, then, implies the following:

- Something exists that is undesirable.
- Many people are affected by this problem (it is relevant).
- Unambiguous aspects or parts are easily identified.
- It can be changed or "fixed."
- There is a mechanism or procedure for fixing the problem.
- The change or repair agent and process is known (usually the government).

The problem frame is a feature of information technology (IT), news media formats, and a pervasive media-source relationship that fuels rocket-like expansion of sources attempting to transform misery, cruelty, brutality, and so on into a particular kind of problem. The driving force of the news coverage, however, can actually distort understanding of the issues, leading politicians, funding agencies, academic disciplines, and even agency personnel who actually deal with the alleged problem to make adjustments that are counterproductive and make matters much worse.

The clear narrative structure of an event stressing an unambiguous problem may be contrasted with an underlying ambiguity in everyday life, especially complex circumstances that are highly contingent. An awareness of the underlying ambiguity of actual social situations is essential to developing pragmatic awareness of what can be done, but ambiguity is not very entertaining. Morality plays are built on the audience's familiarity with narratives that spell out simple and clear truths.

As these morality plays—grounded in media logic—become more widespread and shared, they are becoming part of everyone's basic common sense and awareness of what everyone who is competent knows. Media logic, formats, and the ability to follow news reports presented with machine-gun rapidity (and occasionally sound effects) are now part of our cultural capital: "'Cultural capital' refers to the knowledge, skills, habits, values, and tastes that are acquired in the course of socialization, and which can be turned to one's advantage in particular social settings" (Bourdieu 1977). The formats and recurring reports generated through these frameworks, including fear, are also becoming part of our taken-for-granted cultural capital. This process is the essential foundation for a cumulative impact of fear reports in popular culture and the mass media on perceptions of self, others, and our future. With repetition and packaging as just part of news and information, the language, semantics, syntax, and, above all, problem frame promoting fear simply is to be taken for granted, but used cumulatively to view and interpret other experiences. My suggestion is that news of crime influences our perceptions of fear more generally because the same process and format is used. It doesn't matter, for all practical purposes, whether the report is about terrorism, murder, theft, a school shooting, traffic problems, water pollution, or a missing child who actually just went to a classmate's house.

The problem frame and its logic are becoming critical components of an aware citizen's store of knowledge, including more sophisticated awareness of formats involving split screens, editing techniques, links between TV newscasts and Web pages, familiarity with shorthand addresses (for instance, DPS for Department of Public Safety), news Web pages (such as AZ360.com), and the syntax of one story's link to another—usually disconnected. This sophistication makes it possible to follow a newscast's coverage of the world in 60 seconds, with 3 to 5 seconds per report, moving across Rwanda, O. J. Simpson, the president, a flood in India, the latest cocaine bust, and so forth.

One example is the way news coverage of child neglect and abuse can systematically distort the situation while at the same time provide entertainment. There are several dimensions. From the standpoint of missing children, research has shown that previous reports erroneously claiming that hundreds of thousands of children were abducted and brutalized by "strangers" fundamentally distorted the multiple dimensions of the issue, including parental abductions and runaways (Best and Horiuchi 1985; Fritz and Altheide 1987). Focusing on "stranger kidnappings," of which there are relatively few each year (e.g., 67 in 1983), sparked an unprecedented multimedia barrage of missing child photos and pleas on milk cartons, billboards, network news shows, in mass mailings, and of course in numerous movies and documentaries. The children of America were reportedly under siege. Such action fueled legislation, policy changes, increased criminal sanctions, and millions of dollars of budget allocations. Ignoring the far more numerous runaway and "throwaway" children left most cities with paltry resources to help and protect the several hundred thousand children "on the road."

Another dimension of child mistreatment cast as a coherent problem involves child welfare agencies and parental mistreatment of children, particularly those cases that result in the death of a child. Michael Shapiro (1996) describes this dimension:

> The death of a child provokes rage, a reasonable response. . . . Have people paid by the state to protect that child failed? We then publish or air those people's names, alongside accusations by the mayor or the governor or a legislator. . . . The case worker is suspended. The punishment offers some satisfaction to the public, and to the journalist. . . . But this approximation of a solution— a solution propelled in good measure by the force of the coverage—sets into motion an entirely new set of problems, and with it a different sort of story. . . . The story now becomes one of a "system" that is "overburdened" with all the new children coming in. . . . Then comes a final state of coverage: the search for The Answer . . . but in truth the experts haven't a clue because there is no answer that is applicable to all the children in the care of the state, let alone one that fits into a headline, or a lead, or a quote of manageable length. (Shapiro 1996, 46)

As this story, like many involving problems, moves into a discourse of blame, the journalists' wit and camera frames mash a multidimensional concern into convenient entertaining news formats. The difficulty is that most children and parents who need assistance are not at all typical of parents who kill their children. It is these people Shapiro (1996) describes as the true story of child welfare, the "screw ups," the majority of cases (46). These are parents who lack some basic and consistent competence to provide what is necessary all of the time, but who nevertheless love their children, and, in most cases, the children love them. Shapiro (1996) continues:

> The stories of martyred children have little to do with the everyday grind of parents, their children, and the impossibly malfunctioning bureaucracy that is supposed to make sure those children are safe. . . . When the death of a child becomes the context in which all subsequent child welfare stories get reported and written, then all the failing parents become the homicidal parent and all their children are in grave peril. (46)

The problem frame is the staple of news that exists within its own temporal parameter: It is most compatible with topics and problems that are "new," "unique," even if they are presented in a very familiar way. Previously, people did not so much learn about problems through abstract symbols as much as they experienced them directly or indirectly through situations or through the accounts of friends. This experience often involved force or experiencing the "obdurate character" of an event or some action. Life was hard and there were many difficulties; and these were discussed as nasty and difficult features of life. But the problem discourse and frame, with a structure, organization, cause, and likely solution, were much simpler then than today.

Today, however, IT collapses, greatly condenses, and even reorders the temporal nature of problems and awareness. Problems and issues carry the signature of a highly accelerated problem process, particularly the role of symbols and information as key features of experience and knowledge of the effective environment. IT carries experience-as-information to mass audiences and more recently in real time as an event unfolds (e.g., the CIA advised the White House to turn on Cable News Network to see reports about SCUD missile launches during the Gulf War).

News formulae emerged with the advent of commercial news and the adaptation of entertainment formats to the news business in order to attract audiences. Such formulae, routines, and techniques were tied to IT and the medium of selecting, organizing, and presenting information as news. At first, these were primarily used by news workers, but in the last several decades news sources—usually those associated with formal organizations, but also interest groups who have become "organized" on a rational basis—have incorporated such formulae and formats (Ericson, Baranek, and Chan 1991). These organizations and groups are the sources of information on which news organizations trade.

The spokespeople, news organizations, and increasingly the audience(s) are tied together through a shared discourse contained in the news formats, which are, in turn, contingent on IT. Figure 3.3 shows how the world of experience is transformed into nonproblems, problems, and solutions.

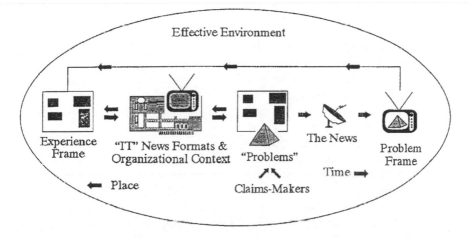

Figure 3.3   Information Technology, News Formats, and the Problem Frame.

Throughout most of human history, people have relied on the "experience frame," which was not mediated by complex IT and news formats until quite recently. The problem frame has been developed and refined with the rise of mass audiences, mass-marketing techniques, and application and refinement of the entertainment formats for sitcoms and news alike. As the process diagram suggests, the problem is routinely applied to various experiences by claims makers espousing problems. As suggested by the example of the news coverage of child welfare, the problem frame is then incorporated into the news broadcast to mass audiences, that selectively interpret the messages within their own experience frames (back to the start). The impact is greater the more the audiences' total stock of knowledge about the particular topic has been derived from other mass media reports also incorporating the problem frame.

The example of neglected children illustrates how news audiences have become so familiar with the problem frame that the elements noted previously do not have to be spelled out by the writer or broadcaster; the audience member applies the perspective to the story and in this sense helps complete it. When certain problems can be cast within TV formats as arenas for disputes, disagreements, or conflicts and struggle, and when these can be visually illustrated, one has the formula for good entertainment, high audience ratings, constant awareness of problems, and a sense of a very troubled world. Indeed, so intertwined is the problem frame with social problems in general that media coverage has become part of the process of turning any concern into a problem or social issue (Surette 1998). The way in which claims makers promote their concerns within the problem frame is suggested by the media-problem process:

1. There is something not liked; people see it as a problem (the claims-making process).
2. The problem orientation is already established for the mass audience, so we fit the concern to that problem orientation.
3. It must compete with other problems and their proponents seeking news legitimacy and coverage.
4. It is either a new problem or a different version (angle) of a previously established problem or issue.
5. Communicating or broadcasting the problem character of the topic is part of the solution but also creates opportunities for those "responsible" for the solution to monitor the problem, as well as be monitored, followed up, and essentially, linked to the problem character of the topic.
6. Mass media publication via news entertainment formats provides information about the topic, the linkages to those responsible, and similar items of concern or new problems.
7. Return to step 1.

FRAMING FEAR

Entertainment problem formats have contributed to the reporting of and fascination with fear. The explicit use of the word *fear* and its multiple derivatives and meanings pervade public discourse. As noted previously, this occurs as part of the routine news process as claims makers learn to cast their statements in a context of fear relationships. The media-problem perspective is quickly understood and resonates with audiences steeped in previous media experiences because they know what a media problem is (Best 1995; Ericson et al. 1989).

The interaction and shared meanings of news workers who follow the entertainment format and audience members who "experience" the world through these mass media lenses promote sufficient communication to achieve the news organization's goals of grabbing the audience while also enabling audience members to be informed enough to exchange views with peers. Shared knowledge about the social world in a mass-mediated society tends to be about bad news. Nearly two-thirds of a national sample talked with friends and neighbors about crime several times a month (General Social Survey, National Opinion Research Center 1994).

AN OVERVIEW OF FEAR

Every society teaches its members many things, including what to worry about (e.g., money, status, sin/salvation, personal relationships, health, crime, or cellulite). There are several aspects of this process that should be stressed before further discussion of the data. First, the target of fear is socially constructed—but this does not mean it is not perceived as real and does not have consequences. Second, fear is built on a foundation of social interaction and communication. Currently, this includes mass communication as part of our effective environment within an ecology of communication (Altheide 1995). Third, there are many individual fears, of course, but my concern is with those that are reportedly held in common.

People do not just read and hear about fear, but they are more familiar with it as a characteristic attributed to their effective environments. Earlier we discussed how information technology and media formats collapse topics, problems, and procedures so that when we are aware of doing one thing, we are often addressing several others. Cultural meanings also change as they become more taken for granted and folded or collapsed into other symbols and contexts of use. For example, when "violence" collapses into "anger," then certain emotions are more directly played out in certain behavior. Likewise with fear.

I suggest that the expanded use of *fear* is collapsing important symbolic meanings and boundaries. More and more topics pass through the problem frame and have "fear in common." The signifier (a topic) and signified (fear) become joined within a context (Manning 1987). The context here is a news report oriented to the problem frame. Public discourse changes when news reports associate fear with certain issues (e.g., crime and drugs). To illustrate, as fear is more closely connected with specific topics, the topic becomes more fearful as a matter of public discourse. Accordingly, if fear is becoming more closely associated with certain topics, this should be apparent in news media reports, and changes in symbolic (word) proximity should be apparent over time.

Private life is closer to public concerns and issues than ever before. This is because both wear the style of popular culture. And this looks like fear. Life is problematic and uncertain, but in the postindustrial United States it is the heightened expectations of predictability and order at a time when many institutional arrangements are in flux (some would say unraveling) that seems to be the culprit. If Jack Katz (1987) is correct that "the experience of reading crime news induces the reader into a perspective useful for taking a stand on existential moral dilemmas" (71), then personal concerns are being perceived as more frightening. Fear provides a common level for the cascading confluence of reports in certain formats that are good for entertaining news, social control agencies, aspiring claims makers seeking public legitimacy, and the transformation of a putative trouble into an issue.

Indeed, it makes good sociological sense to suggest that we have a "problem machine" in much of the mass media. TV news formats favoring short, dramatic, conflicting, visually exciting reports are ripe for treating events and circumstances as problems. Thus, the problem frame has been developed rather

rapidly as a feature of news formats, and we are becoming increasingly familiar with them both. What we take for granted has changed; problems, risks,
and even damage or injury are no longer routine, but they are expected nevertheless. It is the anticipated exception and the societal affirmation of this
exception that we celebrate through countless news reports joining us to
politicians. Fear provides politicians with agendas, dramatic scripts, and news
media pronouncements of remedies to "make us safe" (Gusfield 1989). The social landscape is littered with failed programs and reactive public policies proclaiming the litany of deliverance from an effective environment defined by
fear. One example is a mayoral campaign in Los Angeles in 2001 between An-
tonio Villaraigosa, and the victor, James Hahn. This campaign, like most po-
litical-media spectacles, invoked standard fear frames to persuade voters. Hahn
depicted his opponent as being "soft on crime." One account of the election
states:

> But for all his efforts to present himself as the face of the future, he [Vil-
> laraigosa] fell victim to campaign tactics rooted in the past . . . a task made eas-
> ier by Villaraigosa's 1996 letter requesting presidential clemency for a convicted
> drug dealer. With an ad featuring the letter, a crack-cocaine pipe and a dark por-
> trait of Villaraigosa, Hahn made his rival appear sinister. The image was so
> murky that . . . it seemed an intentional effort to make the Mexican-American
> swarthier, to evoke [as Villaraigosa's team saw it] nebulous yet potent fears of
> dusky drug-addled immigrants menacing civilized society. (Close 2001, 32)

Carried with the message of fear are images and targets of what and who is
to be feared. Attached to these ideal types of villains and threats are formal
agents of social control associated with the available solutions to these problems. We see them occupying the same space in our newspapers and on our
TV screens. Claims makers seeking to promote a trouble into an issue turn to
the news media for help, often wrapping their concerns in an attractive fear
package. Thus, the problem frame reproduces itself.

I have suggested that an ecology of communication has contributed to the
construction and routine use of a problem frame and expansion of fear in public discourse. Researchers are invited to explore the problem frame as well as
clarify its dimensions and articulate its relevance to everyday life. As the mass
media continue to be a major window for shaping, viewing, and addressing
concerns, careful work is required to clarify the process, mapping, and career
of particular issues and problems. Little change is likely without an awareness
of the current meta communication, including current news formats celebrating crime and other constructs of the problem frame. Indeed, the modest suggestions offered here could contribute to a renewed interest in journalistic
education and reform and, hopefully, may promote a dialogue that seldom occurs between communication scholars and practitioners. Journalistic education and awareness offers some hope for reflection, particularly if mistakes can

be recognized and if journalists undertake a fundamental shift to avoid format recycling. As Shapiro noted in his reflections about journalistic distortions of child welfare:

> To cover child welfare properly is to set aside your instinct as a journalist, the urge to find an overarching answer, and your instinct as a person, the attempt to save the innocents, and to accept a more realistic goal—that of raising a series of increasingly difficult questions . . . the right questions can move public debate closer to the messy and individual realities of these families. (Shapiro 1996, 47)

There is another dimension of fear in news reports. Fear is usually associated with specific problems that have been processed through the problem frame and entertainment perspective. If the problem frame is relevant in news coverage, then we might expect that a key symbolic part (e.g., fear) would become associated with topics over time, but also that it may move or travel from one topic to another. We look at this process in Chapter 4.

CONCLUSION

Everyday life is increasingly mediated by information technology as we experience events in an ecology of communication. Information technology and its varied communication formats (media logic) are part of our effective environment that we become accustomed to and take for granted (Pfuhl and Henry 1993). And just as humans in new environments learn to behave differently and soon do it routinely, postmodern media users learn to adjust to new information technology and communication formats, soon taking them for granted.

Media materials contribute to public perceptions, albeit in less than precise ways, whether as "priming" (Iyengar and Kinder 1987), agenda setting, or the shaping of public discourse through news formats. It is all part of our culture, and the task is to continue to map conceptually the symbolic connections we make between our everyday lives, popular culture, information technology, and the news of the day.

The cultural changes promoting the problem frame and the generation of fear are organizational and informational and increasingly electronic. Organizations have adopted electronic media formats that promote an entertainment orientation to problems and their solutions. It is a methodological challenge to investigate for four reasons: First, there has not been a strong theoretical interest in the ways in which the mass media and popular culture have altered the communication of meanings in social life; second, it is important to understand how organizational practices and messages incorporate these entertainment formats; third, until recently, the information produced by these new formats was not easily studied because of limited computer hardware and software that allowed for qualitative and quantitative analysis. A fourth factor is a research design such as "tracking discourse" that would provide a comparative rationale for a systematic study of changes in cultural symbol systems over time. Much of what has been examined in this chapter is of necessity trend and change oriented. Methodological conceptions such as tracking discourse and others (Hertog and Fan 1995) follow from an awareness of the shifting symbolic meanings and reconfigurations I have suggested. These changes cannot be understood one document at a time, or even with a few hundred documents; thousands of documents over several years are essential. But these methodological approaches are very difficult to pursue without the use of electronic processing tools. Media logic cannot be empirically captured without access to research aids compatible with that logic. Resources like LexisNexis, for example, are becoming more widely available and used by social scientists in ways that permit questions to be asked that previously could not be answered. However, careful scrutiny of theoretically sampled documents must be combined with additional resources.

News perspectives and practices, including the organizational context and use of entertainment formats, promote the problem frame that in turn produces narratives of fear. Fear is more visible and routine in public discourse than it was a decade ago. Perceptions of safety, security, and relative ease of everyday circumstances are not uniform throughout American society. Many people perceive the world as very problematic, dangerous, and demanding of extreme measures for protection. Indeed, one of the few things Americans seem to share is the popular culture that celebrates danger and fear as entertainment organized with canned formats delivered through an expansive and invasive information technology.

4

The Discourse of Fear

No passion so effectually robs the mind of all its powers of acting and reasoning as fear.

—Edmund Burke
The Origin of Our Ideas of the Sublime and Beautiful

It is not easy to make people afraid. The word *fear* shows up in a lot of news reports and popular culture. I do not think that this is part of a natural general trend, nor do I think that it is an accident or inconsequential. Fear is the groundwork for the emergence of victimization and the victim identity that is now quite commonplace. My argument is that fear has been transformed by an entertainment-oriented popular culture, including news organizations as well as public agencies and officials who have a stake in fear and who serve as news sources for the insatiable news-programming market for entertainment. And it is fear that makes for good entertainment.

This chapter argues that fear has undergone a profound shift from a time when fear was seen in terms of specific instances or events—parallel fear—to a time more common today: Fear is cast as pervasive, as part of the context of specific acts; I refer to this as *nonparallel* fear. This form of fear is the essence of what I call the discourse of fear. In this chapter, the movement from the parallel use of fear (in the 1980s) to nonparallel use of fear (in the 1990s) is explained. The trends are emphasized to show how public discourse reflects this shift.

More and more scholars acknowledge the fact that fear and entertainment are joined, albeit in complex ways. I wish to emphasize how the entertainment media have aimed a fear machine (discussed in Chapter 3) at audiences who have come to expect entertainment.

Moreover, claims makers and news sources use the concerns about safety and even death to promote the "story" and make the typical news reports about crime even more interesting and enrapturing. My approach to examining fear emphasizes its use and place in culture as indicated by cultural documents such as news reports, the topics and issues with which it is aligned (e.g., crime), and the social effects on decisionmakers and other audiences. One of the last points that I make in this chapter is that fear is now "fun" and people "play" with it, albeit in serious ways and often with deadly consequences.

Nearly everyone knows how to read the news of the day. But using news as a resource for everyday life is different from treating it as a topic with which to understand how social reality is ordered, maintained, and repaired. On the one hand, news reports as resources serve to set the emotional tones for the rhythms of life and to act as reminders of ideals of order and the disorder threatening peaceful neighborhoods and the cosmologies of normal order. On the other hand, news reports as topics provide a window into organizational frameworks of reality maintenance and their relevance to broader societal definitions of situations, courses of action, and assessments of a lifeworld. News reports, as a feature of popular culture, become intertwined in everyday life, political speeches, and other entertainment forms such as movies. This chapter reports on the way fear is being used to provide entertaining news that also benefits formal agents of social control and promotes distrust among the audience. The way the production of entertaining news shapes the content of news can be clarified by looking at the role and use of fear over time and across social issues. When fear is the prevailing framework for looking at social issues, other competing frames and discourses lose out.

When President Franklin Roosevelt said, in the context of the Great Depression, "Let me assert my firm belief that the only thing we have to fear is fear itself," he had not envisioned American news media. Roosevelt cautioned against fear; today fear is embraced and constitutes a major public discourse through which numerous problems and issues are framed. A discourse of fear may be defined as the pervasive form of communication, symbolic awareness, and expectation that danger and risk are a central feature of the effective environment or the physical and symbolic environments as people define and experience them in everyday life (Pfuhl and Henry 1993, 53).

The prevalence of fear in public discourse can contribute to stances and reactive social policies that promote state control and surveillance. As noted above, fear is a key element of creating "the risk society," organized around communication oriented to policing, control, and prevention of risks (Ericson and Haggerty 1997; Staples 1997). A constitutive feature of this emerging order is a blanket reminder of fear. "Fear ends up proving itself, as new risk communication and management systems proliferate" (Ericson and Haggerty 1997, 6). While fear is commonly associated with crime, I suggest that fear provides a discursive framework of expectation and meaning within which crime and related "problems" are expressed. Media practices and major news sources (e.g., law enforcement agencies) have cooperatively produced an organizational machine, fueled by entertainment and selective use of news sources, that simultaneously connects people to their effective environments even as it generates entertainment-oriented profits (Altheide 1997). As one law enforcement official stated about Arizona's televised crime stoppers dramatizations, "If you can have a little entertainment and get your man, too, that's great." This discourse resonates through public information and is becoming a part of what a mass society holds in common: We increasingly share understandings about what to fear and how to avoid it. The consequences are felt in numerous ways but particularly in accelerated negative perceptions about public order (e.g., the streets are not safe, strangers are dangerous, the state must provide more control and surveillance). In commenting on everyday life features of mass society, Stanford M. Lyman (1997) observes, "Such a fearful disunity undermines the general conditions of trust and order, encouraging intrigues, deceptions and interactions that are strategic rather than spontaneous" (294).

My approach tracks the rise of fear in selected news media in order to demonstrate its expanded use, on the one hand, and to show how a discourse of fear moves across topics over time, on the other hand. *Mapping* refers to where the word and related references to fear occur throughout news reports. *Tracking discourse* (Chapter 2) involves locating changes in usage, particularly with different topics and issues, over time. The focus is on the term *fear*, but we are also interested in where it appears, with what meaning, and the themes derived from it. Fear is salient when we apply it to a situation as a relevant meaning. It involves an interaction between an individual and a situation, but it can drastically alter how we deal with that situation and, ultimately, the nature of the situation itself. Indeed, fear may be most important when it is implied as part of a general framework through which events are cast. When fear is used in this way, it becomes a matter of discourse (van Dijk 1988). As an institutional construction of knowledge that is reflexive of "territories, material objects, people, rules, formats, and technologies," the discourse stands for its own foundation and interpretive framework (Ericson and Haggerty 1997, 84). My approach is consistent with important contributions by language analysts and semiotic authorities on the underlying structure of language and the cultural understandings that are encoded. As one authority notes:

> News values, then, are to be regarded as intersubjective mental categories. In determining the significance of events, the papers and their readers make reference, explicit or more usually implicit, to what are called, in cognitive psychology and in semantics, "frames," "paradigms," "stereotypes," "schemata" and "general propositions." . . . A stereotype is a socially constructed mental pigeonhole into which events and individuals can be sorted, thereby making such events and individuals comprehensible. . . . Now, it is of fundamental importance to realize that stereotypes are *creative*: they are categories which we project on to the world in order to make sense of it. (Fowler 1991)

The rise of a discourse of fear is due to its taken-for-granted relevance as an appropriate feature of the effective environment. While fear is different from the specific topics with which it is associated (e.g., crime), I suggest that the expanded and pervasive features of the word *fear* across news sections illustrates a more profound acceptance of fear into everyday discourse that transcends specific topics. Fear is more expansive and pervasive than crime, although the former can clearly include the latter.

My analysis of fear in the news media crosses several theoretical perspectives including symbolic interactionism, structuralism, and cultural studies. Symbolic interaction suggests that the impact of any message is its contribution to the definition of the actor's situation. From this perspective, the ultimate meaning of any text turns on an actor's interpretation of cultural materials, such as news reports (Crane 1992; Maines and Couch 1988; Snow 1983). However, the process and consequences of social definitions extend well beyond face-to-face interaction to include the interstices where major decisions are made that shape the contexts of meaning in which day-to-day decisions are made. Peter Hall's (1997) analysis of meta-power is central to any discussion of the impact of mass-mediated discourse on social life: "Meta-power refers to altering the type of game actors play; it refers to changing the distribution of resources of the conditions governing interaction" (405). Structuralism, while not completely disinterested in the situation at hand, stresses the cultural contexts of messages, suggesting that the most meaningful communication resonates with deeply held and taken-for-granted meanings and relationships between a symbolic signifier and its referent, or the signified (Eco 1979; Fiske 1987; Manning and Cullum-Swan 1994). Cultural studies, drawing on a Marxist view of the production of reality, draw attention to the essential role of mass-mediated messages in sustaining the status quo, including the interests and perspectives of media managers and the interests they serve, which are often at odds with the everyday life experiences of audiences who use this popular culture content (Hall 1977; Kellner 1995; Kidd-Hewitt and Osborne 1995).

The effect is more pronounced when media reports are reproduced in other messages. This process has been described by Peter Manning (1998) as a "media loop": "[w]hen an image is shown in another context, reframed by the media. . . . Media images are constantly recycled, reproduced in a new context, and reexperienced" (261).

Broad effects of mass media presentations include the ways in which public perceptions of problems and issues (the texts they construct from experience) incorporate definitions, scenarios, and language from news reports (Altheide and Snow 1991; Bennett 1988; Comstock 1980; DeFleur and Ball-Rokeach 1982; Ericson 1995; Ferraro 1995; Snow 1983). Linda Heath and Kevin Gilbert (1996) note in a review of more recent research on mass media's relevance to crime: "Because the media often distort crime by overrepresent-ing more severe, intentional, and gruesome incidents, the public overestimates its frequency and often misperceives reality" (371). Indeed, how the mass me-dia report risk suggests that journalists need to be more conscientious and in-formed in their accounts (Willis and Okunade 1997).

While crime and violence are part of the fear story, there is more to it. For example, the constant coupling of crime and other aspects of urban living with fear have produced a unique perspective about our effective environment. While crime is certainly something to be concerned about, as is any poten-tially dangerous situation, the danger, per se, does not make one fearful, just cautious. Fear is not a thing but a characteristic attributed by someone (e.g., a journalist) to something. Often associated as an attitude pertaining to dan-ger, fear is multifaceted in its actual use in popular culture, especially the news media.

Examining the impact of subjects' perceptions of crime on their orienta-tions and behavior, Ferraro's (1995) research on "fear of crime" distinguishes between perceiving a "risk" and being "fearful":

> Fear of crime is an emotional response of dread or anxiety to crime or sym-bols that a person associates with crime. . . . To produce a fear reaction in hu-mans, a recognition of a situation as possessing at least potential danger, real or imagined, is necessary. This conception of potential danger is what we may call perceived risk and is clearly defined by the actor in association with others. (12)

An actor has options.

> Fear is only one of several reactions to judgments of potentially high risk in a situation. Others may include constrained behavior, community or political activism, compensatory defensive actions, and avoidance behaviors including re-location. Perceived risk and the possible reactions to it are viewed as always be-ing developed in an environmental context replete with socially constructed meanings. (Ferraro 1995, 12)

Ferraro notes that people take precautions in everyday life to avoid situations that are perceived to be potentially risky, but not at the same moment feared.

PERCEPTIONS OF FEAR

Fear has become a staple of popular culture, ranging from fun to dread. Americans trade on fear. News agencies report it, produce entertainment mes-sages (other than news) about it, and promote it; police and other formal agen-cies of social control market it. And audiences watch it, read it, and, according to numerous mass entertainment spokespersons, demand it (Clover 1992). As explained in Chapter 2, these considerations informed the methodological approach of tracking discourse developed.

A theoretical sample of nearly two hundred articles from the *Arizona Republic* was analyzed, along with samples from several other media, including the *Los Angeles Times, New York Times,* and *ABC News.* A few points are in order about the major data sources used in clarifying the discourse of fear.

The Arizona Republic *in Perspective*

How much coverage has the *AR* has given to fear over a certain several-year period? We discuss this here as both a conceptual and methodological issue in order to locate this case study within a larger population of newspapers. Figure 4.1 provides a basic description of *fear* in headlines and text in the *AR* from 1987 to 1996. The use of *fear* nearly doubled in both categories: it was in headlines 123 times in 1987 and 232 times in 1996; it was in text 1,379 times in 1987 and 2,209 times in 1996. In order to gain some appreciation for the relative position of the *AR* in the use of *fear* in headlines and text of news reports, comparisons were made with ten major newspapers in the United States: *Atlanta Journal and Constitution* [ATLJNL], *Boston Globe* [BGLOBE], *Chicago Tribune* [CTRIB], *Dallas Morning News* [DALNWS], *Kansas City Star*

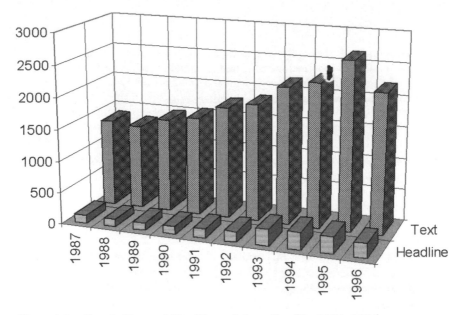

Figure 4.1.   Fear in Text and Headlines, *Arizona Republic,* 1987–1996.

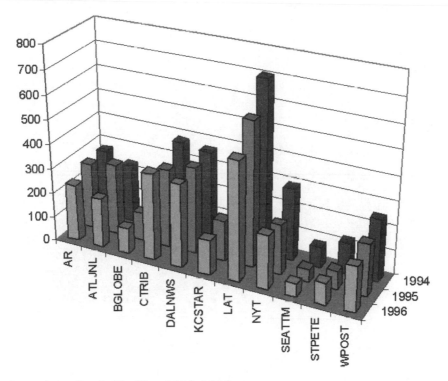

Figure 4.2. *Fear* in Headline, 1994–1996.

[KCSTAR], *Los Angeles Times* [LAT], *New York Times* [NYT], *Seattle Times* [SEATTM], *St. Petersburg Times* [STPETE], and *Washington Post* [WPOST].

There are several points to stress. Fear is no stranger to major metropolitan newspapers in the United States, although the newspapers vary considerably in their use of the word. The use of *fear* in headlines and text increased from 30 to 150 percent for most newspapers analyzed over a seven- to ten-year period, with 1994 the peak year (data not provided). Many of these increases were associated with more emphases on crime reporting (data not presented). Figures 4.2 and 4.3 present data for 1994–1996, which shows that the *AR* is similar to these other newspapers regarding the use of the term *fear* in text of reports as well as headlines. Figure 4.4 shows that between 1994 and 1996, the *AR* ranked eighth (eleven is high) among these papers in the use of *fear* in headlines and fifth with *fear* in the text. It was also one of the leaders (seventh—there were several ties) with *fear* in headlines as a percentage of reports with *fear* in the text. This indicates the relative significance of fear for a newspaper when it is used. Thus, the *Kansas City Star,* compared to the other papers in our study, uses *fear* relatively little in either text or headlines. However,

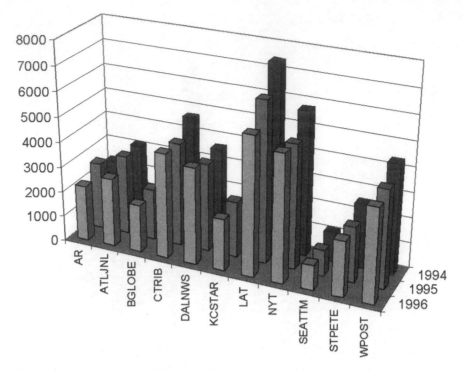

Figure 4.3.   *Fear* in Text, 1994–1996.

when *fear* is used in a report, it is more likely than the other papers to be used in a headline. It should also be noted that the "prestige newspapers" (the *Washington Post* and *New York Times*) used *fear* in headlines comparatively less in terms of the total number of stories they presented in which fear was mentioned.

These data are important to understand part of the process for gathering reports that appear in the *AR* since newspapers not only share wire service reports (e.g., reports with an Associated Press byline), but also information. Thus, what appears in the *Los Angeles Times* or the *Chicago Tribune* may also show up in *AR*. Further, it is widely understood that newspapers, like other media outlets, share perspectives on news and look to each other for guidelines about formats, topics, and emphases. And reporters and editors move from one locale to another. Not surprisingly, then, reports about certain topics (e.g., "carjackings") may start in one part of the country and find their way into news coverage in other regions and cities, even if the particular "crime" has not drastically increased.

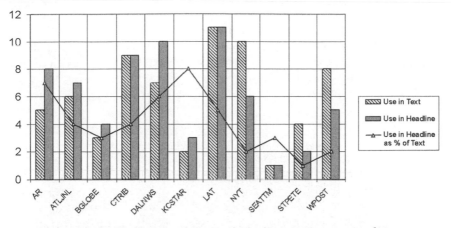

Figure 4.4.   *Fear* in Headlines and Text and Headlines as Percentage of Text,
1994–1996

Arizona Republic *Sections and Formats*

News is a business, a commodity. Newspaper organizations earn revenue in
two basic ways: selling an audience of certain demographics to advertisers, who
purchase space for ads to reach that audience, and selling the newspaper to cus
tomers. While the relative amounts of revenue from these two sources vary
from one newspaper to another, the former surpasses the latter in all cases.

The *AR* enjoys a position not unlike other dailies in many American cities:
There is little competition for readership. For years, Phoenix Newspapers
owned and operated two papers, the *AR* and the *Phoenix Gazette,* but the latter has now been incorporated into the former, leaving one major newspaper
in the area, although there are some other options, mainly in the East Valley
(e.g., from Tribune Newspapers).

As a business, the *AR,* like most major U.S. dailies, must adjust to a changing audience that is constantly being cajoled and approached by a massive popular culture industry, particularly television, which adds a visual dimension to
an entertainment format displaying emotion (Altheide and Snow 1991). Indeed, TV news has been credited with declining newspaper readership during
the last twenty years. This requires that newspapers, in turn, attend to audience interests and perspectives. Thus, newspapers have become more entertainment oriented, and, particularly, more attuned to the lifestyle preferences
of readers. Major format changes have taken place in the *AR* and most other
U.S. dailies as a result.

The *AR* has numerous sections marked off by substantive focus, such as
"hard news," "features" or less timely news, comics, sports, business, and so

on. Historically, fear has been associated with the hard news sections. Tracking fear across various sections over time shows fear as a more general orientation to events and topics beyond specific content. Like most metropolitan dailies, the *AR*'s international and local news coverage has decreased in favor of providing materials deemed worthwhile by market research, such as personal finance, computers, lifestyle, business, and, of course, an expanded sports section.

I examined how news reports featuring fear were arrayed across some of the major sections (see Figure 4.5). Fear is more widely distributed across the various sections of the newspaper than I anticipated. From 1994 to 1996, fear was a staple of numerous sections, albeit to varying degrees, in the *AR*. I examined fear in text and headlines in seven sections of the *AR*: front, valley/state, sports, business, community (of which there are at least thirteen subsections), life, and editorial (see Figure 4.6). Even in sports, the section touted by some as an "escape from real life," an occasional headline with fear appeared. There is surprisingly little variation over time. This is very important for the argument about the emergence of a discourse of fear.

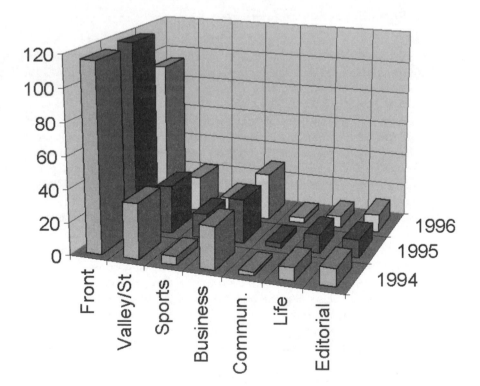

Figure 4.5.   Fear in Sections, *Arizona Republic,* 1994–1990.

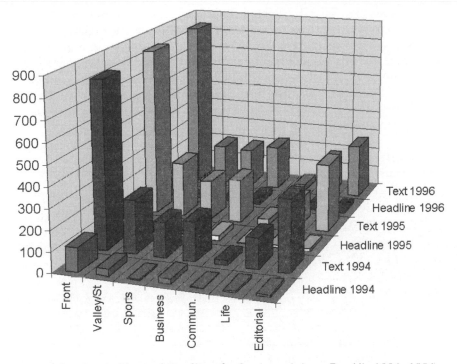

Figure 4.6.   Fear in Text and Headlines by Sections, *Arizona Republic,* 1994–1996.

Figures 4.5 and 4.6 illustrate a general stability of fear in text and head-lines, respectively, during this time period. The ratio of fear in the body of news reports (or the text) to fear in the headlines varies across the sections, from 7:1 in the front section to 29:1 on the editorial/opinion page. The latter dis-crepancy is partly due to the inclusion of numerous letters (as text only) that often do not have their own headlines. The biggest increases in fear in head-lines occurred in sports, while the largest increase in fear in text over this three-year period occurred in business. Although the largest proportion of reports and headlines featuring fear occur in the front section of the *AR* (for example, 55 percent in 1996; see Figure 4.6), it is noteworthy that fear appears through-out the other major sections, particularly editorial, valley/state, and business. This is partly due to the use of *fear* as a noun, verb, adverb, and adjective.

THE TOPICS OF FEAR

The substantive focus of fear also varies widely over time and across topics. Indeed, this is certainly as important as the increased use of fear, since other terms are used more as well. As noted previously, the substance of tracking discourse is to delineate the nature and extent of this change. Reports were sought across sections on a dozen topics that have been useful in earlier analyses of media formats and emphases (e.g., violence, crime, community, neighborhood, schools, drugs, gangs, retribution, children, terrorism, environment, and immigrants). The intent was to see how the relative association of fear with certain topics varies over time in order to examine public discourse about topics and important social issues.

Fear Travels

A key point in this research is that fear "travels" across topics over time. Fear is not exclusively associated with crime, but rather numerous topics "appear" with fear, although their relative strength varies over time. Over a three-year period, more than 21 percent of these reports associate fear in some way with the topics presented in Table 4.1 and Figure 4.7. It is apparent that the use of fear has almost doubled during this decade, although other work documents that fear has nearly tripled in headlines in the *Los Angeles Times* and in ABC television news reports. I also examined the association of fear with the topics of AIDS, homelessness, and cancer. On an average day, a thorough reader of the *AR* would read six to seven reports containing fear and approximately one headline with the word *fear* in it.

Table 4.1 presents a thumbnail sketch of several issues between 1985 and 1994. The raw numbers indicate that topics vary, to some extent, over time. Tracking the modal categories for each issue for the three time periods also suggests the trendiness of certain topics vis-à-vis the entertainment payoff for the problem frame. Thus, AIDS peaked in its association with fear in 1985, the environment in 1992, and so forth. Other points worth noting are as follows:

- This mode of analysis of discourse is partially supported by the collapsing of fear within the topic of cancer, which was included as an in-

Table 4.1. Los Angeles Times Headlines from 1985, 1992, and 1994: *Fear* within *N* Words of *AIDS, Cancer, Crime, Drugs, Environment,* and *Violence*

Topic	Within Two Words			Within Ten Words		
	1985	1992	1994	1985	1992	1994
AIDS	9	2	3	21	4	6
Cancer	0	1	1	1	2	2
Crime	3	5	22	5	18	42
Drugs	0	1	1	2	3	7
Environment	0	0	5	3	8	9
Violence	0	9	12	12	15	25

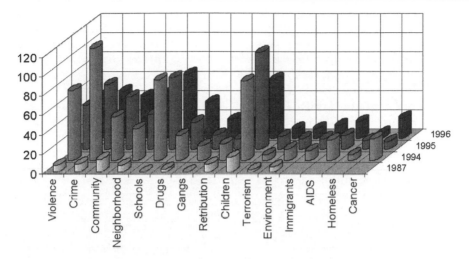

Figure 4.7. *Fear* within Ten Words of Topics, *Arizona Republic,* 1987 and 1994–1996.

tuitive test or control topic. It is axiomatic that cancer is to be feared, and its pervasive use has made the words *cancer* and *fear* redundant; thus, even before 1985 this connection had been established. Analysis suggests that the same thing is occurring with drugs, a topic that has been scoured by official agents of control who have been news sources promoting the isomorphism of drugs/crime/violence/fear/danger. Drugs and fear have become one.

• While the closest association with fear in 1985 was AIDS, this shifted to crime and violence in 1994.

In brief, then, certain problems and issues are more closely associated with fear than others. In 1994, it was crime and violence. Moreover, examining the materials indicates that the problems/issues included drugs as well as gangs. An archetype headline combines all three: "*Crime* Cut by Bikes, Barricades, Law Enforcement: The Neighborhood Was a *Drug* Haven until New Tactics Were Implemented. The Two-Wheel Patrols and Barriers Have Made a Dent in the Danger but Some Residents Still Live in *Fear*" (July 5, 1992.) The increasingly common association of several of these terms with another menace, gang, is illustrated in the headline "Anaheim *Fears Drug* Turf Wars among *Gangs*" (February 6, 1992).

In general, fear "looks" more and more like crime when it comes to news media, but other issues get folded into the mix. Crime and fear are good entertainment. Drugs, gangs, and immigrants are topics that are often associated with crime, or, rather, the crime angle is used to discuss each as an issue. The same is true of homelessness. Crime rates are down, but public concern with

crime is up, way up. While mass audiences are depicted as fearing criminals, the communicative logic joining what the feared are afraid of is worth
examining.

Feared and Fearing

News formats tend to be "tight" and "closed" rather than "loose" and "open"
(Altheide 1985; Schlesinger, Murdock, and Elliott 1983), so they seldom permit the context and very significant background information that is essential
to understand an event rather than just appreciate a dramatic aspect of it. As
Cerulo (1998) suggests, most news reports focus on the victim or the accused/
agent while very few look at context or extenuating circumstances. Since the
major sources of news for crime and most problems are official agencies that
claim ownership of such issues, seldom are journalists provided the breadth of
information that would at least make certain events more understandable (see
Chapter 6). The upshot is that news reports tend to treat the feared aspects of
those accused of crimes as well as those afflicted with AIDS and other social
ills. But it is also true that many of the feared are also fearing of people and
their environments. The materials and the perspective used in tracking discourse permit comparisons of what is feared as well as who is fearing. Brief
summary comments about thirteen examples covered by both the *LAT* and
ABC News were classified as describing people who were both feared and fearing. The groups/categories of people that could be classified as both feared and
fearing include the following:

- Japanese immigrants
- Persons in abusive relationships
- Poor people
- Muslim immigrants
- Blacks
- Homeless persons
- Minorities
- Teenagers
- Gang members

These groups are largely those that are also feared the most by audience-citi-
zens and are often prominently featured in news reports that stress their feared
identities.

Following are two reports from the *LAT* about immigrants illustrating
feared and fearing :

From the *Los Angeles Times,* March 1, 1992 (1500–3000 words)
Headline: Kato slaying raises fears of hate crime; Racism; Japanese community
worries that economic resentment is being expressed through violence

What is most significant about this report is that it is fairly clear what the reasons for the fear are on both sides. Japanese are feared because of economic relations between the United States and Japan. The Japanese are fearful of becoming victims of crime because of this fear. The reasons behind the fear of those committing the hate crimes are not always expressed. The connection between hate and fear is not always clear, but it is a little more clear in this report.

From the *Los Angeles Times,* February 18, 1992 (501–1500 words)
Headline: Share Our Selves finds peace in new neighborhood; Charity: Business owners say fears about crime have not materialized. Now some volunteer to help the needy

Poor people, and especially homeless people, are feared because it is assumed that they will be accompanied by crime, vandalism, and heavy traffic—things that cause a neighborhood to deteriorate. However, through comments made by those who were fearful of the poor, some of the fears that poor people have can be seen. The poor need food, so they are likely fearful of how they will survive or where they will get their next meal. This report helps put different fears in perspective—which fears are really more important?

ABC News, on September 1, 1994, aired a two- to four-minute report dealing with gangs. What was unique about this report is that most reports take a negative stand against gangs. This one, however, allowed gang members to be seen as fearing as well as feared. Gang members are feared for the crimes they commit because the crimes appear to be perpetrated at random; but gang members may also be fearful of other gangs. This report portrayed a gang member who was wanted for murder and who was in turn murdered.

On June 6, 1992, a report about kids carrying guns implies that the teenagers are feared because they carry guns, but they may be carrying guns out of fear. "[I]t's escalated to the point where they feel they need weapons because they're not sure if the people that they're dealing with might have weapons."

Immigrants and gangs are feared and fearing, particularly the latter, even though the reports about fears of young gang members seldom get much play. ABC featured several reports on these topics, and one of the most explicit was in the *LAT* in 1992. This report described an incident in which an individual, who had just been released from jail, was shot and killed. It was stated that even though neither he nor his friends were members of gangs, they had friends who were. It was believed that the shooting was done by members of a rival gang, and police feared retaliation would occur. The shooting was essentially labeled "gang-related." This raises questions about how something gets to be defined as gang-related. Is a crime gang-related if individuals who are members of a gang commit a crime on their "own people"? Does labeling a crime as gang-related escalate the fear involved, especially when certain segments of the population are more likely to be identified as gang members?

EXPLICIT AND IMPLICIT FEAR

Topics become associated with fear through a process. Problems (and associated terms) have a "meaning career," often beginning as something that is deviant or immoral and later becoming more accepted—although not necessarily desirable. This occurs in part through public communication and includes the journalists who write about such topics, as well as the sources who supply them with information and understanding. These sources can be said to essentially own the meaning of the problem or issue (Surette 1998). We communicate differently about things as they become more familiar because taken-for-granted notions incorporate what is obvious. For example, when reports routinely stress suffering and mayhem, fear becomes incorporated into the meaning: Signifier and signified are essentially joined and taken for granted. In this manner, I argue that a clear indication of public familiarity with a topic, as well as how it has moved from one body of experts to another, is the prevalence of fear associated with it.

One example from previous work is *cancer,* a term that seldom appears in conjunction with *fear* in mass media reports. This is not because cancer is no longer feared, but, to the contrary, it is so overwhelmingly undesired—yet familiar—that it has been recast repeatedly into other discourses, such as medicine, health, and education. This has occurred because the sources for reports about cancer tend not to be police officers or public officials but professionals trained in medicine, public health, and education. (However, the fear of cancer has been appropriated by politicians, who use *cancer* as a metaphor referring to *crime.*)

To speak metaphorically, fear has traveled across all the topics we examined since 1987, although children, crime, and schools have remained the top three categories. As Figure 4.7 indicates, the association of certain topics with fear expanded, particularly with children and schools. This is common with the mass media across the United States, but the extent of change is noteworthy. For example, in 1987, there were 8 and 7 stories, respectively, with the terms *violence* and *crime* occurring within 10 words of *fear.* By 1996, the association of *fear* with *violence* and *crime* had increased sixfold. Indeed, since 1994 those topical associations of fear with children and schools have exceeded violence, drugs, and gangs. While other work has suggested that people still associate gangs with danger, fear, and undesirability, the connotation of gangs now contains fear and danger, so it is no longer made as explicit.

Fear travels in public discourse as it becomes associated with topics over a period of time. Frames are akin to boundaries and borders; and like border incursions, we are most aware of them when they expand into other territories or contexts of meaning. But when the incursion occurs subtly and accompanies well-traveled issues such as crime, the adjustment is most likely noticed as a nuance, if at all. Over time, with repeated usage, nuances blend, connotations become denotations, fringes mix with kernels, and we have a different perspective on the world.

The point I am stressing is that fear is a dominant orientation that is shown and lives through certain topics. I examine children and the discourse of fear more closely in Chapter 7, but a few points can be noted here. Headlines about children were associated with fear (topic-as-fear, TAF) in only 8 percent of the reports in 1994 (Figure 4.8). However, nearly a fourth of all reports with *fear* in the headlines (fear-as-topic, FAT) referred to children in the body of the text in 1994, 1995, and 1996. Essentially, the same magnitude was apparent with community, but also note the position of schools. A comparison of FAT is offered with the *Los Angeles Times* (*LAT*) for 1994–1996 (Figure 4.9). The similarity in profiles is striking in the way fear is associated with certain topics, particularly children, community, schools, and police. The argument to this point is that these are not merely words used for a matter of convenience to communicate effectively but have come to be linked to an orientation and course of action implying danger, avoidance, proactive precautions, and threat. These relationships can be illustrated by themes in a sample of articles.

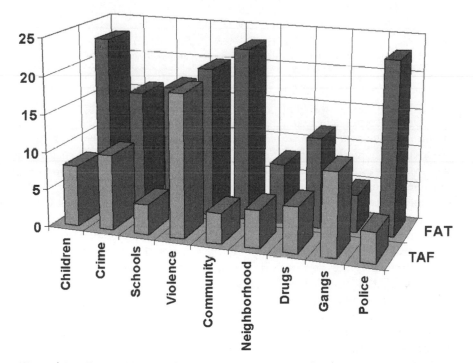

Figure 4.8. Fear-as-Topic (FAT) versus Topic-as-Fear (TAF) by Percentage, *Arizona Republic,* 1994–1996.

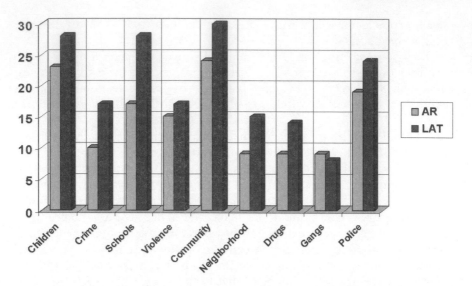

Figure 4.9.   Headline of Fear and Focus on Topic in Text by Percentage, *Arizona Republic* and *Los Angeles Times,* Three-Year Average, 1994–1996.

THEMES OF FEAR

Fear becomes a matter of discourse when it expands from being used with a specific referent to use as a pervasive problem and more general orientation. Several points stand out about the changing role of fear over time. I refer to the two ideal types of fear use as parallel and nonparallel. Figure 4.10 contrasts a shift from parallel to fear discourse with the example of children and fear. Accompanying the development of the discourses of fear are several themes, or parts, of this expanding perspective: fear as resource, reactive fear, proactive fear, fear as a topic, and the reality of fear.

As Figure 4.10 suggests, in 1987, usage of fear can be characterized as localized, momentary, individually experienced, and often urban as opposed to suburban. I call this parallel fear and suggest that these characteristics mark journalistic reporting outside of the problem frame. For example, "'We fear for our children on the streets as they walk to the elementary school,' Steichen said" (*AR,* April 27, 1987). The use of the word *fear* in this instance relies on a first-order connotative value related to a specific issue at a specific time.

Accounts in the *AR* in the later years of the study can be characterized as moving to a problem frame (fear frame) consistent with fear as a discourse, characterized by a more generalized, pervasive, unfocused standpoint. For example, "Hers was the name that shattered the innocence and security of small-town life and glued it back together with fear. Nickie Fater. Loving wife.

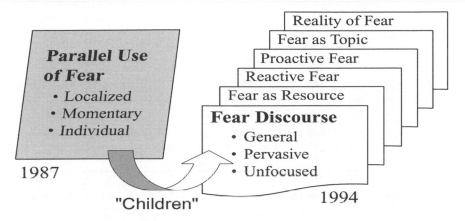

Figure 4.10. An Emerging Discourse of Fear.

Dedicated mother. Gunned down while loading groceries into her car" (*AR,* October 21, 1996).

The following example shows how fear has come to frame the notion of children and schools and illustrates the lengths to which school officials must go to abate these fears:

> The academic challenges are being made more difficult by the disturbing presence and growing fear of crime and violence in our schools. To fight back, police forces are beefing up patrols of schools, and nearly 20 percent of surveyed communities now regularly use metal detectors to detect weapons. (*AR,* November 2, 1994)

This emphasis became more apparent in reports several years later about the growing popularity of Catholic schools in the Phoenix area. The article "Catholic Schools Reviving in Valley," *Arizona Republic,* May 17, 2001, examines this growth. Parochial schools were growing in number; there were thirty schools, with 13,613 students, the most since 1960. Reasons given include higher academic standards, but a compelling theme cuts through the story about safety and fear. One mother who works at St. Matthew's elementary school stated, "I'd like to say people are returning to morality, but that would be a hoot. . . . It's a kinder, gentler atmosphere, and I think that's a big draw."

The authors note that large public high schools

> were perceived by some parents and students as intimidating and unruly. Gang violence, high dropout rates, low achievement and lower teacher pay made the headlines. Bad-mouthing public schools became politically popular. By the time guns and murder came to suburban campuses, fearful parents had the

money to pay tuition and were already knocking on the doors of Catholic schools.

The principal of Chandler's Seton High School claimed that the difference is the "common thread" of religion that binds the community and parents who want the best and expect the best for their kids. "In public schools you have that same group of parents . . . but in public school you have that other group, which doesn't have those same expectations." A fifth grader added, "[Y]ou don't worry about people bringing guns 'cause you know they all want to be here."

Keeping in mind that the focus is on fear rather than, say, "crime," it is helpful to understand how the format of entertaining news embraces reports about fear-as-crime (or children's problems, etc.). Analysis of numerous reports involving fear and the most prominent topics (e.g., crime, violence, and children) suggests that what is thematized as fear depends on what the main frame is.

Materials from *LAT* illustrate the nature and pervasiveness of certain frames. A search for archetypal reports from 1994 to 1998 with the words *children, school, community, gangs, police, violence,* and *fear* provided nine articles relevant to the discourse of fear. Examining these articles to ascertain what the problem is, who cares/who benefits, the role of law enforcement, and whether a social context, for instance, poverty, is discussed suggests the following.

The common problem is violence, or fear of violence, attributed to gang activity. In five of the nine articles, the emphasis is on gangs as the cause of homicides, not social conditions or conventional conflicts and disputes that are historically associated with urban living. Consistent with the literature, the criminal justice system is both faulted for not doing more and praised as a viable option if more resources were available (Surette 1998). Other articles simply identify fear as the problem. "Gang Turns Hope to Fear" documents the huge growth in a certain gang, producing fear, drug dealing, committing assaults, robberies, and homicides: "'What you get from gangs like 18th Street, on a large-scale basis is fear . . . an army in the community'" (*LAT,* November 18, 1998, A1).

The proposed solutions range from changes in police and prosecution tactics and deployment to gun and drug control to family intervention. Most of the discussion centers around whether the police need more money—the mayor says, "Police can do a better job with existing resources," while others say, "The situation will not improve without more resources" (*LAT,* December 16, 1998, A1). Police and prosecutors are presented as doing everything they can with the resources they have. One police commander comments, "The fact that they continue to come to work day after day is amazing, because they are never going to win" (*LAT,* December 16, 1996, A1). Otherwise, law enforcement is only connected to the problem as the primary solution. The only related problem mentioned is the fact that the gang had its roots in the neighborhood's struggles to achieve economic renewal. This issue is actually introduced not as part of the cause of the growth of the gang, but rather from the victims' perspective. In other words, the gangs mostly victimize the various businesses established in the area by immigrants trying to get ahead: "One of the sad truths of 18th Street's ascendance is that the gang's deepest roots— and its broadest impact—are in neighborhoods struggling to achieve economic renewal" (*LAT,* November 18, 1998, A1).

Several articles suggest a limited contextualization, reflecting popular culture images of gangs, violence, convicts, and poverty, situating poverty, violence, gangs, and high incarceration rates within a political economy of race and class warfare. The resources in short supply involve criminal justice agencies and an occasional victim. Indeed, one article on housing problems reflects an absence of any structural analysis. A dire state of affairs in a housing project is due to the residents' lack of respect for their living conditions. The article cites the housing department's director of housing development as saying that "the fresh surroundings will encourage residents to take pride in—and take care of the property" (*LAT,* May 14, 1995, B1).

These materials support the view that the use of fear has changed. Themes of fear suggest that the coverage of fear after 1987 moved beyond mere events or specific topics to a more expansive fear frame consistent with discursive practices. Within this discourse there are two frames that guide or screen fear: fear as a resource and fear as a topic. The former refers to the way in which the meanings of fear are drawn on in order explicitly or implicitly to illustrate or associate an event as an extension of the problem frame (i.e., as something we know about), while the latter examines the character and justification of the way fear is associated with events.

FEAR AS A RESOURCE

Most articles use fear as a resource incorporating fear with accounts structured as narratives that personify morality plays. The focus is on individual misfortune perpetrated by an evil agent, (and/or) who is pursued (or tried or punished) by an agent/agency of righteousness—usually a formal agent of social control—(and/or) who is celebrated by members of the chorus (audience) proclaiming their preference for the righteous over the culprit. (It is estimated that law enforcement officers threatened or used force in encounters with more than a half million Americans in 1996 [*AR,* November 1997]). Reactive and proactive fear are two major types.

Reactive Fear

The majority of topics, problems, and issues presented as news involves those framed as problems. Suffering, misfortune, distress, and inconvenience are the stuff of contemporary news, but they are not the problem. The problem characteristics are part of a format organized around a narrative that begins with a general conclusion that "something is wrong" and we know what it is. An example of audiences participating in a newspaper's morality play is the following letter to the editor published in the *AR* on November. 16, 1995: The headline reads: "How Long Must We Live in Place Where Fear Is Dictator?"

> I was appalled and sickened by the senseless killing of a kind, decent man who did the right thing by helping a trick-or-treater on his own block. A 15-year-old who had no business carrying a gun (Does the NRA really support such craziness?) shot him.
>
> I didn't know this 41-year-old humanitarian, but I do know that he could have been me, or my husband, or any one of you. He did what adults are supposed to do: He protected children! He did not cower in a society plagued with violence and fear.
>
> How can we continue to live in our community, where fear is the dictator and love the enemy? How can we raise our children to be decent, helpful human beings if it means them risking their lives?
>
> I am disturbed by the dilemma we face. When an innocent person is killed for doing something good; when teenagers can't go to the mall without fear of being stabbed; when a convicted child molester can write and produce a major motion picture (*Powder*); and when criminals have more rights than victims, then we must realize it is time for goodness to become militant. . . .

It is as though the audience members—with the aid of editors, who select letters for publication—show their competence by hanging the right script on the fear framework. Thus, something cast as crime or some other subset of evil is acknowledged with an account implicating fear. Taking common sense precautions in a changing effective environment may be of interest, but it becomes more relevant and connected to other news events about life when it is dropped into the problem frame stressing key elements of the morality play. An excerpt about people's adjustments to crime illustrates:

> Fear is starting to run our lives. . . . They are watching for suspicious motorists and pedestrians, taking the minimum amount of money or credit cards, staking out the safest possible parking space and, along the way, leaving stranded motorists in the dust. (*LAT,* December 21, 1993, E1)

The focus is not on a specific act, but rather the act is embraced as merely an example of a larger more insidious problem—fear. Thus, in order to avoid being victims, people who need assistance are passed by. And victims abound in the problem frame.

Proactive Fear

Fear as a resource is provided by news organizations that produce reports within the problem frame of the entertainment format. Audience familiarity with a general scenario lends familiarity and credibility to a specific event. Another theme that is less common than reactive fear is connected with the victim, but it is in anticipation of some event or activity. The idea here is that one does something in order to avoid being a victim or avoid engaging in an activity or issue already tainted by fear. Paradoxically, Ferraro (1995, 63) notes that when people take steps to alter their lifestyles and avoid situations, they actually increase their perceived risk. Exploring news coverage of such accounts has conceptual relevance for the salience of news reports for individuals' perceptions and behavior. For example, there are numerous reports about someone taking proactive or preventive action to shoot or kill or avoid or leave someone or some place because they were "in fear of" something. For example, "More than a third of state residents—37 per cent—interviewed in a poll for the Arizona Republic and KSAZ-TV (Channel 10) said they had changed their routine in the past six months just to reduce their risk of being a crime victim" (AR, May 22, 1994, A1).

More typically, reports are presented about what officials and social institutions are doing to "protect" the public from threats to them or their children. While Chapter 7 examines reactions about children, it is helpful here to make some comments about preventive steps taken by law enforcement people and how this affects children and parents. Following several tragic and widely publicized school shootings, encapsulated with such shorthand referents as "Jonesboro" and "Columbine," Arizona schools, like numerous school districts across the United States, have taken draconian measures against any threats of violence ("'Zero Tolerance' Being Questioned," Arizona Republic, May 19, 2001, 1). Schools and safety are a "flash zone" and represent one of the most successful efforts to promote fear in parents and students. Notwithstanding widespread documentation that schools are one of the safest places for children to be, including home, concerns are raised continually. One Gallup poll reported that 47 percent of adults believed that the chances of a school shooting happening in their community was "very likely" or "somewhat likely" ("'Zero Tolerance' Being Questioned," Arizona Republic, May 19, 2001, 1). Like officials across the country, Arizona politicians have sprung into action to deal with these perceptions. Touted as "zero tolerance" policies for threats and the show of weapons of any kind in schools, Arizona law requires that children be expelled from school, reports be filed with police, and that punishment follow for infringements. This has had a major impact on Arizona schools. "School districts say community fears, brought on by high-profile shootings, have led to an increased awareness of threats. Incidents that likely wouldn't even have gone to the principal years ago now are going to the police." Police referred 241 students to face possible felony charges in Maricopa County Juvenile Court in the first year a new state law allowed prosecutors to file felony school interference charges against kids who make threats. Kids explain their actions as a way to get bullies to leave them alone, or to be "cool for friends," or to win a dare. One boy, who was bullied, said: "I didn't want this to happen. . . . I just wanted to scare them, so they didn't do it again." Ultimately, charges were filed in 37 of 241 cases; prosecutors filed 14 more felony interference charges in cases in which the police didn't ask for it. While only one case has resulted in jail time, the kids' lives—and their parents'—are disrupted as new schools must be sought. According to a spokesperson for the county attorney, "We don't care if they were serious or not. It's a zero tolerance."

Charles Baker, director of security for the Mesa Unified School District, says:

> We have to report them. You report them out of fear that this might be something. You don't want to see things fall through the cracks. . . . I think the problem with zero tolerance is it takes away discretion. It's cut and dry. Each is similar yet they're different. Some of these kids have never been in trouble before. Ever. ("'Zero Tolerance' Being Questioned," *Arizona Republic,* May 19, 2001, p.1) (

A presiding Maricopa County Juvenile Court judge said that kids are better off if problems can be handled outside the court system. "We don't need 13-year-old and 14-year-old felons."

A mother of a boy who told a junior high school teacher "Watch your back. There's a bomb in your class," said that her son was very sorry and that when she was a kid they used to do pranks, but no one ever went to court for it: "People are tired of living in fear. . . . They do live in fear now because you don't know what's going to happen next."

A discourse of fear is promoted by audience familiarity with and use of the word *fear* in everyday life. *Fear* is used as a noun, verb, adjective, and adverb. *Fear* is increasingly substituted for words with much different connotations, such as *concern, relevance, trouble, query, issue, item,* and many others. It is as though the size of the symbolic pot containing fear has expanded exponentially compared to conventional language use; it is more familiar, convenient, and perhaps more forceful in making points. Regardless, it has made its mark on news space.

Fear is associated with topics and events that exist in the space of fear and are often found in topics-as-headlines (FAT) as noted previously. A parallel use of fear has also emerged. For example, an article entitled "End Overcrowding, Juvenile Jails Told" (*AR,* June 24, 1994, B4) began, "Arizona's juvenile-detention facilities have been ordered by a federal judge to eliminate overcrowding by November, and some officials *fear* hundreds of *youths arrested for violent crimes* will be released if no solution is found by the deadline" (emphases added). Note in this instance that it is neither the "crimes" nor the "youths" that are feared, but their release. It is as though the object of the verb (youths) carries weight in deciding what the verb shall be. This discursive labeling joins the object to the action and ties it together with fear.

The Discourse Process

My emphasis is on the way that fear comes to be associated with other symbols, meanings, and activities. For example, when *fear* and *crime* are used together repeatedly, their meaning, when used in certain contexts, can be easily joined. The general model is rather straightforward: When a word is repeated frequently and becomes associated routinely with certain other terms and images, a symbolic linkage is formed. For example, fear is a pervasive meaning and symbol in American culture. Frequently associated with crime, fear is more expansive, and research shows that it covers a much wider symbolic territory than crime. Tracking discourse permits gauging how closely together similar words appear as part of thematic emphasis and discursive practices. Indeed, after repeated usage together, the initial meaning of a word, for example, *gang,* can incorporate fear as a connotation.

Crime has begun to imply fear and no longer must be stated as "fear of crime," but only "crime." Figures 4.11 and 4.12 indicate how this process may operate. Figure 4.11 shows a process that can occur over time, as a particular problem or topic is used closely with fear. Essentially, the argument is that they become blended, and denotation of, say, "drugs" carries the connotation of fear. The same process can be used to discuss the association over time of *fear* and *crime* or *crime* and *violence.* An issue initially used as fear-as-topic (e.g., *fear* of crime) can merge into a topic-as-fear (e.g., fear of *crime*). With the former, *fear* is added to the word *crime* to make it explicit that they are connected, while the latter—through repeated use—simply implies that crime involves fear. Over time, the blended meanings are adopted by public media and various speech communities (aided by popular culture products, including music and movies). When this happens, public discourse has changed, as one symbol implies the other. The social impact becomes more important when that auxiliary term is *fear.* No term is naturally associated with *fear,* although repetition can join them.

Figure 4.13 illustrates the decline of newsworthiness that may accompany the blending of a topic with fear. If we think of fear as having the heaviest, densest news value, then anything with which it is closely associated becomes potentially more newsworthy within the context of the problem frame. However, when the terms are repeatedly used and the meanings merge, for example, "drugs are fear," then *drugs may* become less commonly used with the word *fear* because it would be, in a sense, redundant to state "fear (drugs) are fear." The routinization and expansion of fear would be complete, at least as far as

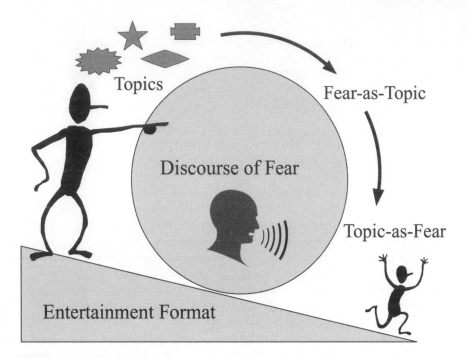

Figure 4.11.   Transforming Fear and Topics.

drugs or crime are concerned, and considerable effort would be required to un-pack or disentangle drugs from fear. Yet there are two ways in which this has been done, and both involve claims makers and moral entrepreneurial efforts: (1) the term, essentially, is taken over by another institutional discourse, for instance, medicine took over *cancer*; or (2) a massive public education campaign may be conducted that finds some redeeming value or worth in the symbol. For example, prevention efforts require some neutralization of negative sym-bols in order to provide some hope for the sick, normalizing a condition (and removing it from moral responsibility), including removing certain stigma. Several decriminalization efforts have taken this route, including alcoholism, gay rights, and dwarfism (Pfuhl and Henry 1993).

To summarize, then, topics can move from fear-as-topic to topic-as-fear over time. This occurrence marks a change in discourse. My analysis of news reports suggests that *children, community, schools,* and *police* are widely used in associa-tion with *fear* or as fear-as-topic. In this sense, *community* and *schools* are "new to fear." This means that when *fear* appears in headlines, one or more of these terms is likely to appear in the text of the article. They are, in effect, joined. Moreover, violence, gangs, and crime are three topics that have moved beyond

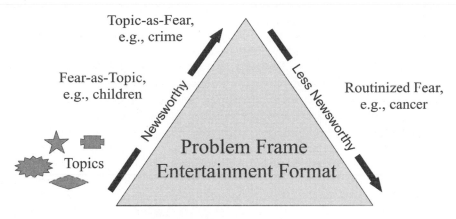

Figure 4.12. The Newsworthiness of fear.

this association and now imply fear; when these terms show up in headlines, the word *fear* is more likely to be used in the body of the article. Stated differently, these terms now carry fear with them. When this happens, words change, meanings change, and their referential social objects and activities also change. Description, prescription, and proscription of language, actions, and orientations can change accordingly, as we have seen happen with fear.

To continue the overview of Figures 4.11 and 4.12, topics are less newsworthy when they have been transformed into topic-as-fear. Several things appear to happen when this transformation occurs. First, the activities are less

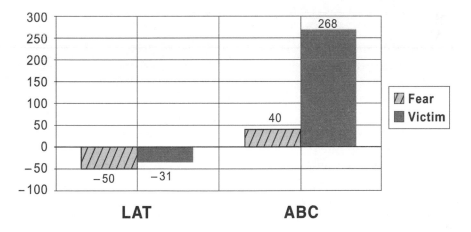

Figure 4.13. Percentage Change in Use of *Fear* and *Victim* by *LAT* and *ABC News,* 1990–1997.

likely to be newsworthy unless they can get recombined with another topic. Thus, as we see in Chapters 6 and 7, crime is more newsworthy when it is associated with *new crimes* and *victims,* rather than *crime* per se. Gangs are less newsworthy than they were a few years ago, meaning that the word is used less often. Second, these topics may become part of another discourse that is owned and controlled by another social institution of elites. Cancer is one example. Cancer is seldom associated with the word *fear* today. The medical discourse does not sanction cancer as fear but rather as a disease, illness, something to be prevented or studied and even cured. While cancer is surely something to be avoided, it is not to be feared, as such. There are, after all, responsible parties, medical elites, scientific controls being used with cancer; it is not the province of public reaction or public officials. We are invited to "seek" the help of cancer experts.

A similar approach is used with fire. Firefighters do not fear fire, but rather, they embrace it. And they want the public to understand fire and to teach their children about it, not simply frighten them. This distinction is seldom made in news reports, which tend to use fear. An example of a rare report seeking to uncouple risk from fear focused on fire. The following excerpts are offered to illustrate what is seldom seen when it comes to crime:

> Take A Positive Approach: Teach Kids to Respect Fire, Not Fear It
> Look to Child Life for answers to your child-rearing questions. Call the hotline at 1-800-827-1092 with any questions or tips you might have. Or write to Beverly Mills, Child Life, 2212 The Circle, Raleigh, NC 27608.
> Question: Our 3-year-old grandson has become very curious about cigarette lighters, candles and other fire. We wonder what would be the best way to instill the danger of fire so he won't get into trouble.—Karen Dennis, Phoenix
> Answer: Especially with young children, take a positive approach to teach respect for fire rather than try to instill fear, parents and fire safety experts advise. And now is the time to childproof your home if you haven't already.
> Lots of parents who called Child Life say once fire is no longer such a mystery, children tend to lose interest. (*AR,* November 8, 1994, D1)

The report recommended particular methods for teaching children about the hazards of fire and offered tips to parents for acquainting children with potential dangers and how to avoid them. The focus was on education and proactive action. This is a rare treatment of fear.

When a term is so firmly established in everyday discourse, it does not need to be embellished; its status and significance changes as a feature of the surrounding and emerging social contexts, auspices, and control. News specialists handle cancer today; it is part of a "medical beat," staffed by reporters with expertise. Unlike police beats, which are often staffed by rookie reporters, no rookie reporters begin their careers as medical reporters. It is a higher level, often demanding higher salaries. It requires expertise, something beyond what "everyone knows." Police, crime, and fear reporters, presumably, have less-challenging tasks. Everyone knows about crime and fear; they have grown up with it before they became journalists, so not surprisingly, police and crime stories continue to be told in much the same that audience members have learned and expect to hear them: There are good guys and bad guys; the job of the police is to protect us; courts and technicalities make their job difficult; when they do finally convict someone, the soft corrections (e.g., jails and prisons) do not really punish the culprits adequately (Surette 1998).

FEAR AS A TOPIC

Another dimension of the discourse of fear outlined in Figure 4.10 is the role of fear as a topic. Fear is very rarely treated as a topic. It's brief appearance tends to focus on the way the term and examples are used in news reports, often contrasting either a claim in a news report or a social impact of news reports—such as fear of crime—with other authoritative standards which may call into question the original concern. These reports tend not to be news reports per se but perspective pieces that are very analytical. More often than not, these reports, like most academic analyses of risk, conclude that our society is relatively safe and healthy.

An important part of the context of fear is the worldview people have about the danger and riskiness of their lives. We get a lot of reports about risk, and many people take them to heart. Here's one example, with the headline: "What we fear most isn't necessarily what's most dangerous."

> "Events that are common in our daily lives are underestimated in terms of the risk they present to us," said Mary Wilson, an assistant professor in Harvard's public-health department.
> "Strange and bizarre things that conjure up images of the unknown cause great anxiety.
> "We end up spending enormous amounts of money on problems that may pose a trivial risk."
> As Europe forks out $2.4 billion to defend itself against "mad-cow disease," which may have infected 10 humans, psychologists and risk-management experts try to understand what makes people afraid. Those fears drive public policy, and picking the "wrong" ones can distract us from bigger killers. . . .

HELPLESSNESS FUELS SCARINESS

Risks over which people have no control, or no sense of control, are scarier. Airline passengers feel they can do nothing if their plane crashes. Car drivers can do nothing, either, if they crash into a guardrail at 60 miles an hour, but the sense of being in control is greater behind the wheel. . . .

"A lot of natural disasters are regular," said psychologist Frederick Koenig
at Tulane University in New Orleans. "If you understand what it is, you don't
have unstabilized or paralyzing kind of fear." (*AR,* April 5, 1996, A1)

Thus, analysts revel in noting that one's risk of getting cancer from cigarettes
(1 in 3) is seldom at the cognitive forefront as a smoker denounces the lack of
police protection in the neighborhood. However, the reports about fear as a
topic are not consistently presented and rarely occur alongside crime reports.

An exception is illustrated by a front-page article in the *AR* on October 24,
1993, "Crime Wave Across Nation Called a Mirage; Despite Fears, Figures Indicate Rate Isn't Rising," obtained from an affiliated news organization:

> Stories of criminal mayhem fill the evening news. Crime sets the agenda for
> state and local politics from Florida to California. Polls regularly rank crime
> alongside the economy and health care as the nation's most pressing con-
> cerns. . . . The president promises federal action; the first lady declares the fight
> on crime to be her next big issue. It is as though the country were confronting
> a devastating new wave of theft and violence.
>
> It isn't. There is no new national crime wave. . . . In the words of James
> Lynch, an American University demographer and crime specialist, "The people
> who are most anxious are the ones least at risk. Of course, for those places where
> things are bad, they are bad. . . ."

Rare is the confessional such as the one that appeared in the *AR* on December 27, 1998. Written by a "an elementary school teacher guest columnist," "Stranger Danger Sometimes Just Plain Hysteria" described a young
mother's concern when she permitted a well-dressed door-to-door salesper-
son—"a young, good-looking man"—to come into her house and clean a spot
from her carpet. As the young man worked, she became anxious lest she and
her daughter be killed and took pains to inform the carpet cleaner that her dog
"bites all the time." The job finished, the carpet clean, she bought the product, musing:

> With no small amount of relief, I showed the young man out the door, peer-
> ing closely for any distinguishing marks in case I would later need to identify
> him in a police lineup. Ah, hysteria. As a society, we have become fearful of
> each other and everyone's motives. Strangers especially. . . . Several weeks have
> passed. No one has broken into our house. Nobody strange has stopped by.
> Nothing has happened.

Nevertheless, we continue to receive a preponderance of news reports about
topics that are relatively infrequent, compared to those problems that are more
likely to harm us.

This is certainly the case in terms of crime versus cancer. Consider, the death
rate alone from cancer in Maricopa County, Arizona, is 121, compared to the

crime rate of 88 (both per 100,000 population). But crime is constantly big news, as are the formal agents of social control who claim they can "do something about it," while "soldiers" against cancer receive scant mention. Crime rates have been steadily decreasing in Maricopa County for several years, but the number of news reports about crime has increased. The name of Maricopa County Sheriff Joe Arpaio has become a news/household word in Arizona and much of the country as his "tent-city jail," "posse patrols of mall parking lots," and other visible crime-fighting activities are covered by hundreds of news reports. His 85 percent popularity rating, according to opinion polls, is one of the highest registered by local opinion takers. By contrast, Arizona State University Regents' Professor George Robert Petit barely appears in any news index. He and his cancer research group have discovered natural compounds that have proven in some cases to be 95 percent effective in combating certain kinds of cancer. This pervasive use and expansion of a discourse of fear opens up a social space to be filled by victims. It is important to focus on how fear promotes victims.

FEAR AND VICTIM

Fear and victim (and victimization, etc.) have expanded drastically during the last decade. Figure 4.13 summarizes analysis of news reports referring to *fear* and *victim*. An initial examination of actual changes in the use of these terms in such major news media as the *Los Angeles Times* (*LAT*) and ABC newscasts (ABC) reveals substantial shifts that parallel, essentially, the data about fear, with one major exception: While the appearance of *fear* and *victim* increases in both the *LAT* and ABC from 1987 to 1994, the *LAT* usage declines overall from 1990 to 1997; ABC newscasts dramatically expanded use of *fear* by 40 percent while *victim* increased by 268 percent during the same time period. This expanding attention by TV to the notion of victim undoubtedly accompanies the growth in the genre of programs (e.g., news magazines, talk shows, reality TV, etc.). Clearly, victim is a powerful and growing symbol in the social landscape.

Victim is a status and not a person, a location in a set of relationships, with expected rights, duties, and obligations. The discourse of fear involves victims, indeed, requires them. After all, victims—especially visual depictions—are required by the problem frame. As the discourse of fear expands, the popular culture apparatus that contributes to group identities seems to find more types of victims. Victim is a desirable status in American life. Talk shows feature battles royal between contestants claiming they are the true victims, the deserving victims. Victims are but the personal side of crisis; a crisis is where victims reside. A personal crisis may affect one victim, but more generally *crisis* refers to "social crisis," involving numerous people. All take place in a time of fear. All of this requires that citizens have information and constant reminders of the pitfalls and hazards of life, whether potential or realized (Ericson and Haggerty 1997). News reports, talk shows, news magazine shows, and a host of police and reality crime dramas seem to proclaim that everybody is a victim of something, even though they may not know it.

There is a cultural script of victimization. The Eagles' popular song "Get Over It" scolds individuals who seek to blame others for their circumstances. Most Americans would not agree with the member of an outlaw motorcycle gang who explained to one of my students about his experience of being beaten by a club-wielding police officer: "I wasn't a victim of anything; I was just fucked!" He took his beating, but he remained in control of his self. The notion that "life is hard" and things don't always work out the way we'd like seems to be lost on popular culture audiences who clamor for justice, revenge, and, of course, redemption, often in the form of monetary rewards. And this happens not just in the United States, although it is commonplace in American culture.

> It is in the USA that victimhood is most developed as an institution in its own right. . . . Victimhood is one of the central categories of the culture of abuse. . . . Celebrities vie with one another to confess in graphic detail the painful abuse they suffered as children. The highly acclaimed BBC interview with Princess Diana symbolized this era of the victim. (Furedi 1997, 95)

Just as our culture has become obsessed with fear, it has also become accepting of victim and victimization. My analysis of news and popular culture indicates that these two terms are linked. We even use the term *victim* when we don't have a victim—for example, "victimless crime"—although reports are far more likely to stress the victim status. And certain domestic violence "presumptive arrest" policies define people as "crime victims," even though they do not perceive themselves as such and refuse to press charges. We even have "indirect victims":

> Victimhood has also been expanded through the concept of the indirect victim. For example, people who witness a crime or who are simply aware that something untoward has happened to someone they know are potential indirect victims. . . . With the concept of the indirect victim, the numbers become tremendously augmented. Anyone who has witnessed something unpleasant or who has heard of such an experience becomes a suitable candidate for the status of indirect victim. (Furedi 1997, 97)

Victims are a by-product of fear and the discourse of fear. I contend that fear and victim are linked through social power, responsibility, and identity. The linkage involves concerns about safety and perceptions of risk. I refer specifically to the role and identity of victim as held by numerous audiences who expect victims to perform certain activities, speak a certain language, and, in general, follow a cultural script of dependence, lacking, and powerlessness while relying on state-sponsored social institutions to save and support them.

> The precondition for the emergence of the victim identity was the consolidation of the consciousness of risk. In the UK and the USA, the growing fear of crime and the growing perception of risks have contributed to the sentiment that everyone is a potential victim. However, crime and the fear of crime are only the most striking manifestations of the kind of insecurity that strengthens the belief that everyone is at risk. (Furedi 1997, 100)

Fowler (1991) and others have pointed out that language and other symbolic representations are not simply presented in literary forms, such as news reports, but also exist in audience members' values and expectations. The texts and effects are mutual.

> It is obligatory to select a style of discourse which is communicatively appropriate in the particular setting . . . and the accompanying ideas follow automatically. . . . The fundamental principle is that . . . the writer is constituted by the discourse. Discourse, in the present usage, is socially and institutionally originating ideology, encoded in language. (42)

Formal agencies of social control (FASC), particularly national decision-makers and local police agencies, benefit from the context of fear. Victims provide evidence of the reality of fear, the source of the threats. Indeed, without victims there would be no credible fear, so they would have to be created even if they did not exist. This, of course, is the work of propagandists (Altheide and Johnson 1980; Jackall 1994; Jackall and Hirota 2000) and the news media that produces news accounts about fear and promotes the discourse of fear without adequate elaboration or explanation. "The promotion of fear and the propagandist manipulation of information is often justified on the grounds that it is a small price to pay to get a good message across to the public" (Furedi 1997, 25). This helps produce "state terror," as citizens seek protection from threats to safety, from risks, and to avoid becoming victims.

Just as there are victims, there are victimizers, the actual culprits. It is the state police, usually, to whom we turn for help. Indeed, analyses suggest that citizens seem ready to give up rights and liberties in order to be protected from victimizers.

> The media-induced public conviction during the early to mid-1980s that violent crime throughout America was rising at epidemic proportions (despite statistics to the contrary, also reported in the media) enabled Ronald Reagan to expand police powers beyond anything Richard Nixon could have dreamed of. [Author uses missing children as an example of other crises that were promoted by mass media reports.] The enemy is not "out there." Once again, "we" are it.

The media short-circuiting of the specificity of the event opens the way for mechanisms of power to reset social boundaries along roughly historical lines—in other words, in favor of traditionally advantaged groups (whites, males, heterosexuals). (Massumi 1993, 26)

Victimization requires an avowed hurt or injury. I contend that the key development toward the acceptance of victim is a cultural context that promotes fear as a common definition of the environment. There is the idea that we are preyed upon by many factors, circumstances, and people: that injuries can occur through direct action, for example, brutal assaults; through the lack of action, such as neglect; as well as numerous contingent circumstances.

One of fear's strongest symbolic pillars is the assumption that individuals are pitted against an unjust and oppressive world that should be just and not as risky. Indeed, we are constantly faced with questions about risk. "The term *risk* refers to the probability of damage, injury, illness, death or other misfortunes associated with a hazard. Hazards are generally defined to mean a threat to people and what they value" (Furedi 1997, 17). Another assumption is that the outcome of such contact between individuals and the oppressive world is, on the whole, negative, harmful, and illegitimate. A third assumption is that such run-ins with the unjust world are noteworthy, sanctioned, immoral, and illegitimate.

A seminar project (fall 1999) used "Tracking Discourse" to investigate the ways in which *fear* and *victim* were used in numerous news reports in the United States and abroad, and how this changed over time. Initial examination of the tracking discourse results made it clear that journalists used many different types of victims in their articles, formed by placing an adverb or adjective in front of the term *victim.* Researchers discovered very quickly that uses of *victim* and its relationship with fear required that the initial questions about the meanings of fear and victim be redefined in terms of context, social status, and contested identities within the context of an entertainment-oriented news media. For example, in an article entitled "Forgotten Victim," in *Newsweek,* October 2, 1978, there were seven uses of *victim.* The article used more modifiers preceding the term than any other in our theoretical sample, including: *innocent, pathetic, fighting, crime, state's, elderly,* and *forgotten.* The tracking discourse suggests that the most common modifiers used were *elderly* and *innocent.* The following are other descriptors used in the news media during the period under study: *secondary, indirect, sympathetic, forgotten, remembered, future, potential, hidden, silent, unknown, unknowing, deserving, undeserving, spiritual, false,* and *guilty.* Such adjectives and the more general use of *victim* are used with some discretion in an evocative sense in order to strike a responsive chord in readers. An example of this appears in the article "'Crib Job,'" in *Newsweek,* November 29, 1976:

The victims are old people, often very old. Hattie Erwin, who is 103, was inching down a Brooklyn street with the aid of her walker when she was knocked to the ground and robbed of her groceries—worth no more than $2. The assailants are the young—sometimes the very young. Although some elderly victims do testify against their attackers, a far larger number are afraid to do so—or even to notify police for fear that their assailants will retaliate. . . . The elderly are a young criminal's ideal victims. "They're weak and vulnerable," explained Mark Forrester, a San Francisco social worker. "They always have some money with them and are usually too shaken by the attack to remember things clearly."

The researchers noted that *fear* often appears within a few words of *victim,* and more typically it is infused within the word *victim.* Several research participants speculated that is the reason why the emotion of fear is invoked in the reader when *victim* is used. One could call this type of fear "subliminal fear" or "implicit fear," a level of fear that is always present in the word *victim.* One insight that emerged from the seminar project was that victim, in general, could be anyone, but a victim that is identified elicits a heightened level of emotion in the reader. As such, this indicates that not only are there different types of victims, but there is a hierarchy of victims and a gradation of fear present at all times in the term *victim.*

A Hierarchy of Victims

Discussions suggested that *victim* often implies innocence and helplessness. We explored how this is reflected in the media and viewed hundreds of news reports through an analytical lens coated with such queries as, does the implied innocence or guilt of the victim present the victim as more or less deserving? What role does fear play in presenting the victim?

We concluded, based on the articles, that some victims are more deserving of victim status than others, while some uses of *victim* do not seem worthy of victim status. For example, in a discussion of the National Football League's 1991 draft of college players, a prospect's (Bret Favre) driving mishap was described as: "The sharp, graveled curve outside of Pass Christian, Miss., was an accident awaiting a victim" ("Draft '91: First in a Series Scouts: The Worst Draft in a Decade: Hawks May Consider Taking a Quarterback," *Tacoma News Tribune,* April 14, 1991). Seminar reflections led one member to note that this usage implies that Bret Favre was a victim of a curb awaiting a victim, but that this begs the question of whether it was Favre who caused his car to crash. Therefore, perhaps he is not as deserving of victim status as an "innocent victim." By the same token, a victim need not be human to be a deserving victim, as shown by one report's discussion of koala bears, a species dwindling in numbers: "The teddy bear-like koala, symbol of Australia, has won the heart of humankind."

A feature of tracking discourse is to promote theoretical sampling in which comparisons and contrasts are sought in a kind of "natural experiment." This research process revealed that similar language can pertain to corporations as well as to individuals. For example, in one article about antitrust charges brought against Microsoft, the software corporation, lead defense attorney Paul Maritz was the source attempting to offer an alternative definition of the situation. His portrayal of Microsoft as a victim that feared being run out of business was a clear attempt to alter the reader's thoughts in a specific direction. After all, it would behoove Maritz to have the reader believe that Apple Computer was attempting to destroy Microsoft. Similarly, in an article entitled "Food Firm's Fears Delay Recycler's Permit," the owner of a refuse company seemingly appealed to readers who would be swayed by the claim that he was a victim of legal definition.

In the seminar, we all agreed that the news is filled with victims whose portrayal often determines whether they are important enough to be news. In other words, whether they are deserving enough of the audience's attention. In this way, victims become locked in a battle for attention. Some articles seem to suggest that certain victims have not received the attention they deserve (at least in the journalists' eyes) when they are referred to as "forgotten victims." Also, if the victim is to be considered deserving he or she needs to be perceived as innocent. Three articles of forgotten victims illustrate how innocence was portrayed.

The first case is of the "forgotten victim of Chechnya," the Russian Army. The author refers only to the section of the Russian Army that fought in Chechnya. Since it is difficult to portray a group, the journalist chose an individual. Readers do not know how many soldiers the journalist actually interviewed or how representative this particular soldier is of the Russian Army. Did the journalist choose the representative soldier because he appears more innocent? First, this soldier is very young, and he joined the army to serve his country. He was obedient and did his duty. The soldier says:

> I don't know what it was for. . . . We lost. We never had any guidance. We were lucky to get helmets. Nobody ever told us what our mission was. Nobody ever told us why we were killing the people we insist are Russians. And now we are supposed to sit here and freeze to death until we get the nerve to desert.

Another article was an account of a victim of race hate. The story is about Duwayne Brooks, a victim who survived the attack of his friend Stephen Lawrence, who was stabbed to death by a gang of white racists as Duwayne looked on. Without providing background information or a context for the murder, the article begins with a very brief synopsis of the crime: "He saw his best friend knifed by a gang of white racists. He was helpless as his soulmate slowly bled to death. He narrowly escaped the same fate himself" ("The Death of Stephen Lawrence: Forgotten Victims of Race Hate: The Man on the Spot," *The Observer*).

The last article is a plea for attention for victims of hate crimes. (I present more material on a study of hate-crime reporting in Chapter 6.) The article appeared in *The Guardian* ("Forgotten Victims: A US Gunman Goes on a Murderous Rampage, Shooting Blacks, Asians and Jews," July 6, 1999, 8). The author argues that these victims deserve more attention because of "the rash of violence against blacks, Jews and gays." He also claims that these groups are more deserving because they are vulnerable, and studies show that the victims of hate crimes suffer more emotional trauma than victims of comparable crimes. The author sounds indignant when claiming that "wall to wall coverage of the Kosovo [*sic*] crisis, GM food, and Northern Ireland have pushed them not just down but entirely off the agenda."

Cultural Differences

The research team documented how the terms *fear* and *victim* were used in several different ways. Through this multiple usage, the terms came to mean and represent different meanings from their original. Often the meanings and usage vary based on who uses the terms and in what context. Further, these contexts often vary by region, culture, and the group using them.

An implied weighting or scale to judge victimization is apparent in the establishment of a hierarchy of victims. As noted previously, such a scale suggests that some cases are more deserving of the title *victim* than others. Several of the articles that appeared within the American press reflected this idea and, in addition, questioned who were more deserving victims. The articles also questioned whether one was really a victim at all and whether the "culture of victimization" had gone too far. Perhaps the best support for the idea that the culture of victimization had gone too far in the United States is the fact that many of the U.S. news articles had to define specifically which type of victim was being examined in the report.

Unlike American-origin articles, those composed by Soviet and Russian journalists did not highlight the different types of victims nor did they question the status of victims. The terms *fear* and *victim* were used by the former Soviet government and the current Russian government as political tools. Our interpretation was that these terms were used in certain ways to manipulate the public, based on individuals' former experiences, and to help the government maintain its current control.

Similarly, the Israeli articles in the U.S.-based *Jerusalem Post* did not discuss a culture or proliferation of victimization. Nor did they discuss a hierarchy among victims. Rather, the articles stated who the victims were, what they were victims of, and how they came to be victims. However, like some American articles, two Israeli articles regarding the distribution of leaflets by Palestinian activists implied that there was a distinction between innocent and deserving or guilty victims. In addition to these differences, it seems that the articles from Soviet/Russian and Israeli sources relied on the use of the terms *fear* and *victim* less frequently. Several reports from the former Soviet Union and the Israeli press used *survivor,* rather than *victim,* more often to define those who had gotten out of or lived through bad situations.

Shielding Victims

We discovered various scenarios in which actions taken and those not taken were used to contextualize the frameworks connecting *victim* to certain events. This was very apparent in explorations of the term *shield* and its implication that human agency should have been exercised at a time prior to some event. For example, in an article about a garbage collection/recycling company, a comment was made about how reform would only be "a protective shield for an industry that does not want to police itself and does not feel a responsibility to answer to its victims or the public." Also, the word *shield* appeared in an article about the sexual pasts of rape victims. In Indiana there was a shield rule enacted that was supposed to protect rape victims in court, but it was overturned in the Supreme Court. Another article claimed that Indiana doctors were protected (shielded) from medical malpractice suits by laws. This lead us to suggest that one way to define *victim* is "those persons who need to be shielded or protected from something."

Further analyses suggest that the failure of some external (or potential) controller or protector produces newsworthy victims, and that these victims are people audiences should pity because of the controller's failure to shield them from a situation/person/incident beyond their control, and culture provides members with criteria. For example, an article about the former Soviet Union focuses on a woman who, upon being forced by hostile forces to flee her home, nevertheless disavows being fearful and defines her situation by stating, "No, I was not just afraid, because I knew that all this would happen. . . . But this is not fear. This is not fear. Ones who are afraid now are the ones who stayed behind."

Victim and Blame

Many of the materials suggest that victim statuses were related to the audience's awareness of fear and blameworthy circumstances. This is the basis on which deserving and undeserving, or less-deserving, victims turn. The suggestion is that victim, fear, and a deserving victim create a dynamic that allows audience members to identify with the victim and then to separate themselves from the victim while assessing blame; fear is the glue that drives the dynamic in a circular manner.

The exploratory research provided insights into three key considerations for uncovering how fear, victim, and blame have become part of the discourse in the discussion of whether to allow "Indian gaming" in Arizona, for example. These are (1) how fear is manifested, (2) who assesses blame, and (3) the motives for assessing blame.

Our seminar affirmed what decades of research has documented: Media attempt to elicit emotion, whether it be anger, pity, sorrow, fear, or compassion, to engage the reader. It is the writer who anticipates and fits the proper frame around the report in order to elicit a predictable emotional response, which, in turn, helps determine which victims are most deserving. Accordingly, the account must be presented in such a way that the reader can determine a victim's status based on his or her own emotional response to the victim's story, which, in turn, is based on the victim's perceived involvement (or guilt) in his or her victimization. The more innocent and helpless victims are, the worse the audience feels for them and the more deserving they become of the victim status. Assumptions about fear and fearfulness are key here.

These different meanings have important implications for social justice. Further, this implies that social norms and widely held cultural stereotypes, regardless of whether they are correct, help determine victim status. If these stereotypes and norms are based on out-dated and sexist attitudes, many people (both men and women) who have been victimized, as agreed on in a general sense, may not be considered victims by the public at large and by the justice system. For example, if widely held social beliefs state that men cannot be raped, then a man who is raped while in prison may not be considered a victim. Due to his lack of victim status, he may be denied assistance and recourse.

Our study is one reflection of a growing awareness among social scientists that fear and dread are celebrated in public life and social policy (Best 1990; Ericson and Haggerty 1997; Glassner 1999). Seldom does anyone focus on such questions as part of their day-to-day activities. One exception was when artists were recently attempting to select 100 from 6,000 photos of people killed by the Khmer Rouge for a display at the New York Museum of Modern Art. Regardless of the vantage point from which an artist sees things, the task was similar to that of a journalist or anyone else dealing with finite meanings to capture pain of horrific proportions: Who was the best victim? who would make the cut? They did it; criteria were used, narratives were realized, and points were made. My point is that this is emotional work, seldom done with such avowed pain and discomfort as the artists experienced, but rather, selecting appropriate people as victims implicating fear goes on routinely in the news media. This process helps produce an accepted victim identity.

We communicate best with what we take for granted. Cultures command, convey, and ultimately consist of the discourses they reflect and speak. An expansive discourse of fear in public discourse can contribute to stances and reactive social policies that promote state control and surveillance. Fear is a key element of creating the risk society, organized around communication oriented to policing, control, and prevention of risks (Ericson and Haggerty 1997; Staples 1997).

CONCLUSION

Fear is a pervasive word and meaning of everyday life. It has become a prevalent discourse in the United States and is expanding in Europe as well. More and more Americans perceive life to be fearful and risky, particularly due to crime and violence but also a number of other causes as well. Most importantly, we talk fear and experience victimization in numerous ways. Examining news reports about fear in major news media for a several-year period affords an opportunity to assess the character and extent of news coverage pertaining to fear. Casting this inquiry and relevant findings within a theoretical framework about the nature and role of the news media operating in a changing context of an ecology of communication contributes to a more comprehensive awareness of news reports about fear, as well as extends our understanding about the communication process and the role of the news media in creating social reality. This research suggests that fear is not used by itself but is increasingly part of a discourse of fear, or a way of focusing on the fear-related features of most events.

A fear perspective is implied with a discourse of fear. Numerous topics and issues are reflected in fear. Indeed, our materials suggest that status dimensions give fear an identity. Race/ethnicity, social class, and gender concerns are implicated with fear, particularly in the context of change and disorder in a pluralistic society. The poor, dispossessed, and most recently franchised segments of society are disproportionately associated with the largest fear application—crime.

Several associations are particularly noteworthy. Headlines with the word *fear* tend to be associated with children, community, schools, and the police. Frequent associations are related to changing meanings of these words as topics in their own right, as certain kinds of issues, with implications about the source of problems, and, perhaps more importantly, the kinds of solutions warranted. Analysis of frequent news topics such as crime, violence, and drugs suggests that crime news and fear news are parallel but different. Fear is more expansive and pervasive than crime, although the former can clearly include the latter. Fear is bigger news than mere crime or even violence. Fear has become a standard feature of news formats steeped in a problem frame oriented to entertainment. Entertainment abhors ambiguity, while truth and effective intervention efforts to improve social life reside in ambiguity. It is this tension between entertaining and familiar news reports, on the one hand, and civic understanding, on the other hand, that remains unresolved.

Fear is no longer simply attached in parallel fashion to a particular event or problem but is used in sweeping, general ways as a topic that surrounds a particular event or problem. I indicated that reports involving children, community, and schools illustrate a change in accounts from an emphasis on localized, momentary, and individual experiences to a more generalized, pervasive, and unfocused fear frame. The discourse of fear is often presented as a resource and seldom as a topic, with the former branching into reactive and proactive fear.

Fear is more prevalent in news today than it was several years ago, and it appears in more sections of the newspaper. This is particularly true of headlines. Moreover, tracking the topics with which fear is more closely linked demonstrates that fear travels across topics over time, albeit to varying degrees in different news media.

5

Journalistic Interviewing

> There is almost no circumstance under which an American doesn't like to be interviewed. . . . We are an articulate people, pleased by attention, covetous of being singled out.
>
> —A. J. Liebling

Journalism is as useful as its interviewing practices are sound. The discourse of fear emerged from an entertainment format that emphasized evocative reporting. This included dramatic visuals, showing people in conflict. Television interviewing had a large impact on all other forms of journalistic inquiry. This chapter examines how the meaning, use, and impact of the interview have been transformed into an entertainment vehicle driven by media logic that has developed since the early days of print journalism. The main focus is on the use of the interview in contemporary journalism, talk shows, tabloids, real TV, movies, and, of course, political reporting. Particular attention is given to TV as a key constructive player in institutionalizing the criteria for a "good interview." My basic thesis is that a major reason that interviewing is so relevant and popular today is due to its transformation from information to an impact orientation that is more characteristic of our media culture. Of course, fear is a central part of this. These points are set forth in sections examining the growth of media logic, the postjournalism turn, the changing context of interviews in journalism, information technology and entertainment, the professionalism of journalism, and prime-time TV interviewing.

In the modern age it is journalists who have used interviews the most and whose work contributes significantly to how social scientists, reformers, and other investigators employ interviews. Bear this in mind when some social scientists suggest that cultural observers are journalists. (Marcus 1997) Contemporary interviewing is about the mix of answers, since texts are nearly always edited to illustrate certain themes that were known in advance of the interview. Attention is given here to how the institutional framework of contemporary journalism, including its commercial environment, changing in-

101

formation technologies, and adoption of entertainment formats, has led to important changes in the meaning and use of interviews. With an emphasis on evocative answers and the fleshing out of questions that provide answers to fit entertainment formats, contemporary journalists are not isolated in their use of such techniques.

MEDIA LOGIC

The form and content of communication are much different, although quite related. The way in which messages are mediated and formatted shapes their character. How we communicate in daily interaction is a fundamental statement about social order. What we communicate, or the nature of the specific content, helps define a specific situation. Key analytical terms of mediation, media logic, and format are useful in understanding how elements of communication contribute to social order (Couch 1984; McLuhan and Fiore 1967; Simmel and Wolff 1964; Weingartner 1962). Cultural change is signaled in part by the appearance, style, organization, and use of various media. A plethora of work demonstrates that formats of communication constitute the selection, organization, presentation, and content of messages (Altheide 1985, 1995; Altheide and Snow 1979, 1991; Ericson, Baranek, and Chan 1987, 1989).

Mediation refers to the channeling, transport, and molding of information as experience. Intuitively associated with major mass media, such as newspapers and television, a distinction is made between print and electronic, on the one hand, and the various organizational cultures that shape and mold information, on the other hand. *Media logic* refers to the assumptions and processes of constructing messages within a particular medium. This includes rhythm, grammar, and format. Format, while a feature of media logic, is singularly important because it refers to the rules or codes for defining, selecting, organizing, presenting, and recognizing information as one thing rather than another, for example, "the evening news" and not a "situation comedy" or a "parody of news." An example of the latter is when an entertainment program, such as *Saturday Night Live,* presents parodies of news in the news format. It is the distinctive media logic and format of television news reports that separate them from newspaper reports. More specifically, the former deals with electronic visuals in time while newspapers deal with print (linear) representations in space, for example, column inches. The former signals importance temporally by the order in which an item is placed in the newscast and by how much time it is given. Newspapers and print, in general, show importance by location (e.g., on the front page), number of column inches assigned, and the presence of photos.

Media logic influences how organizations operate, particularly communication media. Media logic is most easily recognized by shifts in culture, when something new seems to be added to a previous experience or activity. For example, sports arenas now include big-screen video monitors for replays, advertisements, and even TV programs. The visual materials are now incorporated into the rhythm and flow of athletic contests. Indeed, time-out commercials for basketball and football games are now taken for granted; the contest is altered to accommodate the commercial messages being sent to mass audiences, while those who are actually attending the event live are presented other commercial messages in the stadiums.

Virtually every aspect of life in the United States of America, and in an increasingly large part of the world, is influenced by media logic. Popular culture is the arena in which media logic plays out, but popular culture is being transformed and integrated into most major institutions of life, including politics, education, religion, business, health, and family. These impacts entail not only mere technology, such as the use of computers in daily life, but also the temporal and spatial orientation, rhythm and pacing, and, above all, the major expectation: entertainment. And most of this integration "looks like" television. Marked by an emphasis on evocative meanings—as opposed to more linearly oriented referential formats—it is the emergence of the entertainment format and the technologies that have transformed it and normalized its presence in most daily routines that heralds the most fundamental, yet often subtle, changes in postindustrial life. Journalism, in general, and especially journalistic interviewing, is in the middle of these fundamental shifts.

THE POSTJOURNALISM TURN

In stressing how interviewing has changed for journalists, I wish to emphasize that this is due mainly to other changes in the context of information gathering, preparation, and delivery. Not only has the organizational end of journalism undergone major changes, but so has the audience, or rather audiences, whose expectations of information have become linked with entertainment, or "infotainment." It is the context of information and news that has changed, but, of course, the practice of journalism and the mass media in general have contributed to these changes. I refer to the complex interaction of technology, communication patterns, and social activities as an "ecology of communication" (Altheide 1995).

Media logic has transformed journalistic interviewing from what was primarily a discovering or information-gathering enterprise into an aspect of entertainment. As journalistic practices and perspectives as well as entertainment formats became more widely understood, the line separating journalists from their interviewees began to fade.

Interviewing changed when politicians and other organizational shells became aware of some of the format changes noted previously. The postjournalistic turn fundamentally challenged the autonomy and relevance of professional journalism's training, ethics, and truth claims (Altheide and Snow 1991). As students of communication worked with advertisers and politicians, for example, it became apparent how robust the media logic was that underlay most broadcasting as well as major print media. Emphasizing entertainment formulae of visual, dramatic action meant that a straight interview providing referential information would take too long and would violate the media logic canon. As journalists and sources shared the media logic and formats for what was a good interview, the occupational and perspective lines that had separated them became blurred. With the rise of this postjournalism era, the interview became a tool for quick answers, narrative-induced emotion, and for a purpose other than getting detailed specifics about particular questions.

As TV news heralded the visual, and especially the entertainment-oriented visual, sources soon mastered the relatively simple logic for "getting airtime." They would simply provide the kind of events that journalistic formats preferred, including the interview scenarios, massaging content to suit. Experts on journalistic interviewing contributed to the booming public relations industry (Ailes and Kraushar 1988). By the 1970s, most companies and politicians had followed presidential candidates' leads and had hired media consultants, advisors, and trainers (Martin 1977). Much of the emphasis focused on how to prepare for an interview, how to cover oneself, how to duck tough questions, and so forth. The underlying thesis was that interviews could be damaging and should be managed. News sources learned how to shape events and interviewing opportunities that suited them. All that was necessary was to provide the right mix of visual opportunities and, of course, timing. Michael Deaver (1988), Ronald Reagan's media advisor, was one of the best at using media logic to "take control" of interviews. He stated his approach in an editorial in the *Washington Post,* "Sound-Bite Campaigning: TV Made Us Do It" (1988, Oct. 30, C-7):

My own contribution to campaign innovation resulted from observing the medium as we prepared for the 1976 presidential race. I noted how the people who run television news were reducing a candidate's thoughtful and specific speech on an issue, say, an upturn in the economy, to a 10-second sound bite, which was then followed on the screen by an effective visual of someone, usually in the Midwest, "whose life remains untouched by the prosperity claimed by President Ford," as the voice-over told us. The point is that rather than inventing the effective visual or the 30-second sound bite, we simply adapted an existing TV news technique that was already widely used. . . . So, in our morning issues conference, a meeting much like those held in the editorial offices of newspapers and television networks and stations all over the country, I decided to "lead" with the housing story. But rather than have White House Press Secretary Larry Speakes hold up charts or issue a press release, and thereby bury the story in the business segment, we took the president to a construction site. There, wearing a hard hat and standing in front of homes under construction, he announced the housing start numbers and what that meant to the American people and the national economy. Naturally, the story played big on the evening news.

THE CHANGING AUSPICES OF INTERVIEWING

In this section I discuss briefly how other social changes, including the rise of new electronic media, contributed to the changing use, character, and meaning of journalism and interviewing. Some general comparisons are offered in Table 5.1. The content of communication is reflexive of the form and communication process. All modes of inquiry are influenced by the dominant institutions of the day as well as information technologies and the role and significance of certain communication formats (Couch, Maines, and Chen 1996). Putting information processes and information-gathering techniques in context, then, raises questions about the underlying logic, control, sponsorship, and oversight, or *auspices of interviewing*. When viewed as part of an ecology of communication, or the communication process in context, the fate

Table 5.1. The Changing Auspices of Interviewing

Interviewing Steps and Process	Newspapers and Print Media (Traditional)	Television and other Electronic Media
Information Technology	Print; linear and referential; collect complete interviews; "get the facts"	Electronic; visual; reflexive and evocative; collect thematic interviews; get some feelings and "emotions"
Formats	Inverted pyramid; narrative report	Entertainment; drama, action, and emotion
Time to Gather Information	Extended	Short
Use of Interview in Report	Extensive	Very brief
Interviewee's Knowledge, Experience	Usually minimal, especially prior to TV	Extensive, local officials
Audience's Knowledge and Expectations	Limited to previous news reports	Extensive; previous reports; movies; and personal experience
Perceived Impact of Interview	Limited to report and issues	Including the issues, personal, and legal implications
Impact on Interviewing	Moderate	Major

and utility of journalistic interviews is unsettling (Desmond 1978). The meaning, use, and significance of interviewing by journalists reflect changes in mass media, popular culture, organizational frameworks, marketing, and journalistic professionalism (Bensman and Lilienfeld 1973). Together, these suggest some guidelines for tracking the changing auspices of interviewing. Some of these changes are due mainly to electronic media that are visual and operate according to entertainment formats, such as TV news. Newspapers and magazines have adjusted their own approaches to fit more closely with these formats (Altheide and Snow 1991; Bailey and Hale 1998; Maines and Couch 1988). Table 5.1 summarizes some of the changes discussed in the following sections. Contrasts are drawn between the more referentially oriented newspapers and the more evocatively oriented TV styles. Journalistic interviewing now reflects shifts in information technology, formats, time and work schedules within which to gather information, the use of entertainment-oriented themes, and the journalists' desired impact.

There are several important differences that suggest changes in contexts as well. While the larger context involved development and elaboration of markets within and between print and electronic journalism, interviewing practices oriented to getting the "right" message out differed in more profound ways. As a print-based medium, journalism's history embraced the tools of writing and the market orientations of paper news (including magazines). Reporters worked by finding people who could tell them about events. They would pose questions, write answers, and then draw on these notes and impressions in writing a story. The writing was descriptive, attempting to set a tone that would interest readers. This took time.

The relationship between the interviewer and his or her subject has changed in the age of television. Primarily due to adjustments in commercialism, entertainment formats, and reporters' responsibilities to produce more reports in less time, journalists seldom spend as much time interviewing. Previously, interviewing involved more discovery time, information gathering, refinement of a perspective, and perhaps the need to learn more about the subject matter before further questioning.

INFORMATION TECHNOLOGY AND ENTERTAINMENT

Journalistic interviewing practices now reflect the shifts in information technology and entertainment formats. Interviewing orientations during the print era were informed by entertainment values, but as noted, with an emphasis on using the interview to learn about the events in question. While journalists may have had an idea about where the story would go before conducting the interview, it was not uncommon for this to be adjusted following revealing interviews. And while print journalists also faced space restrictions on the length of their articles, TV journalists, with exceptions, face even more severe limitations in terms of time.

Electronic technology permits and stresses visuals over aural information, impact and emotion over referentially derived meaning, and brevity over elaboration. As news formats emerged that essentially began with the end of the report in order to keep the viewer watching for the parts to be filled in, writing styles became even more inverted than the traditional approach used in headline writing in newspapers. Videotape recording and editing equipment meant that two or more visuals could even be superimposed at the same moment, set to a dramatic tempo. Items selected for reporting and the nature of reporting changed accordingly.

TV journalists are trained to focus on certain themes and angles of topics for interviews. This means that they enter the interview with a well-defined sense of what the story is, what the parts will be, and, with exceptions, the individual being interviewed is merely playing a part in completing the picture. As noted previously, when TV news and other mass media programs adopted the entertainment format, emphasis was placed on selecting interviewees and events for coverage and on presenting them in certain ways as to hold audience members' short attention spans. Presentation stressed short, visual, action-oriented reports. This meant motion on the camera and the display of compelling emotions throughout. When typical news reports last less than two minutes, there is not much time to capture—let alone explain and elaborate—on complex points. The TV journalist knows this and seeks to elicit key points from the interviewee in a very brief time, focusing on the most emotional bases. While actual interviews might last an hour or more, the interviewee could not expect to see more than thirty seconds of comment on the aired report. And, as many interviewees can attest, those portions that are used may not include the most significant point made during the interview or the complete version of the point the interviewee was trying to communicate. This is the bane of referential information: Limited time and focus on emotionally salient material cuts out most information.

The format of many TV news reports calls for a response, the other side, or an expert view on a topic. The interviewee is approached with questions and answers in mind. The main role of the interviewee is to provide the appropriate piece within a limited time. For example, I am known as a person who is critical of news practices, and I am asked occasionally to provide a statement about a particular aspect of news coverage. When the U.S. Marines "invaded" Somalia in December 1992 and were met by an army of journalists, cameras, and so forth, some people were outraged, calling for harsh actions against these interlopers. When a local network affiliate asked for my views, her initial questions suggested that I would be critical and would attack the news media for being so crass and interfering. The reporter was surprised when I stated that the media were doing exactly what was expected of it, that Pentagon "leaks" helped stage the entire operation in an attempt to enhance the image of the military and to improve public opinion of this very questionable military adventure. As a result, the network used an even smaller segment of my statement than usual on the evening news!

The organization of interviews has changed as well. Previously, what was said and meant would suffice for print journalists; they could get the information, interpret it, and write a report in a narrative, linear fashion. It was referentially based, even though it might have been an emotional report. This changed in the age of television. With more emphasis on entertainment and the capture of emotionally charged aspects of a topic and less time in which to produce the report, there was no compelling reason to invest a lot of time in an interview that might play for fifteen seconds on a news report. Emphasis shifted to getting emotional signatures or reactions.

Radio and television brought the emotional context of an interview to audiences. Capturing a sob, seeing tears flow down cheeks, looking into the eyes of the interviewee during tight camera shots merged as critical features of the message and, in some cases, the most important part of the report. It would not take long for spin doctors to realize that how something is said can be as important and compelling as what is said.

Broadcast journalists quickly dubbed the print journalists' format the "talking head" and something to be avoided. Not only did this further promote the penchant for visual action to mark time in news reports, but it resolved an impasse that had grown between journalists and their sources. For years, most journalists resented the public relations emphasis, back-stage preparations for interviews and events, and laundering of accounts by sources.

Entertainment-oriented interviewing has produced what may be termed the "talk for pay" syndrome, or the assumption that famous or important people deserve to be paid for a conversation before an audience. Numerous actors in the modern world have requested and received pay for talking; the price tag grows the more notorious the personality, as with Frank Sinatra, who reportedly turned down $250,000 for an interview (Brady 1976). The interface of interviewer and interviewee has become a viable format for profit in the changing face of this media age.

Journalists such as Barbara Walters are known for conducting interviews with well-known people, and, to her credit, occasionally this includes world leaders. However, most interviewees are important popular culture types, for example, movie stars, TV talk show hosts, or professional athletes. The topics are virtually always personal, career-oriented, or about conflicts with a spouse and are very promotional for both the interviewer and the interviewee. The broadcasts are well advertised and may even be featured in several parts. There is a very clear sense in such interviews that the interviewer is helping the interviewee tell his or her story and, indeed, is providing a valuable service to the interviewee as well as the audience. The "inside" look at power and fame remains a compelling fiction of our popular culture industry. One analysis suggests that the depth, detail, and slow-moving coverage of programs such as C-SPAN's *Booknotes* illustrates how things have changed in interviewing and the journalistic turn away from history.

> The broadcast network interviewers ask mostly about emotions and feelings. On many of the cable talk shows, the host is the star so the questions are really rococo essays that render the answers superfluous. And when you cast your eye out to the broader culture, you see even more than curiosity about simple facts has been submerged amidst the more sophisticated interested in theory and perceptions. (Brooks 1999, 22)

Celebrity talk can be expensive, but in the big picture of TV production expenses, talk is cheap. Interviews have also been influenced by the rise of talk shows. Having a well-paid host hoist celebrities into the spotlight to promote a movie or upcoming event may cost mere thousands of dollars compared to the several-million-dollar price tag on most prime-time shows. And talk shows have adopted pure entertainment formats that originally developed in vaudeville and were refined over the last forty years on such TV shows as *Laugh-In* and, two decades later, *Saturday Night Live* (*SNL*). Politicians showed their "accessible selves," their "human selves," by appearing to have a sense of humor. Even Richard Nixon played himself in a *Laugh-In* segment. Other presidents would travel through the last third of the twentieth century by stepping on quips and sitting in "guest" chairs reserved for movie stars and athletes. Presidential candidate Bill Clinton played a saxophone on TV. The 2000 presidential campaign saw the emergence of talk shows, such as *The Tonight Show with Jay Leno*, develop regularly appearing segments featuring Angela Marie Ramos seeking hugs from the candidates.

Recalling that the basic formula for most popular culture programs is to pursue those formats and topics that attract the largest audiences for the least amount of money, it comes as no surprise why talk shows have flourished. Most are relatively inexpensive to produce, that is, get interviewees, and, depending on their emphasis, they can attract relatively large audiences. The most salient point, however, is that interviews are used to promote entertainment via personality exposure. Talk as action is merged with onstage fighting for the enjoyment of all, for example, the *Jerry Springer Show*. The interview in TV-land has become a pretext for emotional display, even violence (Gamson 1998). Such staged in-studio battles have then been discussed on other talk shows, using interviews.

THE IMPACT OF JOURNALISM BECOMING A PROFESSION

Interviewing changed when journalism became more professional. "Older" print journalists often did not attend journalism school, but learned their craft

as apprentices, moving up through the ranks. The interview as a method of information gathering wasn't so much an option during print-oriented journalism as a necessity; everyone used it, and you just did it, learned it, and made
adjustments. The story was greatly shaped by what the interviewee told the
journalist. Studs Terkel (1974, xxv), a print journalist, gave this account of his
approach:

> I realized quite early in this adventure that interviews, conventionally con-
> ducted, were meaningless. Conditioned clichés were certain to come. The ques-
> tion-and-answer technique may be of some value in determining favored
> detergents, toothpaste and deodorants, but not in the discovery of men and
> women. There were questions, of course. But they were casual in nature—at the
> beginning; the kind you would ask while having a drink with someone; the kind
> he would ask you. The talk was idiomatic rather than academic. In short, it was
> conversation. In time, the sluice gates of dammed up hurts and dreams were
> opened.

As noted previously, this type of work took time.

As journalism became part of major media conglomerates and helped expand information-for-a-profit opportunities, the entertainment formats and
communication styles that attracted audiences and commercial advertisers
contributed to changing interviews. Changes in journalism accompanied
shifts in information technology, organizational adjustments, and, above all,
the fragmentation of large markets into smaller niches controlled by a few conglomerates. There was more competition for audiences who had more choices
(cable TV, specialty magazines, etc.).

Journalism schools had to adjust to new technologies and job markets. Students had to know how to write, of course, but also how to conduct interviews
in different contexts in varied media. "J schools" expanded the point stressed
by Bensman and Lilienfeld (1973) about taking into account the audience:

> The journalist, hemmed in by the periodicity of publication, and by the fact
> that he is selling some kind of media or publication, is forced to anticipate the
> response of his audience in terms of what the journalist calls newsworthy, or "hu-
> man interest." He must anticipate what will excite, stimulate, and titillate an
> audience at the time of publication. This means that the flow of his attention
> must be consistent with the "natural flow of attention of his audience." He must
> drop stories and his interest in events as events themselves shift either in their
> dramatic impact on audiences, or in the journalist's estimate of the audience's
> rhythm of interest. (208)

Acquiring information remained important, but the meaning and message
had to be cut short. Many journalism schools today do not even require a course
in interviewing, but often include it as part of a more general survey of methods or information-gathering techniques. Interviewing has been integrated

into the new professions of journalism by melting its distinctive edges to accommodate faster, more evocative visual formats. This does not mean that
quality journalistic interviews do not appear; they do. Nor does it imply that
there are not very good interviewers in journalism; there are. It does suggest
that the changing character of the look of information, and access to it, has had
a profound impact on how we gather information, assess it, and reflect on related ethical practices.

The filing of false reports is a case in point. When journalists submit com-
posite sketches of various interviews as a "real person," or simply make up
cases, there is far more than mere ethics of reporting involved: These practices
reveal a crack is opening in some epistemic contradictions of journalistic interviewing. Every case of false reporting with which I am familiar involves fictitious detailed accounts and understanding of everyday life situations that
resemble thoroughly executed interviews. The stories offered, made up as they
are, are reflexive of a process of data gathering that, were it carried out, might
paint a similar picture. When false cases win awards (e.g., Janet Cooke's
Pulitzer Prize–winning fictitious account of an eight-year-old heroin addict,
"Jimmy's World"), there is an even sharper implication that authentic interviewing is the kind of reporting we should strive for, including such depth,
detail, and understanding (Eason 1986).

Fortunately, journalism's ethics and standards continue to insist that no
matter how compelling the printed version, no matter how "essentially" it
touches on "typical" scenarios and processes, it is not good enough if it is not
real. Indeed, an editorial in the *Washington Post* (April 16, 1981, A18) about
"Jimmy's World" included an assertion about journalistic credibility:

> In fact, it will be an error and a shame if serious students and critics of the
> press take the "Jimmy" episode as the model of what's wrong with us or as ev-
> idence that stories are largely fabrications. The fact is that the shortcomings we
> in this business are continually fighting against, the shortcomings that can
> threaten our prized credibility and that we recognize in all their danger are far
> more subtle and insidious than some out-and-out made-up story.

In other words, the line between the interviewer and the interviewee is a pragmatic substitute for authenticity. In the journalistic perspective, it separates
reality from other alternatives, no matter how true they may be. That line is
more distinct in a print and linear world than in an electronic age that operates more temporally than spatially, more emotionally than rationally.

INTERVIEWING AS A CULTURAL PHENOMENON

Interviews are everywhere in postindustrial society. Interviews are seen and
heard throughout popular culture. As suggested, popular culture changed

interviewing from a method of data gathering to an evocative presentation of another story. Compromised veracity accompanied this shift. Whereas the questions asked always had implications and the face-to-face situation carried nuances which might inform the exchange, the impact of the situation and the occasion of the interview itself made things different.

Another significant change that has governed the use of interviews by journalists is that the compelling context of commercialism has contributed to the blurring of distinctions between journalist and entertainer. Interviewing has multiple meanings in popular culture, but that is not as clear when someone is doing what looks like an interview but it is really for promotional purposes. More is involved than merely whether the subject matter is serious or not serious. The issue concerns what happens to the interview when it works both (or all) sides of the street, so to speak. This opens up the big issue about the nature of the interview itself and suggests that, in popular culture, the interview is several things. While interviewing is merely a vehicle for other purposes, it is so ingrained in our culture as a framework (Atkinson and Silverman 1997) for acquiring information that I argue it has contributed to the expansion of popular culture and has lent its credibility as an information vehicle to transforming news and blending other programs.

In earlier periods, participants and audiences differed in their experience and expectations of interviews compared with the contemporary electronic scene. Most of the people interviewed in a primarily print-oriented culture might never have been interviewed previously and certainly had not experienced a lot of interview presentations except for perhaps something read in a newspaper. In the current age, it is much different. The question and answer format, with a clear purpose of being read or heard by others, is familiar in everyday life, and most people today are aware of the utilitarian side of interviews. In earlier days, newspaper audiences differed from television news viewers. The former's base of experience for reading and understanding news reports was everyday life and other newspaper experiences. TV audiences see many interviews on the news, magazine shows—where "stars interview stars"—as well as entertainment programs and movies.

The meaning of interviews changed as more people acquired a broader understanding of how they were changing. They grasped not only the utility involved (e.g., will I get the job?), but also the significance of power and identity as well. The person asking the questions is acting from a position of power, even if he or she is employed by another for this purpose. As more people became aware of interview procedures and the way that answers could be edited, interviewees began to add an "editing" perspective to answers, especially when interviews were conducted by journalists. Framing of answers, considering different interpretations, avoiding strong adjectives or naming specific times and places became the hallmark of this new awareness. This is particularly true of politicians and public officials. Many organizations established press relations officers, public relations arms, and so forth to provide information and "comment" when contacted by journalists. Many contemporary organizations, such as police departments, permit only designated officials to provide interviews to reporters.

The practice of framing responses took on an added dimension, however, when expertise in framing messages began to develop. Known as "spin doctors" and by the negatively tinged designator "PR," comments by organizational actors are widely acknowledged to be less than accurate, self-promotional, and always utilitarian. Indeed, it is becoming more common for journalists to "retire to" public relations positions in large organizations. Hunter Thompson's approach to "gonzo journalism" took into account how interviews would be arranged and managed on "their terms" in order to control the outcome. A gonzo journalist would take a direct approach, often pushing aside civilities that were manipulated for an interviewee's advantage. His approach was different. He explains why he would call movers and shakers in the early morning hours:

> In Washington, the truth is never told in daylight hours or across a desk. If you catch people when they're very tired or drunk or weak, you can usually get some answers. So I'd sleep days, wait till these people get their lies and treachery out of the way, let them relax, then come on full speed on the phone at two or three in the morning. You have to wear the bastards down before they'll tell you anything. (Brady 1976, 8)

In view of the multiple interests that may enter a journalistic interview, it seems cogent to ask about different meanings called forth by a particular interview. Keeping in mind that most people who are interviewed by journalists have witnessed numerous interviews and, in many cases, have been interviewed on numerous occasions themselves, what does the interview tap? When one considers that the interviewee may have various agendas to set forth, different audiences in mind for each one, and perhaps a history with a particular interviewer, it is not altogether clear what answer a particular question will call forth. For example, most claims makers, advocates of certain positions or policies, fashion their opportunities for journalistic interviews toward convincing particular decision-making audiences of perhaps four or five people. They are not interested in merely going on record, feeding the public information store in some way, but rather, they are targeting decisionmakers who often view TV newscasts in order to get a sense of what the public is thinking.

As decades of social science methodology have taught, interview "answers" reflect much more than simply the question and the truth of the answer (Cicourel 1964). This is particularly important to keep in mind when using interviews as a method of data collection and interview transcripts as data. Indeed, this is why it is often very risky for social scientists to use interview transcripts alone in attempting to capture what an individual interviewee "really, really" thinks about a certain issue (although it is a legitimate data source for delineating public information and reports about a particular topic).

PRIME-TIME TV INTERVIEWING

The nature, use, and meaning of interviewing has changed within popular culture. As used in entertainment programs as well as news "infotainment" programs, interviewing is powerful because it is evocative. Shaped by media logic, media interviews cut to the chase, ask the big questions, help the audience anticipate the answers, and evaluate them. As one of my colleagues put it, in prime time, testimony becomes evidence. This perspective can be seen in several genres of news and public information shows. All feature the interview as star.

> The development of the "evocative interview" and the perspective that fostered its use by stars and, in turn, its adaptation by audiences is a major development in the history of interviewing. It was the widespread adaptation of media logic and entertainment formats that fostered such a perspective and orientation among actors as well as audiences. In becoming more evocatively packaged and presented, the emphasis of interviewing has shifted from information gathering to satisfying production values stressing impact, shock, morality play scenarios, and "big conclusions." Searching for big conclusions has led journalists to push for the big question without obtaining the background information necessary to recognize what a range of appropriate questions might be. Such appropriate questions often emerge from lengthy conversations and engagement of the interviewee while learning about his or her world and experiences and then locating an initial journalistic interest in this context. This takes time and experience. It is an approach that experienced journalists and other ethnographers cultivate. There is a style of interviewing that develops from such practices, sometimes referred to as "deep background," "depth interviewing," "focused interviewing," or "active interviewing". (Holstein and Gubrium 1995)

TV news formats do not permit much time to present more than a few minutes of interviews, and only then when interviews follow entertainment formats. The focus is on impact, and impact on TV had to be seen, heard, and felt by the audience. One genre that developed to meet these needs was the news magazine show, for example, *60 Minutes*. These shows are known for probing controversial topics and for presenting "bombshell" interviews. A journalist commented on the way that *60 Minutes* producer Don Hewitt helped increase viewer ratings:

> Hewitt's regrettable legacy in this regard is that modern news magazines focus obsessively on "the get"—the first interview with a person of the moment, like Kato Kaelin or Monica Lewinsky. News is rarely got from the get [regard-

ing: Diane Sawyer asking Marla Maples] "Was it the best sex you ever had?" . . .
The get is about the correspondent's charisma and power, not the subject's view.
Hewitt understood that the audience wanted the same thing that had drawn
him to journalism in the first place: the movie version. . . . So he turned his correspondents into movie stars. (Friend 2001, 92)

Topics for these shows involve a substantial team of field producers and reporters who develop report ideas, pursue them, engage in preliminary interviewing with subjects, and basically set forth a script for the "stars" (e.g., Mike
Wallace) based on a lot of background work. However, audiences see only the
star reporter asking a few probing questions, for which the answers are usually
already known. Like the tip of an iceberg, what the audience sees is part of the
illusion of showbiz and not the bulk that supports it. It is an edited investigation and interview, essentially camera work capturing large amounts of eye
candy presented to viewing audiences—not the complex series of interviews
and other background work done in preparation for show time.

What the news magazines rely on is the iconography of television. This
means a lot of visual busyness: split screens; sepia dissolves; "cookie cutters"
(which throw exciting shadows behind the interviewee, such as a louvered window or a vertical slash); and cranes that swoop to capture the correspondent's
standup. (Friend 2001, 92)

This genre presents three to six investigative reports during thirty to sixty
minutes. There are several advantages of this approach. First, more time is
available for preparing and presenting reports. Without focusing on breaking
news (or timely news), these reports may be planned well in advance. Second,
the genre permits longer reports to be aired. This affords the opportunity to
present longer excerpts of interviews. Another strength of this approach for
entertainment purposes is that they are cast as investigative reports, focusing
on social problems, but more typically on some aspect of corruption that could
be personalized or located in and around particular organizations, offices, or
individuals. While only segments of longer interviews are broadcast, they tend
to be provocative and "smoking gun" interviews that are often framed in tight
shots of the subject's face, focusing on eyes, and so forth. With exceptions, the
intent is to pursue an angle as part of a more general theme.

In most journalistic enterprise, the preparation and background work of actually collecting information is not presented as part of a report. This helps
the credibility of journalism since it hides the fact that most news content can
be described as information transmission (or "information mechanics") rather
than information gathering, sifting, challenging, interpreting, and presenting. So, if the typical interviewing process were shown, the readers or viewers
would see that most reports come from institutional news sources such as businesses, government agencies, and law enforcement agencies (Holstein and

Gubrium 2000). Viewers would see that journalists receive press releases or monitor police radio transmissions (with scanners) and then select events and activities to cover.

A different approach is used with investigative journalism, also known historically as muckraking, which spans newspapers, magazines, and novelists. Interviews play an important role in this work. Investigative journalism did not begin with TV investigative reports, but the TV format took on the added dimension of providing compelling visuals of the "guilty look." A key part of this presentation is to open up part of the interviewing process for viewers to see as part of the context of the overall message of guilt and guile. The news magazines incorporate those parts of the interviewing process into the presentation that are consistent with the theme of the report. This is done through the "ambush interview," in which a subject who has not granted permission for an interview is surprised by the reporter at an unexpected time. With the reporter thrusting the microphone in front of the target, the two verbally spar as they walk. Startled, and still not wanting to be interviewed, the individual invariably says something or acts in an untoward way, which could then be used as evidence of the person's refusal to cooperate and that he or she has something to hide. Showing this process on camera has become part of the overall report and is consistent with another underlying theme of some magazine genre shows: that the reporters are helping us.

The push for evocative formats in TV news was accompanied by the widespread availability of technologies permitting "action news" or "going live," which subsequently led to the development of numerous other TV shows. The hosts of these shows, often respected journalists in their own right, all suffered the metamorphosis of successful mass media: They believed their own propaganda, or more directly, they began to see themselves as the central figures in interviews and, eventually, the events that were covered.

A prime example is *Nightline,* a popular ABC late-night news show that focuses on both current events and issues raised in the news media. *Nightline* thrives on crises. Indeed, it began with a crisis in 1978 with a mission to follow the daily developments of the Americans who were taken hostage in Teheran, Iran. Several dozen Americans held hostage hardly strikes the chord that a "nation held hostage" does. So that's what *Nightline* called it: "America Held Hostage: Day X." The 444-day run of the hostage crisis seemingly discovered late-night audiences interested in news and crisis updates. The host, Ted Koppel, was a good interviewer, who, during a relatively brief on-air conversation, could ask provocative but basic questions clarifying issues and moving the discussion beyond the mere headlines of the topic. This skill and emphasis gradually merged into a more directive role when it came to interviewing. By the mid-1990s, *Nightline* became a more active player in events, not merely reporting on them, but actively seeking resolutions. It became entertainment. The sense of a public mission was invoked on numerous occasions as Ted Koppel evolved from an energetic curious journalist seeking information to one approaching omniscience, and, in several cases, blatant arrogance. This all transpired through interviews.

A case in point is Koppel's approach to the "story" of "kids shooting kids." Violence in schools has become a major flash point for concerns about fear. School shootings have been cast as a "crisis" as well as an "epidemic." Numerous efforts (e.g., armed guards, metal detectors, "locker sweeps," hot lines) have been taken across the country to tighten control of school buildings, often resulting in less freedom for students and teachers. *Nightline* provided extensive coverage of each school shooting, but did very little to put the activities in perspective.

One such shooting occurred at Columbine High School in 1999. In the aftermath, Koppel and his crew returned to Jonesboro, Arkansas, the scene of a similar shooting some thirteen months earlier. On April 22, 1999, the *Nightline* crew met in a church with several dozen Jonesboro residents, including the mother of one of the boys who did the shooting and the husband of a school teacher who was killed. *Nightline*'s self-proclaimed role was to promote "healing" by letting the residents of the Jonesboro community talk with those of Columbine. So emotions were running high, and they got more intense when the husband of the slain Jonesboro teacher objected to the presence in the church of the youthful gunman's mother, indicating that he had been "sandbagged" by the *Nightline* show. He went on to explain that he had never received an apology from the mother, even though he was aware of how badly the parents of the shooters felt, how devastated their families were. A few excerpts from the transcript show what ensued. These can also be seen as an illustration of what has happened to the journalistic role, the use of interviews in evocative formats, and the active participation of the journalist in the event being covered. The discussion includes several speakers, including Mitchell Wright, the husband of a slain woman, and Gretchen Woodard, the mother of one of the assailants. Illustrative comments of the strong, directive role of the journalist to promote a certain answer are given in italics.

> Ted Koppel: *You said at the outset that it's been 13 months and you have not received any kind of direct communication or apology from either of the families. Mrs. Woodard would like a chance to get up and speak. I don't want you to feel blindsided again. May I call on her?*
>
> Mitchell Wright: I don't mind you doing that, but here's the thing. Just like I said earlier, don't, in Colorado, don't make the victims have to ask for an apology.
>
> Ted Koppel: I heard you and I hear you now. Mrs. Woodard?
>
> Gretchen Woodard: I guess I feel I need to say that I did not come here and I would not want words from me to ever hurt anyone any more than anyone has already suffered. *I do know that I come here with good intentions and to let the people know that we all do have to work through this and we take a day at a time*

and sometimes it's a minute at a time. I have really struggled with coming here tonight because I did not want to cause any pain. I just did feel it was very important to know that there are people all over this world that are scared, that took five minutes of their busy life to say that we're also in their thoughts and prayers. And it's enough when I look in my other children's eyes to know we do have to go on. Where in the world would we ever go? You know, this went national. Someone wouldn't know . . .

Ted Koppel: But I can't begin to know what Mr. Wright is going through. I don't pretend to know what you're going through. I really don't. But I do know that *I've just heard an anguished cry from one man saying it's been 13 months and I haven't heard an apology yet and I, I don't, I don't want to be the one to lead you to it. That wouldn't be appropriate either. If you don't feel it, you shouldn't say it.*

Gretchen Woodard: No. And I can't help what someone feels in their heart and I don't begin to know what Mr. Wright has gone through either. I do know what I live with every day of my life and like I said the rest of my family does and I guess that I don't feel it is my right to be here and cause any more hard feelings and it is important to me to say that standing here and pointing fingers at someone and saying you're a bad person or you're this or you're that, there isn't a quick fix answer.

[Note: Mrs. Woodward has made her point, but it is not sufficient for the evocative reply required by this interview format that is framed by Koppel's intent to be a "healer."]

Ted Koppel: I don't think anyone was asking for a quick fix. *I'm going to ask one more time, do you feel it is appropriate, right, to say to the families of those who were killed by your son . . .*

Gretchen Woodard: Yes.

Ted Koppel: And how sorry you are?

Gretchen Woodard: I have [said] many times and I have in the papers and I have in the local media. There were many times.

[Note: Her contrition is not strong enough for the dramatic finality called for by the entertainment interview.]

Ted Koppel: *But not to them.*

Gretchen Woodard: I haven't reached out. . . .

[Note: As though he becomes aware of how painful this is for Mrs. Woodard, and the breaching of a traditional journalist's interviewing role, Koppel retreats.]

Ted Koppel: I mean I'm not saying, I'm not saying that that's necessarily something you should do, but clearly Mr. Wright feels you should.

Gretchen Woodard: And I do feel that with my heart and I have said many times that I'm sorry. I don't know what I could say or do to help. Is there words?

> I mean there just isn't and I just know that it did take all the strength I had
> to come here tonight and . . .
> Ted Koppel: That I surely believe. I really do and I know a lot of you do.

[Note: Gretchen Woodard is not an experienced interviewee; she is not merely performing according to *Nightline*'s grammar and flow of the interview. She is struggling to convey her feelings, but it is not her timing that counts. It is the entertainment format that matters here. She didn't take her "cue" to quit, the way someone familiar with TV interviews would.]

> Gretchen Woodard: And I am very sorry. My family's very sorry and my son lives
> with this every day, struggles with this, Mitchell does.
> Ted Koppel: All right.
> Gretchen Woodard: And that is the most I guess I can say.

Following other comments, including parents thanking Koppel for letting them speak, *Nightline* signed off.

Cringing at the crass sensationalism of this production, I crossed the line from being a media analyst to a media critic—very directly. I sent an e-mail to the *Nightline* producer (they have a Web page). My comment and his reply follow.

> From: David Altheide
> Sent: Friday, April 23, 1999, 12:04 p.m.
> The Nightline show on Thursday, Apr. 22, 1999 was one of the worst displays of sensationalism on TV news that I've seen. You just dug the infotainment hole deeper and helped articulate further our postjournalism condition—where the line disappears between those covering an event/story and the event itself. As a long time viewer of Nightline (remember, America Held Hostage, Day X?), I am chagrined that Ted K. and company sought to outspringer Jerry Springer and the soap opera emotional shows by trying to set up a confrontation between the mother of one of the Jonesboro "shooters" and the husband of one of the deceased, who skillfully plays out a TV victim role. And, in a church? Have the egos and media logic supporting this program gotten so bold as to think that you can "heal" something? Reverend Ted! Faaantastic!
> —David Altheide

The reply from the producer:

> We have had an unusually high volume of e-mails following our two-hour town meeting from Jonesboro, Arkansas. They have been thoughtful, provoking and very constructive. Please understand how difficult it is to answer each one individually. Please know each one is read.
> Our objective was to perform a public service in the midst of crisis—to allow the people of Littleton, Colorado, to hear from members of a community

who had gone through a similarly horrific event thirteen months ago. What can they expect? Who do you tell the kids about returning to school? What do you do about the media circus that puts down its tent after every one of these tragedies?

It was one of the most intense experiences anyone connected with NIGHT-LINE has been through. The people in Jonesboro recently marked the first anniversary of the school shooting at Westside Middle School, churning up emotions and when the Littleton shootings erupted on Tuesday, it sent Jonesboro reeling, forcing the community to relive its worst nightmare.

Our *fear* [my emphasis added] was that by going to Jonesboro at this vulnerable moment, we would be adding to their burden. But many people told us they wanted to turn their grief into something positive and were eager to provide whatever help they could to the people of Littleton. In fact, the people in Littleton were so touched by the folks in Jonesboro that they stayed after the two-hour broadcast to talk with NIGHTLINE correspondent John Donvan. Their conversation was so riveting, it will be broadcast tonight.

The most common complaint we heard from our viewers was the frequent breaks for commercials, forcing Ted to interrupt some of the guests. It is irritating and frustrating, but the nature of the beast. The commercials allow us to send a team of people to Jonesboro and produce a two-hour town meeting with 36 hours notice. Can we make a more graceful transition to commercials at times? Of course, but understand on a live broadcast packed with emotion with all kinds of chatter in Ted's ear, it can be rocky at times.

As always, we value and encourage your feedback. Hopefully, we will act on your suggestions in a way that conforms to your vision for NIGHTLINE.
Sincerely
Richard Harris
Nightline Senior Producer

There are several points about this production that can also serve as a summary for this chapter.

1. The media people see that an opportunity to let the people speak can be beneficial to us all and, of course, to them. This is significant, since *Nightline,* like most national media programs, seldom moves beyond a handful of locations in its coverage of many issues and virtually never lets "regular people" express their views.
2. The entertainment format of drama, emotion, confrontation is present. *Nightline* draws on the relatively recently developed formats of daytime shows, such as Springer, to have confrontations, to apologize face to face. It is about generating conflict and drama and emotional tugs that touch audiences and let them participate: a public degradation ritual. It is about ratings and money. A statement by the Jonesboro school superintendent, who remained silent during the ABC *Nightline* telecast from Jonesboro said, "It stirred up emotions that were becoming lightened.

We'll have to deal with that tomorrow. But they [ABC-TV] made their money" (*Arizona Republic*, April 25, 1999, A1).

3. Even the "accuser," who dislikes the media setup of the confrontation— that an individual he obviously blames for the tragedy was present—is cooled by Koppel's questionable assertion that he did not know she would be present. The commercial enterprise that promotes this type of program is referred to by the show's producer as a necessary evil to be tolerated in the midst of the emotional outpouring; by this admission, we are given a glimpse of the real motivation and foundation for the coverage in the first place.

4. The victim role is celebrated and promoted, as several actors (e.g., Mitchell Wright) repeat their performances. The spatial, temporal, and symbolic lines and spaces separating public from private are smashed. Sense making, reconciliation, and the all-too-human quest for meaning, comfort, and solace are appropriated by the visual coverage so that we all can share in their suffering.

5. Placing this event and its coverage in context is challenging but necessary since "what it is" is largely a feature of the meanings and definitions that are made of it. The interviews by Koppel did not do this. There is much to be said about the event(s) themselves, and only a few points will be mentioned here about it, including the role of the high school social structure, that some kids were not shot, presumably, because they had a better relationship with the shooters, including the possibility that they were also the butt of oppressive high school social structure. A genuine interest in understanding the situation would consider the perspective and findings of social scientists and psychologists who could conduct relevant field studies and interviews to provide a scenario about how these events emerged. While no single cause would be found, understanding would be developed that may help inform others seeking to prevent similar activities.

CONCLUSION

Journalistic interviewing reflects changes in culture, information technology, marketing and commercial interests, and the ways in which these have been folded into an ecology of communication guided by media logic. Entertainment formats rule the day in politics, sports, religion, education, and journalism. Fear is but one consequence of this perspective.

I stated at the outset that journalism remains as useful as its interviewing practices are sound. Journalistic interviewing practices are sound for the things they reflect: Journalism is very useful for making money; it is very useful for getting public attention; and it is very useful for having a very focused impact.

But it's less useful for understanding social problems and keeping audiences informed about their everyday lives. The nature and meaning of interviewing has profoundly changed over the last seventy years and has provided a paradox of interviewing in our media age: The journalistic interview has been transformed via media logic to provide evocative scenarios that are quite effective. Such changes make interviews more interesting and more entertaining. But, with exceptions, such evocative approaches are less useful for truth seeking. With changes in information technology, particularly TV news, and the mushrooming growth of popular culture industries, journalism has become more entertainment oriented. Veteran journalist Daniel Schorr (1993) reflected on this now less familiar look of journalism:

> I have this sense that somehow journalism has to separate itself from the media. I'm not sure how it is going to happen. But reporters have to somehow draw back from being part of the great performance and say there are responsibilities that we have. (22)

The uses of interviews to fill in an established thematic point or to complete a requisite role, such as that of an expert, are well established and are likely to continue. Interviews as referential points for any purposes other than personality insights or material to be incorporated into a documentary format are not very common. It seems clear that interviewing has a steadfast hold on entertainment and infotainment as well as a host of reality shows in which "real people" tell their stories about "real problems," and often act out their differences with "real violence."

When audience members and performers have experience with standards and criteria of a good interview, how to conduct it, and how to participate as a competent member of popular culture, interviewing moves beyond the occupational borders of journalists, social scientists, and others into the popular culture comfort zone that pads affect within an ecology of communication. Interviewing in this context becomes a social activity to be done right, grounded in effective dramaturgy of everyday life. Useful information may occasionally be provided, but can only be evaluated within the criteria appropriate to its time, place, and manner.

> Indeed, when you step back far enough you begin to appreciate that C-SPAN is so far out of tune with the times that it has become an intellectual counterculture. Especially on the weekends, the people who fill its screens seem quaintly and bravely out of step. . . . C-SPAN is factual in a world grown theoretical. It is slow in a world growing more hyper. It is word-oriented in an era that is visually sophisticated. With its open phone lines, it is genuinely populist in a culture that preaches populism more than it practices it (Brooks 1999, 22).

The credibility of journalism hinges in part on the place of interviewing in its craft. It is no coincidence that the decline in public respect for journalism has been accompanied by a fundamental shift in interviewing techniques and uses. Notwithstanding that false reports, propaganda, and distorted views of reality can always come from selecting sources of information no matter how "well" they are interviewed, it is the interviewing process as a way of engaging and confronting social life more directly that greases the way journalism will slide in the future. To reiterate a *Washington Post* editorial statement about the shortcomings of journalism, "[they] are far more subtle and insidious than some out-and-out made-up story."

6

Policing Crime and Fear in the News Media

No topic illustrates fear better than crime. This chapter examines how domestic crime and war is packaged by news sources representing criminal justice agencies, in the case of crime, and the military, in the case of war. The focus is how both generate fear by proposing "solutions" to fear. A critical part of this process involves being a news source that gets to define situations, the essence of power in modern life. I examine how the military works with the media to define situations on the international scene, and then I turn to the domestic and more local crime scenes, where various criminal justice agencies work closely with journalists operating within the problem frame of entertaining media logic. Brief case studies are presented of the role of news sources in news reports for three events: (1) an execution of a convicted murderer; (2) advocacy for hate-crime legislation; and (3) press coverage of a widely publicized female sex offender.

Crime refers not only to certain illegal acts, but also to the language, images, and symbols that are used in discussing kinds of behavior and activities, often condoning acts to prevent crime. Of course, there are different kinds of crimes. We usually associate crime with street crime, and this generally refers to our internal domestic scene. But there is also a range of white-collar crime, as well as seemingly innumerable misdemeanors. External threats to U.S. citizens or our allies may be viewed as international crimes (e.g., aggression) or acts of war. Defense and corrective action is required in both instances: Police are assigned to domestic crime, while the military is expected to police the international arena. The policing activity in the domestic and international realms involves massive organizations with millions of workers, requiring considerable resources. These must be provided and legitimated by elected officials who serve the public interest. This requires the consent of the governed—and this is where the news media and popular culture come into play. The mass media provide the information as news to the audiences, and thereby engage in policing activity in its own right:

> A substantial amount of reporting consists of accounts of "policing" under-
> taken by one organization in relation to other organizations or individuals. . . .
> The news-media emphasis on organized life, and its policing, means that they
> focus on aspects which violate expectations about organized life of which sug-
> gest tendencies towards disorganization, and the social control of policing ef-
> forts to deal with these. Furthermore, because news organizations are entwined
> in the organizational nexus of policing they report on, in some instances they
> themselves take on a policing (fourth-estate) role with social effects. (Ericson,
> Baranek, and Chan 1987, 47)

The basic way that such policing occurs, of course, is through working closely
with spokespersons, honoring their scripts or claims of authority, and through
interpretation of various events.

> More than anything else they do, the news media attend to the definition of
> social problems and the preferred solutions of accredited bodies. . . . The ad-
> vantage of the news media for promoting one's cause is that they have the aura
> of being somewhat removed, a third party. Moreover, by translating them all
> into the common sense, the causes which are conveyed appear naturally to be
> the case. This makes the news media a much better vehicle of communication
> than printed or broadcast material put out by a particular interest group to get
> its message across, because in comparison that material appears explicitly to be
> bureaucratic propaganda. (Ericson et al. 1987, 36)

THE MILITARY-MEDIA COMPLEX

Propaganda promotes fear as well as justifications for battling against the
source of fear. This usually means that something or someone is going to be
attacked. Propaganda has become fused with the entertainment format in forg-
ing a renewed relationship between news and entertainment, the major networks and the military, and foreign conflicts and domestic policy. Fear is part
of the entertainment process today. Those who share information and media
logics trade on common operating procedures and perspectives.

Much has changed since social scientists like C. Wright Mills joined President Dwight D. Eisenhower in the 1950s in urging caution for an emerging
military-industrial complex. Their concern was that the military and big
weapons manufacturers were pursuing common interests to the detriment of
the political process. The connections were managed as high-ranking retired
military personnel found lucrative jobs as lobbyists and advisors with major
aircraft and arms manufacturers. The weapons industry was becoming a
stronger lobby for the defense department, as well as fostering hard-line political decisions compatible with military deployment around the world. This
changed as the Cold War ended, and also as more military brass retire to serve

television and cable networks. While arms manufacturers still benefit from military buildups and wars, so do the news media.

The mass media play a significant political and cultural role in numerous social relationships, particularly support for the military. And, conversely, the media and the military have been involved in a reciprocal relationship trading on entertainment topics for movies and news, on the one hand, as well as technological access and development, on the other hand. Jackall and Hirota's (2000) provocative account of George Creel, the role played by the Committee on Public Information (CPI) at the start of World War I, and the amazing transformation of the role of public relations in public life led them to conclude in other work that "the rationalization of advertising and public relations in the twentieth century was largely a product of war" (12).

Only on rare occasions, such as in the waning years of the Vietnam War, did major American media reflect displeasure with foreign policy and military operations. An adversarial relationship with the military was apparent in some media outlets until the 1980s when government censorship and restrictions first separated and then reintegrated the media. The Gulf War in 1991, Desert Storm, was enthusiastically supported by most media outlets, with celebratory coverage of well-orchestrated—although often invalid—visuals of dramatic success and kills (e.g., the impression that most Patriot missiles hit their targets). The scaled-down ("billion-dollar special") four-day version of missile attacks on Iraq in 1998 ("Desert Fox") was not hindered by congressional hearings or media-generated debates.

How did the media stance on military operations change from support to challenge back to support in a mere two decades? A very brief look at the role of the mass media, information technology, and the military in an era of unprecedented growth of entertainment as an industry and perspective can answer that question.

The military-industrial complex is an artifact of the Cold War era during which Congress, the media, and the public took for granted that the Soviet threat and the numerous sparring bouts (brush-fire wars) needed constant military expenditures. Notwithstanding the significance of yellow journalism in promoting jingoistic adventures, the media were a minor—albeit a supporting—player in the rules and strategies of national and international dominance. Print and movie media served governmental interests, often as explicit propaganda outlets for hot and cold wars until the 1960s. Reliant on governmental licensing and regulations, the fledgling TV industry, save for a few journalists, lacked the markets and the infrastructure to boldly challenge governmental initiatives.

The military-industrial complex changed when the Soviet Union disintegrated. Champagne celebrating the victory had hardly stopped bubbling when it became apparent that the arms industry would have to take another tact to assure its future growth and prosperity. The defense budget was slated to be cut, a process that was exacerbated as an army of claims makers jumped on domestic threats to garner congressional and public opinion support for sundry wars on crime, drugs, gangs, and, more recently, immigration. The major networks promoted such efforts by airing a number of reality TV shows emphasizing crime, violence, fear, and danger.

The debacle in Vietnam cost the United States some military credibility, and it took more than two decades of Hollywood movies and entertainment efforts to bolster claims that the United States had actually *won* that war—or *would have* won it had it not been for the political defeat at home, which refers to the domestic protests and the politicians' (e.g., Lyndon Johnson's) reluctance to "hit 'em with everything we had." The mass media, particularly TV journalism, was blamed for the negative public opinion and the political decisions that led to U.S. withdrawal. Subsequently, it took a number of military victories against such adversaries as Grenada, Panama, Iraq, and Somalia to redefine losses as victories and get the military back on target in public opinion and political influence.

> In the face of a 25 percent decline in defense spending since the end of the Cold War, and with the Joint Chiefs of Staff warning of readiness concerns, many military officials believe a robust public affairs operation is one of their best weapons in selling their needs to the public and Congress. "Today, when you get an opportunity to stand up and represent your command, you've got to hit a home run," Army Maj. Bob Hastings told the students in his public affairs course. (Vogel 1998, 6)

The military-media complex is a feature of programming in an entertainment-oriented era which is dominated by popular culture and communication forms that share sophisticated information technology promoting visual media and evocative content. The media are a major player in this chapter. It was not until the 1960s that TV surpassed print media as a cultural force. With an expanding revenue base, the emergence of the concept as well as actual target audiences, and sophisticated marketing techniques, the mass media—and especially television—flexed its technology muscles and discovered that not only did visuals sell products, but they also conveyed powerful messages about social issues. A flood of information technology—from CDs to cable to VCRs to the Internet—produced a popular culture inspired by entertainment forms and the visual image. These technological and organizational changes influenced the renewed convergence of military and the mass media.

Several parallel developments to the winding down of the Cold War were critical to the resurgence of American military in foreign policy. One was the expanding use of satellites for military and commercial purposes (e.g., surveillance and communication). Another significant development was the rise of cable TV, particularly the rise of the "fourth network"—the Cable News

Network, CNN—and 24-hour news. During the 1990s, the fourth network was followed by a fifth (Fox), as well as conventional networks' expansion (e.g., MSNBC). Together these contributed to expanded global coverage, including the terrorism and war niches. With costs rising for the big three networks and mergers treading across bottom lines, ABC, NBC, and CBS sliced news staffs and began relying on satellite feeds as well as the work of stringers stationed throughout the world rather than fully staffed foreign bureaus.

> A tightening economic climate for broadcasters has also led to cost-cutting initiatives at the major networks, diminishing their presence overseas. CNN, meanwhile, has staked out international news as its competitive turf, proudly noting that it is the only western TV news organization with a regular presence in Iraq, including five correspondents in Baghdad. (Lowry 1995, F1)

International coverage declined, save for reactive crisis coverage, which was often live. The junior network(s) filled in and showed remarkable capacity to adapt with mobile units. As the new networks helped initiate and refine the cable/satellite information technology, they were essentially using very similar technology to the military, whose increased use of sophisticated missile and other weapons systems relied heavily on satellite communications. Military operations changed with this technology, but so did its public relations and war-broadcasting capabilities.

The Gulf War with Iraq in 1991 was very important for the resurgence of the military and the military-media connection in this postjournalism era. Despite initial proclamations by media pundits and some academics about media control and censorship, this war contributed to the shared use of entertaining visuals by the Pentagon and the major networks in the United States and throughout the world. Generals and journalists joked as they led global audiences through bomb-sight videos of explosions and hits, complete with "oohs" and "ahhs" and, occasionally, laughter when, as in one case, a motorist crossed a bridge just moments before it exploded. CNN's round-the-clock live coverage of the missile and aerial bombardment of Baghdad helped establish its future role as an important player in international affairs and coverage. Bob Murphy, ABC's senior vice president for news, told the *Los Angeles Times* reporter Brian Lowry:

> "While others cut back, we have grown and grown and continue to do so," said Eason Jordan, CNN's president of international networks and global news gathering. "CNN takes the world seriously, and that's one of the things that distinguish us from all competitors." (Lowry 1995, F1)

While the initial coverage was by radio, the presence of CNN changed how networks would cover war in the future. Critical, reflective pieces on war and analysis of the consequences on foreign policy and the future all but disappeared. Coverage of the 1991 Gulf War also changed how the enemy would operate, and, perhaps most importantly, it altered how the military would interact with the press.

CNN's Gulf War coverage is significant in several ways. First, it operated in enemy territory with the full cooperation of the enemy, the highly demonized Saddam Hussein. Both sides appreciated the role of the media and gave it privileged status in order to promote and use key visuals—a dramatic hit or civilian casualties—for their own purposes. Despite having its movements restricted, CNN became the signature network of the Gulf War, and over the next few years would add other campaigns to its resume. Second, the real-time round-the-clock coverage meant that viewers associated CNN with live and actual coverage. Indeed, top Pentagon and governmental officials were told to "tune in CNN" to find out the latest about the Gulf War. Third, the technology of warfare combined the use of target-based cameras that could broadcast flight toward a target, as well as sophisticated aircraft cameras that could follow a missile and record its hit. This made for spectacular dramatic visuals, the foundation of the entertainment format. Such visuals contributed to the changing role of military press briefing. Fourth, the journalist's role shifted to one of commenting on the visuals being seen and the technical aspects of weapons systems rather than rationale and strategy for the entire operation. This led to a major change in how the military handled the press.

> After watching some 600 of his troops float down with Russian MIG fighters flying cover above them, the U.S. commander, General John Sheehan, remarked: "It really is a different world." The general was referring to the new relationship with former cold war opponents, but he could very well have been speaking of the changed relationship between the American military and the media. (Topping 1998, 58)

Less adversarial than during the Vietnam War era, the modern press, especially broadcast news, uses new technology that makes it somewhat less dependent on the military for access and information.

> The bitter standoff extending over more than three decades has eased considerably. There has been a relaxation in the attitude of the military toward the press, but not simply as a consequence of some Pentagon revelation. With the end of the cold war and the development of ultra-fast satellite communications, old hard-fought issues such as military insistence on prior review of copy filed from war zones have become obsolete. Reporters roaming war zones equipped with portable satellite equipment are no longer dependent on military facilities to file stories or transmit photographs. Engaged now in peacekeeping and humanitarian operations, such as those in Somalia, Rwanda, Haiti, and Bosnia, the military have concluded that they must treat the media less as adversaries and more as partners. (Topping 1998, 58)

Media logic, or criteria for effective mass media programming, essentially defined the format used by the journalists and the military. News organizations and their sources share knowledge of news criteria and the perspective of journalism. As Army Major Bob Hastings explained to the *Washington Post*'s Steve Vogel (1998, 6):

> Information officers must be ready to take advantage of "media moments" from gauging a reporter's perspective on a story to brushing dandruff off the general's shoulders and, most important, knowing how to get out the "command message": the information or story angle that commanders want the public to know.

The media-military partnership includes shared information technology as well as shared perspectives on the story, emphasizing weapons and strategies. Airtime, or what was allocated to broadcast, which required military experts to narrate, emphasized the visuals of armaments, as did newspaper photographs. The dominant frames and themes of the coverage were about technology and weapons. The *Los Angeles Times* correspondent George Black (1991) noted that the news media treated the initial phase of Desert Storm exactly as the military wanted, "a blur of meaningless press conferences, video-game images . . . and the illusion of news" (M7).

Traditionally, experts were used on a case-by-case basis, but the nearly eight-month planning for coverage of the Gulf War suggested a more permanent relationship between sources and journalists.

> To fill in the gaps left by the Pentagon, every network producer has a Rolodex full of military analysts and retired officers, many of them highly paid shills for the arms industry. CNN is perhaps the worst culprit here. In one egregious case, it turned for an opinion to Richard V. Secord, retired Air Force major general. (Black 1991, M7)

Following the Gulf War, numerous military officials and spokespersons became reporters, correspondents, and consultants for the networks (e.g., Pete Williams, Tony Cordesman, Chuck Horner, and Norman Schwarzkopf). General Schwarzkopf, who gave lectures for fees of $50,000 and sold his autobiography for $6 million, was given his own TV show. In later years, he was interviewed by former subordinates, who also worked for the networks. Most of the discussion about impending war focused on strategies, military goals, and weapons systems. Seldom would lengthy analysis occur about the legitimacy of an operation or its foreign policy implications.

Seven years after the Gulf War, on December 16, 1998, as the House of Representatives was conducting impeachment hearings against President Clinton, the United States again struck at Iraq with a four-day missile and aircraft bombardment, resulting in hundreds of Iraqi casualties and an approximate cost of more than a billion dollars. In opposition to the United Nations charter and all international treaties and agreements, the attack began hours before an official report was received about Iraq's refusal to comply with UN-mandated inspections for weapons of mass destruction. Except for some charges that the president had begun the bombing to detract attention from his impending impeachment, there was virtually no media discussion or congressional debate about this decision, including a raid that was aborted some two weeks previous. Many of the countries that had comprised the UN coalition for the 1991 war withdrew support, and in several cases (e.g., France, Italy, China, and the former Soviet Union) they condemned the assault.

The American news media benefited from the coverage of both events. CNN achieved its highest ratings of the year—up 448 percent, highest ever since the 1991 Gulf War. Fox News Channel's ratings were up 212 percent, and MSNBC's climbed 118 percent between 5 and 8 p.m. The war coverage was carried on live with commentary from several network journalists, who could see "explosions in the distance" and held press conferences with Iraqi government officials, and, in at least one case, visited a family under siege. Notwithstanding the lucrative ratings, some viewers didn't feel that the coverage was as exciting as the last war.

Military-media people commented on problems with assessing the overall impact of the bombardment, the necessity to evaluate effectiveness, and that undoubtedly some retargeting would occur. Several opined that more must be done to get rid of Saddam and that there would probably be more strikes in the future. One example is from Tony Cordesman; he and Chuck Horner were two of the retired military personnel used by *ABC News*. The separate position of the journalist from the government was typically illustrated during the Vietnam War by referring to the government or the United States by their official names rather than "us" or "we." Cordesman's network's standpoint is typical of many of the spokespersons who have worked for the networks since the first Gulf War. In response to ABC's Peter Jennings question about the targets in Iraq, Cordesman says:

> Well, Peter, *we* do know a lot now about the kinds of targets and how many have been hit. *We* know that *we've* hit at the Republican Guards and army barracks. We know *we've* hit hard at command and control facilities, including his intelligence headquarters. (*ABC News,* December 18, 1998, emphasis added)

What "we" have seen develop post-Vietnam is an expansive media culture that provides communicative wraps that essentially dominate minor differences in content. It is entertainment that counts, and it plays well. Certainly, war movies continue to be popular. *Saving Private Ryan,* heralded for its realism and celebration of the costs of violence, yet depicting war-as-heroic, motivated tens of thousands of tourists to storm the beaches of Normandy and seek the grave of "Martin," a fictitious character. A realistic movie (a romance with a great deal of special effects) about the attack on Pearl Harbor followed in summer 2001.

The military-media complex generates new reality. Riding the latest wave of jingoism on an expansive sea of commerce, NBC's anchor, Tom Brokaw, wrote a book about the WWII generation—*The Greatest Generation*—that was, of course, hyped on NBC. Rare is the critical comment about Brokaw's idyllic production, but there are a few. One columnist noted a number of shortcomings of the "greatest generation," for example, racism and sexism, and then added:

> The greatest generation had to come from the United States, where it would get the greatest exposure. And reach the greatest number of consumers. And engender the greatest sense of nostalgia. And have the greatest chance of landing on the bestseller list. (Montini 1999, B1)

The Gulf War productions were accompanied by other programs that had an overriding impact on social order. Playing on the discourse of fear that pervades domestic policies involving crime, drugs, gangs, domestic terrorism— and the need to protect children—President Clinton, with resounding approval from Congress, promised to expand the defense budget in order to take care of our brave men and women in uniform, even as the battle against the likes of Saddam continued. The latest twist, following after several popular movies about deadly foreign viruses, is the notion that the country must prepare itself for biological, chemical, and computer warfare. In a speech to the National Academy of Sciences (January 22, 1999), President Clinton proposed nearly $3 billion to be used to defend the nation against impending germ warfare and unscrupulous computer hackers with the aid of a crack "cybercorps" of computer security experts. He assured the audience that civil liberties would not be trampled as the government continued to organize its military intelligence, criminal justice, and public health agencies to deal with the impending threats.

The reality of the moment is reflected in programs. The impeachment hearings of President Clinton were carried live by several networks, although audiences were not significantly larger than top prime-time shows. A split-screen format originally developed for sports coverage enabled cable news viewers to see live explosions in Baghdad and listen to members of the House of Representatives vilify President Clinton for disrespecting the law. Meanwhile, media consultant Schwarzkopf was asked what a difference the missiles just used on Iraq might have made in the Vietnam War. With a smile, he said that the politicians then may not have permitted the military to use them against Hanoi. Things are different now.

POLICING CRIME NEWS

Policing issues and events take on greater significance as we are exposed to more messages and images about reasons or threats to safety and as life is viewed as more risky, dangerous, and fearful. Many people in the United States have a vested interest in crime and wish to maintain it as an important concept as well as a problem requiring attention. I refer particularly to formal agents of social control (FASC) including police, prosecutors, courts, and corrections personnel, although the plethora of businesses providing fences, security systems, alarms, and numerous protective devices may also be included in this list as well as the National Rifle Association and the massive American gun industry.

There are an estimated 100 million handguns in the United States. The handgun industry has profited immensely from the public's mounting fearfulness. Handgun sales virtually mirror the increase in the use of *fear* in the news media, with a steady increase starting in 1984 and peaking with about 3 million purchases in 1993 and 1994. (The figures in Chapter 4 illustrate a similar rising trend in the use of *fear* in the media.) According to Dennis Henigan, legal director of the Center to Prevent Handgun Violence, "Most people who buy handguns do so for self-defense, so the handgun market is far more responsive to at least the public perception of the prevalence of crime" ("Handgun Sales Worry Industry," *Arizona Republic,* April 15, 2001, A12).

However, the public zeal to embrace more guns has been dampened by the spate of widely publicized school shootings, which increased publicity about the slaughter that occurs in central cities and the all-too-frequent reports of accidental shootings in homes. Gun sellers have responded. Smith & Wesson, for example, trading on the identity and fashion-symbol status of its name and brand, has engaged in alternative merchandising for adults and especially youth. Ten percent of Smith & Wesson's sales come from such merchandise as stuffed animals, jackets, caps, bathrobes, bicycle helmets, license plate holders, watches, key chains, and coffee mugs.

The handgun industry is not the only beneficiary of fear. In addition to numerous businesses, real estate agents touting "safe areas" and developers selling homes in gated communities are also doing well. As are private, charter, and parochial schools, with soaring enrollments.

Granted, there is a lot of crime in the United States, but the most important reason why there is so much emphasis on fear is the way crime is treated in the mass media. No single topic dominates the local news as much as crime (Surette 1998). News reporting about crime and punishment helps promote fear by emphasizing certain characteristics of "abusers" and then showing how policing activities serve to protect the public and other innocent people from such acts. Indeed, *justice* means "criminal justice" throughout the United States and a growing part of the world.

Fear is part of our communication environment. It cannot be separated from the ecology of communication that connects feelings we have with messages we receive through media production techniques and information technology. Crime news, for example, continues to increase despite a consistent decline in crime rates. There are three major reasons for this. First, crime news involves entertainment, and this is a staple of current news formats.

Second, police departments and other agencies have adjusted to news practices and now use spokespersons, who provide reliable information to news agencies. These people are news sources helping to direct the flow of information to news organizations that, in turn, decide what to present as newsworthy on any given day. News sources, as we have long known, define situations, for all practical purposes. This means that what most citizens think and feel about life and issues is informed by popular culture, particularly if they have little personal experience with the issue at hand.

News sources have certain points of view, and when only a few "get to speak," their views dominate; for all practical purposes, they "own" the event, issue, or activity. Moreover, news discourse tends to present facts from sources with opposing recommendations and interests. Yet, a resolution is not likely to be achieved because each source is in a frame in which the facts being articulated are applicable. Consequently, frame conflicts are not likely to be resolved. The issue, then, is of perspectives, and the more perspectives we have, the more "truthful"—although not always "more simple"—the account.

The third factor in promoting fear in news reports and popular culture is the dominance of visual images over other modes of information. When we see instances of fear, for example, a homicide scene, they seem so real and close, even if they occur miles away. Moreover, the image we see appears to be similar to others we have seen—and therefore "know" about—from other news reports, movies, and even newspaper reports. It is this familiarity with the visual side of fear that gives it social significance.

The bias of the visual is that an example of something can quickly become the thing itself. Crime, for example, may be represented by an unshaven, scowling face looking from behind prison bars. Or, it may be a bloody body, partially covered by a jacket and surrounded by yellow police tape. These are specific instances of a crime visual, but they easily can become the basic meaning of crime or icons of crime for audiences (Surette 1998). After a while, whenever crime is mentioned, these images come to mind. Audiences actually "see the scene" as a general picture of crime. These images can soon become the strongest symbolic referent with crime. This is how crime is given a particular meaning for individuals and for entire audiences.

The significance of the visual for our lives, especially crime and fear, is suggested by Denzin's (1991, 1995) work on the visual and the voyeur. His task was to understand the dynamic between action, character, and self while also avoiding acceptance of inauthentic renderings of self. Denzin lives in a world where identity—how we are known to others—prevails, but he would prefer a world where self—especially the expressive self—has more of a place. This world cannot occur visually, but must first be discursively inscribed as a constructed world, built on a visual architecture that does not permit multiple views of the order of things. Seeing occurs after a completed project, but the process of focusing is where the action is, where the emotional energy of self-creation exists, where freedom resides. Movie scenarios can, on occasion, help this, but even their images are harnessed by video logic, the casting of multiple dimensions in two dimensions. The cinema didn't give us ample freedom for temporal order; spatial meanings prevailed, seen narratives overcame imagined ones, and even efforts to make films about imagination succumbed to the visual format. So, we're watching the idea work its way out in a visual form that has little time for temporality.

There are different kinds of visuals, even though many are being folded together within an expanding ecology of communication. While other media are referred to as features of popular culture or as part of the visual emphasis (e.g., television), the deep interpretive readings focus on films. There are several theoretical reasons for this, as well as a few practical ones. Key theoretical and conceptual reasons include the focus on cultural logics as defined and addressed by numerous postmodern theorists, such as Jean Baudrillard. For example, the preface to *Images of Postmodern Society* (Denzin 1991) quotes Baudrillard as saying, "The cinema and TV are America's reality" in support of Denzin's general view that "this society only knows itself through the reflections that flow from the camera's eye." Adapting Baudrillard's thesis that "members of the contemporary world are voyeurs adrift in a sea of symbols," Denzin argues, "They know and see themselves through cinema and television" (vii).

The media images captured by Denzin are consistent with his overall thesis that the postmodern world is characterized by the cultivation of conspicuous consumption, identified by Hollywood genres stressing money, sex, love and intimacy, crimes of violence, passion and greed, race and repression. "Gone are the highest ideals of humanity, including freedom, self-respect, open dialogue and honesty" (Denzin 1991, 149).

When audience members see an event or issue a certain way, for example, as "crime," then this categorization becomes their basic point of reference and virtually all comparisons and topics involving crime begin with this. Even if an individual eventually comes to question this image, the image will remain for some time.

News reports and other popular culture messages provide some very consistent images of crime and danger. This is done with the image process just discussed, but there is an additional element of helplessness and dread. Crime is but one example of a larger array of images that promote the sense that the world is out of control. Helplessness is combined in many reports with a sense of randomness. This promotes incredible anxiety and fear that something might happen (1) which we know about (e.g., violent crime); (2) about which little can be done; and (3) which may occur at any time. The only response we seem to have is to wait and to prepare (e.g., get armed, lock doors, build walls, avoid strangers and public places). This may be a good formula for cinematic thrillers, but it is lousy for everyday life. Moreover, these responses also promote a very strong urge to get help from somewhere, anywhere. This is why audiences seem so willing to accept all kinds of definitions of what the problem is—the causes of crime, what can be done about it, and how limited our alternatives are—which usually involve the police and criminal justice system.

Messages about crime and fear are produced as part of an organizational process that involves news organizations, criminal justice organizations, and public responses. How do these ideas get organized, promoted, packaged, and how do they actually play out in news media reports? For fear to become part of our cultural milieu, it must be produced and packaged; there is nothing natural about citizens expressing unprecedented concern over their own safety, or parents promoting the notion of "stranger danger" with their children, or the massive exodus from public and open spaces in cities and suburbs to gated communities, an oxymoron of our time. This kind of pervasive fear is not just in the wind or part of the times, but is manufactured through symbolic manipulation of language, emotions, and identity.

The following sections offer some examples of the process that connects news reports with entertainment formats and news sources in order to promote certain consistent images of crime and fear.

CAPITALIZING ON PUNISHMENT

Donald Eugene Harding's execution by the state of Arizona on April 6, 1992, marked the end of a thirty-year moratorium on the death penalty in that state. Harding's case was important in order to "prepare" the citizens of Arizona for the execution of twenty-two more Arizona inmates in the following eight years. Harding had been found guilty of killing two men, although he confessed to killing seven people in four states. A career criminal, Harding had a brain disorder marked by "fits of rage" compounded by a childhood of neglect. Don Harding's was an easy case for politicians and other advocates of the death penalty to support for execution. As I stress in previous chapters, this was during the time period that fear was rampant in news media throughout the United States.

The novelty of the event brought out key news sources. Robin Rau (1993), a graduate student in the School of Justice Studies at Arizona State University, analyzed the news coverage of the impending execution. Hers is one of the first studies to examine how sources, themes, frames, and angles are used throughout a story. Just as the materials in earlier chapters indicate that fear travels over time and across topics, the process of defining a situation in news reports also changes over time as different sources tell different stories. Rau investigated thirty-two relevant articles, published between November 1991 and April 1992, using the general procedure discussed in Chapter 2. The major news sources (the number of times they were cited follows each source) included Harding's defense attorneys from Arizona Capital Punishment Representation at Arizona State University (ACPR)—11; the attorney general—11; religious clerics—10; victims' survivors—8; Department of Corrections officials—11; various court spokespersons—9; medical experts—4; Harding—31; his brother Darrell—2; editors/columnists—8; witnesses to the execution—5; and other Arizona citizens—7.

In general, Rau found that organizational points of view "speak louder and more often" than the voices and perspectives of less-organized groups, and that individuals are seldom heard except in letters to the editor. Several themes were identified; these were policy issues—or laws, rules, and alternatives. There were fifty-three of these themes, and they were apparent throughout the coverage, especially just before and after the execution. By and large, the policy perspective was owned and controlled by criminal justice agencies. For example, Grant Woods, the attorney general, described Harding as a "heinous murderer" (*Arizona Republic,* January 4, 1992), a "cold-blooded, cruel, vicious killer" (*Arizona Republic,* March 19, 1992), and a person who "fits the description of the type of person who should get the death penalty" (*Arizona Republic,* April 5, 1992).

Another theme was mitigating circumstances—Harding's impaired mental capacity and cruel childhood. These appeared fifteen times, with their strongest exposure during the week prior to the execution. The defense attorneys were the main owners of this frame. A report from the Arkansas State Hospital about Harding as a boy is an example: "There seems little doubt that we can give this boy what he needs, and without doubt, he is headed for serious trouble, which we can't stop. It is amazing the degree of psychopathy contained in a boy this young of age" (*Arizona Republic,* December 15, 1991).

Pain and suffering refers to the emotions of the survivors of the victims as well as the pain of dying in the gas chamber. There were twenty-one reports of this theme and these also tended to cluster the week before the execution. The main sources for this frame were the "survivors" of the "victim" and the condemned man's family: "It has taken me a long, long time to even recover this far . . . we . . . trusted no one. . . . It made me cautious and a lot more cynical" (*Arizona Republic,* April 4, 1992). These sources emphasize that the "execution brings relief and hopefulness" (*Arizona Republic,* April 7, 1992) that Harding will never be on the streets again and take away other families' loved ones.

Editorial columnists, while not of a single mind, did emphasize revenge. In one editorial, William P. Cheshire referred to Harding as "Mad Dog Harding" and described him as a "maddog killer," "cold blooded," a "reptilian murderer," and a "psychopathic killer" (*Arizona Republic,* December 22, 1991).

> The Wises' daughter was haunted for years by irrational—or maybe not so irrational—fears of death. Mary and Pam Cocannon had been married a little more than a year when Mr. Cocannon was murdered—but forgive me. I know it isn't fashionable to talk about grieving victims. Let's get back to Harding. (*Arizona Republic,* December 22, 1991)

Finally, several frames, or more specific angles on a theme, were identified: The "legal frame" refers mainly to legal matters, appeals, bureaucratic responsibilities, and reports about legislative mandates. The legal frame comprised 60 percent (53) of all frames. These primarily came from defense attorneys, prosecutors, and Department of Corrections personnel. For example, a retired prison guard stated: "Sometimes we feel for the condemned, but this is one aspect of the job. When the law says he is to go, who are we to try and stop it?" (*Arizona Republic,* April 3, 1992).

The "justice frame" refers to source reports discussing moral positions, the victims' emotions, and the morality and equity of an execution. Nearly 23 percent of all reports (20) were consistent with the justice frame, coming mainly from clerics. For example: "As Christian leaders, we want to bear witness that the death penalty cannot be justified as a legitimate tool of society's justice system" (Bishop Heistand, *Arizona Republic,* January 4, 1992).

The "personal frame" (10 percent) and the "public frame" (8 percent) were less frequent, coming mainly from comments by Don Harding about his "pointless life," from his brother, and with some comments coming from the "general public." Don Harding said:

> I just wish that when my execution takes place on April 6 that, somehow, magically it would erase all of that pain for the victim's families) . . . But it won't. . . . Is murder the solution to murder? No, it's not. But, me personally . . . I'm tired of living in cages. It's all I've ever known, and my life has pretty much become pointless. (*Arizona Republic,* April 3, 1992)

One of the most interesting aspects of this study was the careful documentation of which sources dominated key themes and frames. This study clearly shows who owns public definitions of executions in the news media: the formal agents of social control—legal people, particularly attorneys and corrections officials—and the "victims" of the wrongdoing (60 percent of the cases). Their views were dominant, focusing mainly on themes of policy, and, not surprisingly, this carried over into the legal frame. The pain theme was emphasized just before, during, and after the execution and was mostly expressed by clerics and victims, although a few journalists who witnessed the execution expressed dismay at the spectacle. Cameron Harper, a TV journalist with station

KTVK, stated, "We put horses down more humanely. [The execution] was not something you would want to see" (*Arizona Republic,* April 6, 1992). Ironically, perhaps, the justice frame was the province of clerics and victims, often taking opposing views, of course.

The dominant news sources defining crime and capital punishment essentially normalized the event for news purposes. The "novelty" was gone, and editors did not pursue issues related to capital punishment independently of the dominant news sources. One year and three executions later, a journalist commented on the lack of "news interest":

> When multiple-murderer Don Eugene Harding became the first Arizona inmate to be executed in 29 years last April, television stations across the state interrupted regular programming with lengthy, live reports.
>
> TV coverage was less intense last month, when John George Brewer was granted his wish to die, although there still was interest because he was the first Arizona inmate to die by lethal injection.
>
> But when quadruple murderer James Dean Clark was put to death early Wednesday, only one Valley TV station saw fit to inform viewers. The others offered reruns of their 10 o'clock news, the talk show Whoopi, Late Night with David Letterman and the syndicated game show Love Connection.
>
> As Arizona continues to execute condemned inmates—two more are scheduled for this year—it almost was a given that news coverage would dim. (Kwok, Manson, and Leonard 1993)

Those who would provide the justice frame for examining the state's lethal reaction to crime were losing their voice. The following excerpt uses *fear* as a synonym for *concern,* but *fear* is not used to discuss how the state's focus on crime and punishment contributed to the general situation that brought back executions and, in effect, transformed the opposition to capital punishment into a point of view rather than making capital punishment a compelling issue in its own right.

> "We would need a triggering event, most likely an unequivocally innocent person being put to death," said John Johnson, an Arizona State University professor and member of Middle Ground, an inmate-advocacy group. "Otherwise, it'll take time."
>
> Indeed, Johnson hopes Arizona will not go the way of Texas, where executions often are memorialized by a couple of protesters and noted only in snippets buried inside newspapers.
>
> Many death-penalty foes *fear* that public outrage over state-sponsored death will wither now that lethal injection has replaced the gas chamber as Arizona's official method of execution. Voters made the change in November 1992, seven months after Harding took nearly 11 wrenching minutes to die from cyanide gas.
>
> Sherry Simard of the human-rights group Amnesty International acknowledged that lethal injection has taken "the horror out of executions" for some.

"After Don Harding and that terrible 10½ minutes, people decided lethal injection was a more-humane method of execution," she said. (Kwok et al. 1993, emphasis added)

The "policing" of the Don Harding execution news coverage illustrates how different perspectives on capital punishment are distilled into one sensible option. Like the casting of a play, news sources are relegated to certain parts. Dominant news sources gave testimony to the state's capacity to deal with the object of fear—a murderer—by emphasizing the suffering of "real victims," as well as potential victims—everyone else. Policing acts of violence by Harding can also be extended to policing mental states, or intent, as with hate crimes.

POLICING HATE

As suggested earlier, formal agents of social control promote a sense of risk requiring more protection and policing. A common way that this is done is to emphasize tried-and-true threats and dangers, such as crime, and then to show how they can be controlled through punishment, for example, the death penalty. While policing with the death penalty is certainly related to the expanding discourse of fear, there are political differences in support. Typically, liberals do not support the death penalty, while conservatives and even "middle-of-the-roaders" do support it. The discourse of fear runs much deeper and is less divisive when it comes to the policing of hate crimes. Americans of all political persuasions often support it: Liberals like it because it seems to give more attention and credibility to the discriminatory and harmful policies affecting the poor and minority groups. Many conservatives support it because it shows that cruel and targeted crimes against all Americans will not be tolerated and that the law is fair. In this sense, hate crime legislation unites more Americans, who are joined against a common enemy. The important part of the process is who gets to define the situation of hate crimes.

Hate crimes are one of the newest threats to emerge in recent years. A hate crime is defined as an unlawful criminal act motivated by dislike of a certain individual or group based on that individual or group's race, ethnicity, religion, or sexual orientation. Hate crimes have been investigated by several researchers (Jenness 1995), including Tufano's (1998) intriguing investigation of news reports about hate crimes published in the *Arizona Republic* between 1990 and 1997. Tufano's aim was to identify the main issues, themes, and sources used to frame and present hate crimes. In general, he found that articles on hate crimes emphasized certain aspects and particularly those themes already familiar to audiences about fear and danger, including the need for stiffer laws, criminal incidents, the need for more law enforcement, and the need for more public attention to the problem. Not surprisingly, certain sources were connected to these various points of view.

Hate crime news has had a career similar to that of child abuse, in general (Johnson 1995a), and, more specifically, missing and abducted children. Mass media audiences throughout the United States have been barraged by entertainment shows, docudramas, and news reports of missing and murdered children (Best and Horiuchi 1985; Altheide 1995, 144; Fritz and Altheide 1987). Claims about the nature and extent of the missing children problem were structured and communicated in order to be both familiar and relevant to the intended audience. In turn, messages of crime, fear, and danger were intertwined with the issue of missing children, thus making the problem appear more threatening and severe than it was in reality.

The *Arizona Republic* reporting about hate crimes focused on the severity and extent of the problem of hate crimes, rather than offering a better understanding of the true nature of the problem. For instance, Tufano's analysis of the materials revealed that throughout the text of the articles there were four main subtopics discussed: (1) hate crime laws; (2) incidents of hate crimes; (3) initiatives other than legislation; and (4) statistical data on the number of hate crimes committed annually. Further, an emphasis was also placed on discussing the topic through such familiar themes as the need for stiffer laws, accounts of criminal acts committed, the use of increased law enforcement as a solution, and the general increase of the crime reflected through the reporting of statistical data.

Many articles were packaged and communicated to the public through the problem frame outlined in Chapter 3. These reports incorporated messages of crime, fear, and danger in order to both attract and familiarize the intended audience with the overall topic. Use of the problem frame reduces complex social issues to simplistic problems that the public can recognize, understand, and relate to, as well; certain aspects of the problems become typified in ways that are consistent with certain concerns of the public (Best 1995). Thus, the messages that are conveyed through the problem frame tend to reinforce public perceptions about the pervasiveness of fear and danger (Altheide 1997).

Claims makers or interest groups, including politicians, are opportune news sources for journalists, and they seize on topics presented within the problem frame to help propel their causes, corrections, and careers. The Anti-Defamation League (ADL) and Klanwatch are two of the most powerful interest groups claiming that hate crimes are reaching epidemic proportions and that their perpetrators should be prosecuted and punished more harshly than conventional criminals (Jacobs and Henry 1996; Jacobs and Potter 1997; Jenness 1995). These and other groups are reported by Jenness (1995) to "have played a key role in documenting instances of bias-motivated violence, identifying and publicizing harm associated with such violence, submitting proposals for reform, and calling on the law to intervene on behalf of affected constituencies" (217).

Hate crime legislation expands the power and reach of formal agents of social control. This legislation provides lawmakers and public officials an opportunity to fuel the discourse of fear by publicly condemning bigotry and prejudice. Ironically, police departments and criminal justice agencies, which have historically been suspect at discriminating against minority groups and other "outsiders" (through racial profiling, discriminatory sentencing for gang members, etc.), are often quick to support hate crime legislation.

> Politicians are easily convinced to support hate crime laws, because in passing such laws they believe they are sending a message of support to minority communities that demand such signals. They also send a more general message that they are morally correct individuals. (Jacobs and Henry 1996, 37)

In 1990, there were six articles published in the *Arizona Republic* about hate crimes, dealing with laws, incidents, initiatives, statistics, and other data. This number increased by 400 percent to twenty-six in 1997, with the largest number of articles focusing on laws and dramatic incidents. Of course, law enforcement officials tend to play prominent roles in contributing to new sources of fear. For example, between 1990 and 1997, police and other formal agents of social control (FASC) were key news sources in 19 percent ($N = 258$) of the articles, while various public officials' "concerns" were heard in about a fourth of all reports, with other claims makers' statements appearing in 21 percent of the reports. The skillful work of news sources such as FASC is illustrated in a report from the *Phoenix Gazette,* the *Arizona Republic*'s sister newspaper, about County Attorney Richard Romley's plans to push hate crime legislation. The article reflects the stronger voice allowed this news source, the prosecutor, permitting him even to rebuff a critic. The headline: "Romley Aiming at Hate Crimes":

> Maricopa County Attorney Richard Romley planned to launch a campaign against hate crimes this morning, proposing legislation and establishing a special unit in his office.
> The initiative comes two days after teenage brothers from Scottsdale were arrested in connection with a series of cross-burnings. . . .
> An advance copy of Romley's speech said the incidents—at a synagogue and two eateries—exemplify the terror of bias crimes and the need to get tough.
> "Hate crimes are insidious. Apart from the obvious impact on a specific victim, a hate crime intimidates a particular community."
> Romley's statement said he intends to reject plea bargains in hate crimes unless the defendant agrees to jail time.
> The policy will apply to any crime in which a person is victimized because of race, religion, gender, sexual orientation, disability "or any other actual or perceived condition."
> *Romley's office released a packet of sample cases and statistics showing that hate crimes are on the rise in the Valley.*
> *For instance, in 1991 there were 48 incidents reported in Maricopa County, compared with 160 last year.*

Despite several high-profile prosecutions, Romley noted, "The message that we are going to be harsh on hate crimes obviously hasn't gotten through to some."

"The difference is the emphasis on hate crimes has increased," Lotstein said.

Romley also will have a hate-crime hotline in his office (the number has not been established), and form an "anti-hate task force.

He also plans to continue his push for legislation that would make hate-mo-tivated crimes—including those directed at homosexuals—subject to harsher penalties.

Lotstein acknowledged that Romley has pushed for such a measure since 1989 with little success.

Last year, lawmakers adopted a bill providing tougher sentencing for criminal dam-age to places of worship. But the overall hate-crime package died without a sponsor or hearing.

Lotstein said the courts have given hate-crime laws mixed treatment on con-stitutional grounds. However, he added, passing such a bill in Arizona would make a clear statement to bigots and their prospective victims.

Gary Peter Klahr, a Valley lawyer and member of the Arizona Civil Liberties Union board, said the proposal sounds like bad policy, good politics. He said judges are entitled to consider motive as a sentencing factor, and the develop-ment of a statute that penalizes defendants for their beliefs creates a terrible precedent.

"The intent is great," Klahr added. "But you don't need that. What this is is a typical Rick Romley political deal."

Lotstein scoffed at the criticism. "Mr. Klahr's analysis is typically faulty and nonsensical," he said. (*Phoenix Gazette,* April 10, 1994, B1, emphasis added)

Seldom were the voices of victims, the general public, or the alleged of-fenders heard. Moreover, the public impact of interest groups in the discourse of fear and hate crime legislation is apparent when viewed over time. Tufano's (1998) analysis showed that from 1990 to 1997 interest groups prevailed in the early part of the hate crime campaign, followed by a period when police sources and officials were more dominant. There is a temporal order to this, as though the initial interest groups get the message out to audiences, including the police and officials. Next, the police carry the message and become the strongest supporters. With the passage of time and enough reports, the politi-cians are able to test the political waters to see in which direction the audi-ences are leaning, and then they become the strongest supporters.

This shift coincides with increased reports from legislation and national sources about hate crimes on the Arizona scene. Between 1990 and 1993, the majority of the articles focused on the subtopic of hate crime legislation. More specifically, these articles focused on the national debate of whether hate crime laws are unconstitutional. In particular, two of the main stories consistently reported centered around two U.S. Supreme Court cases: *R.A.V.* v. *St. Paul* and *Wisconsin* v. *Mitchell.*

Between 1995 and 1997, coverage shifted from national debate to a more local one. Articles focused on the discussion of whether Arizona should implement state hate crime laws. Although this debate was similar to the argument reported at the national level, what is significantly different is the type of sources cited in the text of the articles. As noted, local elected officials (e.g., Romley) became the dominant sources cited; very few other sources are cited.

Articles that discussed the subtopic of incidents of hate crimes tended to emphasize acts that were committed locally. Thus, it is no surprise that local police agencies (in particular the Phoenix Police Department) were the most prevalent sources cited. It is also no surprise that other types of sources for this topic also represented local interests.

The news coverage of hate crimes changed in a way that is consistent with the discourse of fear. Initial focus and emphasis shifted from discussing the topic at a national level to discussing it locally This was accomplished by further relying on local official sources, which, in turn, provided authorized knowledge establishing both the credibility and importance of the issue. Hate crimes as an example of the discourse of fear present some differences, however. First, fear is more pervasive than hate crimes. Second, interest groups and divergent points of view are brought together with fear. Major social institutions rally to support hate crime legislation and enforcement. Children, as discussed in Chapter 7, become a target to protect and to control. Indeed, just as police departments were "welcomed" into schools to educate students about drugs, so too were they encouraged to develop an education program in Phoenix that would address "hate philosophies": "The solution to prejudice is continued public education and public scorn for those not possessing sufficient intellect to see the error of their ways" (*Arizona Republic,* July 23, 1995).

On the one hand, police departments and social control agencies may benefit from the increased attention to the subject. For example:

> The Phoenix Police Department aims to get a better handle on hate crimes by creating a special squad to investigate incidence of bias. It has set its sights on raising the level of understanding among its officers of the importance of recognizing hate as a motivation of crimes and as a negative influence on the communities they serve. (*Arizona Republic,* January 9, 1997)

On the other hand, police can be criticized if they are not perceived as taking the necessary steps to protect some groups from the consequences of hate. For example:

> Asian-American students from around the state said Saturday that they feel shunned by Tempe police in getting answers about the February beating of an Arizona State University graduate student from mainland China. They said they are unhappy with the way police have handled the beating, saying law-enforcement officials do not recognize it as a hate crime. "We feel the issue has been ignored," said David Tung, president of Asian Students in Action, a coalition

of Asian-American students that met at ASU to discuss issues related to their culture. (*Arizona Republic*, April 18, 1993)

In sum, the discourse of fear plays on a history of audience familiarity with news reports about a range of threats. Hate crimes are a recent example of how politicians and claims makers are able to work with journalists in providing authoritative statements that are consistent with the discourse of fear and entertaining media formats (Jacobs and Henry 1996; Jacobs and Potter 1997; Jenness 1995). The construction of social problems generally reflects a process that entails the interaction and participation of various social activities. The news media depend on the claims makers as official sources of information in order to produce the news. "The activity of making claims, complaints, or demands for change is the core of what we call social problem activities" (Spector and Kitsuse 1977, 78). Although they are not the sole factors in the creation of a social problem, the media play a pivotal and strong role in defining and legitimizing the problem as well as promoting official interventions, policies, and programs. Thus, as social order has become more mediated, understanding the interaction between claims makers and sources and the media becomes key.

FEMALE SEXUAL OFFENDERS AND THE SEARCH FOR A VICTIM

Protecting children from crime and abuse has been a major feature of modern social control efforts (Best 1990; Johnson 1995a). A multitude of reform efforts—ranging from working conditions to family aid—has been justified in various ways as efforts to "save the children." Children, as archetypal innocent victims—and therefore, the most deserving of all victims—become key symbolic pawns in the political chess games of power and domination in the modern age. As noted previously, even wars are justified to save the children. The justification brings children and fear closer together by extending the search for potential harm. Family violence and sexual abuse of children has been recently scrutinized and attacked for its damage to children. News coverage was common in the 1930s about "perverts," who were reportedly obsessed with the corruption and the resulting harm of innocents. Indeed, Jenkins (1998) argues that fears of a criminal threat to children were sparked by the kidnapping wave that peaked with the Lindbergh baby case. Researchers argue that this marked a precedent that was often repeated in the following decades, with notable peaks during 1947–1950 and 1953–1954 depending on the crime rate, in general, and sex crimes, in particular (Soothill and Walby 1991). It was suggested that perverts and covert pedophiles had infiltrated large numbers of institutions at all levels and had earned positions of trust in churches and schools (Chermak 1995). The sanctity of schools and the teachers who oversaw the education and growth of young children were scrutinized.

The discourse of fear as a perspective opens up seemingly unlimited terrain for exploring potential victimization of children. Extending the reach of social control and formal sanctions to actual and potential victimizers requires playing to the discourse of fear, and this often entails challenging previous assumptions about safety and innocence. The creation of the female sexual child abuser is an example.

The focus on schools and day care centers as dens of sexual inequities against young children gained widespread notoriety in the 1980s following the arrests of twenty-four alleged members of a "sex ring" in Jordan, Minnesota, in late 1983 and the emergence of the McMartin Preschool case in 1984. Print and TV news reports covered these cases extensively. Part of the context for the entertainment format was the inclusion of children in the problem frame. Entrepreneurial groups had been working for several years to become the authorities on child abuse, particularly missing and abused children. Several movies, for instance, *Adam,* about missing and exploited children were released, and numerous politicians seized on "protecting children" as a key valence issue, one that joins most political factions. While child-adult sexual relationships have a long history, attention began to shift to sexual exploitation of children. Horror stories about alleged abuse were common during this period (Johnson 1995a). Of course, there was also the rampaging war on street crime and especially drugs. All of this was occurring at about the same as the rise of victimization as a viable social identity. It should also be stressed that news media programs were increasing, thus providing more time to be filled in a very competitive market. This, then, was part of the setting for some rather reckless and destructive work by formal agents of social control and journalists who carried their claims. The McMartin Preschool case was one of the most tragic results of policing fear.

Two proprietors of a day care center, Buckey McMartin, and his mother, Peggy McMartin, 63, were charged on 64 counts of child molestation and one shared count of conspiracy involving eleven youngsters who attended their family-run nursery school in Manhattan Beach, California, between 1978 and 1983. The bizarre testimony of children, who were "prodded" by prosecutorial interrogators, included claims about satanic rituals, sacrifice of animals, and nude photos. The jury trial lasted seven years and cost more than $13 million. The prosecution was led first by District Attorney Robert Philibosian and taken up by his successor, Ira Reiner, an ambitious politician who used the notoriety of the case to mount an unsuccessful campaign for California attorney general. Philosobian's conduct during the trial illustrated crass pandering as a crime fighter:

> When the McMartin Preschool indictments were first issued in March, 1984, then-Dist. Atty. Robert Philibosian, facing a tough electoral challenge from Reiner, tried to exploit the case. During pretrial hearings, he sat at the side of his prosecutors in court, a practice not seen in at least 15 years. During recesses,

Philibosian conducted hallway press conferences to grab some headlines. (*Los Angeles Times,* May 6, 1990, M5)

Reiner's campaign to become California's top lawman was built on "pro-choice, pro-environment, pro-active," including victim advocacy:

Film stars Ed Begley Jr. and Theresa Saldana, neither of whom accompanied Reiner to Sacramento, praised the two-term county prosecutor for his record on toxic pollution and on violent crime.

"He's been very, very open to victim's rights groups," said Saldana, a leading activist on the subject since she was stabbed in 1982. (*Los Angeles Times,* March 9, 1990, A3)

In the first trial, Raymond Buckey was acquitted of 40 charges, and the jury cleared his 63-year-old mother of all 12 counts against her. The jury dead-locked on 13 counts against Raymond Buckey, and prosecutors refiled eight of them. A mistrial was declared in the second trial when the jury deadlocked on all eight counts against him. Eventually, all charges were either dropped or not supported, and the McMartins were acquitted after spending years in jail—Peggy spent two years, Raymond spent five (Beckett 1996; Waller 1991). In the end, they lost everything.

Several journalistic accounts, offered as part of Peggy's obituary, captured what now seems to have been sheer madness:

Buckey's ordeal began in 1983, when the mother of a 2½-year-old who attended the McMartin preschool in Manhattan Beach, Calif., called the police to report that her son had been sodomized there. It didn't matter that the woman was eventually found to be a paranoid schizophrenic, and that the accusations she made—of teachers who took children on airplane rides to Palm Springs and lured them into a labyrinth of underground tunnels where the accused "flew in the air" and others were "all dressed up as witches"—defied logic. Satanic-abuse experts, therapists and social workers soon descended on the school and, with a barrage of suggestive, not to say coercive, questioning techniques (lavishly praising children who "disclosed," telling those who denied the abuse that they were "dumb," introducing salacious possibilities that children had never mentioned), produced increasingly elaborate and grotesque testimonials from young children at the school. . . .

Yet even now, the legacy of McMartin and other cases like it (Wee Care in Maplewood, N.J.; Little Rascals in Edenton, N.C.; Fells Acres in Malden, Mass.) is with us. It's with us—this is the sad part—in policies that discourage day-care workers and teachers from hugging children or from changing diapers without a witness, lest they be accused of something untoward. (*New York Times,* January 7, 2001, sec. 7, 51)

These alleged victims would share the same discourse of fear invoked to "make sense" of homicide victims such as Polly Klaas in California, Megan

Kanka in New Jersey, and Ashley Estell in Texas. Notwithstanding these tragic deaths, the claims makers (news sources) promoted what researchers have documented as the "myth of the missing children problem." Moral entrepreneurs touting that more than 1.5 million children were missing and abducted by strangers succeeded in having state and federal laws enacted to "protect children," as photos of missing children adorned milk cartons, billboards, network and local TV newscasts, and billions of pieces of mail (Best 1990; Best and Horiuchi 1985; Fritz and Altheide 1987). Together, these cases created a public outrage at the perceived inadequacy of the criminal justice system to prevent child molesters from harming innocent children. Laws became more punitive (e.g., castration was an option for punishment in several states), fingerprinting of child care workers was allowed, and teachers were under scrutiny as children and parents were given instruction in "good and bad touching." Perhaps most significantly, a genre of TV realism shows was spawned to enlist the public's aid in "returning children to their parents," as well as capturing a range of fugitives (Fishman and Cavender 1998). These shows received thousands of tips each week from across the country as neighbors reported strange behavior next door, grocery customers saw suspicious-looking people lurking around the watermelons, and motorists reported unsavory types driving pickup trucks in the next lane.

Policing evil against children had been well established, but efforts to expand its reach are illustrated with a case of an accused female sex offender. Barbara Sharp's (1999) investigation of news reports of twenty-four female sexual child abusers centers on the case of Mary Kay LeTourneau, who in 1997, made headlines for sexually abusing a thirteen-year-old boy and former student. Sharp's overview of many news reports reflected the problem frame and the role of key news sources. The coverage illustrated the perpetuation of stereotypical myths surrounding sexual interactions between older women and young boys. On the one hand, the angle of some reports was that LeTourneau had not violated any codes, legal or ethical, and the juvenile male was not harmed in any way by the experience. Other news sources supported the angle that the young boy should consider himself lucky. Other articles, mainly "opinion" pieces, expressed the view that LeTourneau had committed a crime against the young boy and that she was no better than her male predator counterparts.

Sharp's study is relevant to our discussion of policing of fear because it reflects the policing of children and those who supervise them, teachers. Recall previous discussions about the discourse of fear that emphasized how cultural categories are assumed to be opposites, for example, men and women, old and young. Fear lurks in the unstated anticipation that differences and discontinuities will not be breached and that certain consistencies prevail; thus, we have "dirty old men," but seldom "dirty old women." This is refreshing from a social control perspective because we can anticipate and beware of dirty old

men who molest young girls, as well as young boys. Such patterns are not desired, and they may be feared, but they remain predictable and understandable within cultural scripts. The female sex offender, however, does not fit this
mold. She is very disruptive of our ordered categories of conventional sources
of fear, and therefore becomes, potentially, a major source of fear. But first, her
presence must be highlighted and emphasized, must be publicized. Those who
control and supervise young children are culturally the least suspect, yet, as
we have seen in the McMartin day care case, allegations—even when deter-
mined to be untrue—generate a lot of publicity and attention for the claims
makers and news sources promoting them. For a woman teacher to "seduce" a
male student is "unheard of," and that is why it offers a rich opportunity for
social control agents to find cases to promote their protective work. The category that is the primary focus of this study is the "teacher/lover." I have
stressed that the mass media's power extends beyond an ability to transmit information and knowledge; it also represents a capacity to define situations for
other individuals in society, which in turn reflects a capacity to construct social reality.

Mary Kay LeTourneau's case essentially opened up to female sex offenders
the problem frame discussed in Chapter 3. In a sense, it galvanized media attention on other cases involving women sexual offenders. Thirty-five-year-old
LeTourneau, a Seattle elementary school teacher and mother of four, was
charged in 1997 with sexually molesting one of her former students, who was
fourteen years of age. During their affair, she became pregnant; the boy was
the baby's father. LeTourneau pleaded guilty, apologized publicly in the court-
room, was sentenced to six months incarceration plus probation, and received
mental health treatment in lieu of more prison time. Upon her release in the
early months of 1998, she contacted her young suitor and became pregnant
again almost immediately.

Many of the newspaper articles presented a profile of a woman who had
everything, but who risked it all for an illicit love affair. However, Sharp's
analysis suggested that later articles were written with the purpose of excus-
ing her actions for the following reasons: (1) LeTourneau's mental condition;
bipolar disorder made her prone to deep depressions; (2) her heritage as the
daughter of John Schmidt, an ultraconservative politician, whose career ended
abruptly when his affair with a former student and their two subsequent children became public knowledge; (3) her troubled marriage, particularly her
husband's extramarital affairs and their distant, cold relations; (4) other edito-
rials and opinion pieces that placed blame on the victims. All of these articles
are similar in that they place culpability for LeTourneau's crimes outside of her
control.

Dominant themes emphasized in the articles on female sex offenders included the following: (1) Women from abusive backgrounds, often incestuous,
are nearly always willing to do almost anything for acceptance; (2) women who

sexually abuse children tend to be a close relative, a mother, sister, or aunt to the victim; (3) although there are different types of female sexual offenders, Mary Kay LeTourneau illustrated the most prominent category, that of the "teacher/lover/offender type," who get involved with young adolescent males; (4) the familial and maternal supporters of both LeTourneau and the boy expressed remorse and regret. An *Arizona Republic* article from August 24, 1997, quoted the boy's mother: "Mary is a *mother*, and I am a *mother*. And I assumed I could trust her with my son" (emphasis added); (5) there is a cultural norm that a young man could not be "assaulted by a woman," and the young boy professed love for LeTourneau, suggesting that he was not a victim, but also shared responsibility. An article in the *Boston Globe* ("Older Woman, Young Boy," July 9, 1996) stated that "sex with any female—particularly a mature, experienced one—is perceived as good fortune for the boy. Intercourse is rarely considered unwanted [for men]"; (6) the female sex offender and her victim were "in love"; the boy involved with LeTourneau stated that he was not a victim, but that he was in love with his former teacher and was saddened by her conviction.

> Behind LeTourneau trails a tale of doomed romance and ruined lives. The boy with whom she claimed to be "in love" is said to be suicidal at the thought of losing the woman who not only took his virginity, but also gave birth to his child last year. Several hundred miles away in Alaska, the four children of the marriage she abandoned are equally distraught. (*Los Angeles Times*, February 8, 1998)

The teacher-felon also proclaimed her love for the young man and reportedly informed her parents that she was going to leave her husband to be with the thirteen-year-old.

There is little that has been established as "devilish" in cases involving female sex offenders. While the indiscretion is illegal—an adult being involved with a minor—it was only that; culturally, and most importantly, from the perspective of news audiences, it was not implicating evil because there was not a clear-cut victim that would stand the test of many people's commonsense view of order and sexual opportunity. For example, some articles quoted the boy, "I want people to stop seeing me as a victim. My life is going to be fine. Mary didn't harm me in any way." This disclaiming of victim status makes this a difficult case for the problem frame, and therefore, such cases are not as easily formatted to be entertaining problem-frame news. For example, one article printed a portion of a letter from the boy's mother to the judge which pleaded for LeTourneau's release, adding that her son would feel guilty if she remained in custody. As Sharp (1999) states:

> Not surprisingly, LeTourneau placed part of the blame for her crimes onto her victim. *The Evening Standard* published a statement made by the offender on

July 30, 1998, in an article entitled, "The Schoolteacher, the 13-year-old Boy, their Baby and a 'love' that has Shocked America." LeTourneau is reported to have said "people are putting me down, accusing me of being mentally unfit because *I allowed him* to love me." Later, she says, "I felt that *he* needed the relationship." Also, in this article the boy's mother is again quoted for her merciful pleas on LeTourneau's behalf. She said, "I've been asked by many people, how can I forgive her? Mary's not a bad person, just a human being who made a terrible mistake. I do not feel that there's a crime, my son does not feel victimized." In another article, the reporter refers to the victim as a "man" five times within the first few paragraphs, thus understating his inability to consent to a sexual relationship and denying his victimization. The media associated the victim's manhood, and his ability to procreate, as proof that he received no harm.

LeTourneau's lawyer, David Gehrke, argued similarly . . . . [He] said his client should get a soft sentence because the victim doesn't call himself a victim, but a willing accomplice. The lawyer said LeTourneau's crime is "much less harmful" than those committed by other rapists, arguing, "It's important for people to understand that when you say 'convicted of rape of a child,' the image that that conjures is not the case here. The biggest difference is how the victim perceives it." (*Arizona Republic,* November 16, 1997; Sharp 1999, 58–59)

My emphasis in this section of the chapter has been on the process and "fit" of certain topics within the problem frame and the discourse of fear involving children. Female sexual abusers such as Mary Kay LeTourneau do not fit this frame easily, partly because of cultural prescriptions and several decades of heavy entrepreneurial efforts by numerous organizations and claims makers (e.g., proponents for recognition of domestic violence, the glass ceiling) that tend to cast women as victims rather than as victimizers. Quite simply, we do not have a lot of news experience with women culprits, felons, and, particularly, victimizers, mainly because there are not widely accepted victims of such acts. The *Arizona Republic* took a stab at pushing this case into the discourse of fear by implying that stronger and more consistent policing efforts should be used against women as well as men. On April 16, 1998, the *Arizona Republic* published an editorial that compared the case of Mary Kay LeTourneau to that of Ken Lamberton, a Mesa, Arizona, schoolteacher, who was convicted of sexually molesting a fourteen-year-old student and was sentenced to twelve years in prison.

Obviously, Mary Kay LeTourneau received far more lenient treatment from Washington's criminal justice system than Ken Lamberton did from Arizona's. Perhaps that was a result of differences between state laws. Or, perhaps, it was based on the fact that Ken Lamberton is a man rather than a woman. Two cases tried within Arizona indicate that the latter is probably true. In September, 1993, teacher Colleen Taylor was sentenced to only nine months in prison for having a year-long sexual relationship with a 14-year-old student. In June, 1987, librarian's assistant Suzanne Yeager received no prison time after she admitted to having seduced a 14-year-old, eighth-grade boy. (*Arizona Republic,* April 16, 1998)

A related dimension of the LeTourneau case is that *victim* and *victimizer* are cultural terms charged with meanings that reflect audience members' background and experiences, including their exposure to massive amounts of popular culture material and formats. LeTourneau and other women may be viewed as victims, who are simply reacting to adverse conditions or defending themselves (e.g., some who kill their husbands in domestic violence disputes). "The judge in the case reportedly stated, 'A crime perpetrated by a woman on a male child is not the same as a crime perpetrated by a male on a female child'" (Sharp 1999, 70).

A powerful theme, then, in many of the articles is that males are not vulnerable to sexual offense, in general, and, in particular, cannot be raped or taken advantage of sexually by females. This notion reinforces the myth that is nicely captured by the problem frame that states sex offenders are "dirty old men" or "sex-crazed perverts," whose only desires are to seduce little girls or perhaps little boys.

Sharp (1999) concludes her important study:

> The mass media, realizing the entertainment value of this particular type of crime, spent a great deal of time and resources in order to feed their audiences every detail of LeTourneau's life, of the victim's life, of the sexual interactions between them, of the trial where LeTourneau was convicted of child rape, and of her recidivism and return to prison in 1998.
>
> Since this key case played such an important role in defining female sexual abuse as a social issue, and was also the first such case to attract such a substantial amount of media attention, other cases of female sexual abuse have followed. The media have begun to relate other cases of abuse more frequently, especially where the woman is a teacher and the victim is a student, or where the case contains other similarities to that of the LeTourneau case. (88–89)

CONCLUSION

The mass media, especially organized entertaining news, and the agencies of social control are synergistically joined in an ecology of communication. Mass media and popular culture require entertaining programs and periodic crises to gain the attention of audiences that are increasingly fragmented, partly due to the expansion of numerous media outlets and choices. Legitimacy and need are problems for the military and police, particularly if "peace" breaks out, and if crime declines. More generally, if social order overtakes social disorder in public perceptions, the military and police become less important. This poses an organizational challenge that has been partially solved by the mass media and popular culture myth-generating machine, including the on-going emphases detailed in this book about pervasive threats and the discourse of fear.

Policing crime promotes fear by emphasizing the immediate victims, and, more importantly, all those who are potential victims. News organizations rely on institutionalized news sources to provide the routine reports that are re-quired by regularly scheduled newscasts. News sources have learned the news routines and especially the format preferences. This gives them an advantage over less organized and usually "less legitimate" organizations, groups, and in-dividuals who wish to have their voices heard.

The military and criminal justice organizations share more than a hierar-chical structure. They reflect the value structure of society, including cultural preferences, biases, and fears. These are incorporated into cultural myths, nu-merous narratives of valor and bravery, major holidays, and most importantly, the mass media and popular culture. Their very existence reflects pervasive fears about safety and survival. All actions taken by these organizations are thereby cast as relevant to their main mission: to protect citizens.

Each organization points to sources of fear, the "other." With the military, this generally refers to external enemies, although at certain moments in his-tory, the look may turn inward toward enemy agents, spies, saboteurs, and, of course, terrorists. Police and criminal justice agencies focus on domestic crime, which can cross international and ideological borders with such crimes as drug trafficking, arms shipments, and counterfeiting. For these institutions to re-main viable and on patrol—at least in the minds of citizens—the mass media are necessary to not only promote (with appropriate revisions) certain myths, but also to carry reports about the ongoing challenges of maintaining order, both externally and internally.

The threats must be maintained, and as noted, this has become more diffi-cult, especially when some external enemies (e.g., the former Soviet Union) have disappeared. Thus, we have achieved the bizarre situation in which our major external enemy—the former Soviet Union—has become less of a threat. But the military—with a need to stay viable—has made attempts to push stringent foreign defense policies through Congress. Gaining public support for such drastic efforts, both domestically and abroad, is no easy task, but it can be made easier if there is enough fear—not danger, but fear—of other en-emies. The generation of this fear is partly accomplished by news agencies that require entertaining information and scenarios to attract audiences. Playing to fear is lucrative and controlling, and it is exciting and fun for audience mem-bers. Citizens are now asked to watch for criminals, look for missing children, and promote surveillance efforts to reduce and control use of illegal drugs. Policing our lives becomes more acceptable if the risks are great enough, if the messages are repeated often enough, and if the fears resonate through every-day life.

7

Children and the Discourse of Fear

Fear is the path to the dark side.
—*Star Wars: Episode 1: The Phantom Menace*

INTRODUCTION

Fear changes with historical periods and with the information technology that influences our identities and how we relate to social life. The communication order changes the meaning of things and the symbol systems that we use to "make sense" of our place in the world. We have seen that news reports and social control work have become joined through mass communication organizations. Print and electronic news media use entertaining news formats that make their work more predictable and manageable while also delivering entertaining information that news consumers have come to expect. Many of these reports originate with institutional news sources, including formal agencies of social control (FASC), such as police departments. The combination of entertaining news formats with these news sources have forged a fear-generating machine that trades on fostering a common public definition of fear, danger, and dread.

This is most apparent with children and fear. Children are a powerful symbol for protection as well as punishment of not only those who would hurt children, but also children who are blamed for other social ills. As powerful symbols, children have been joined with fear in entertainment as both victims and victimizers. The former may be recognized as child abuse, while the latter appears as juvenile crime, gangs, and so forth. This chapter examines the ways in which fear has been coupled with certain issues, particularly those involving children as both victims and victimizers in the modern discourse of fear. The fear emphasis is consistent with the agenda of social control agencies that often serve as major news sources. This point is illustrated in two ways: First, I focus on how children became part of an emerging discourse of fear.

Materials from news media reports illustrate the shift that occurred in the way that fear was used (from more specific or parallel fear to more pervasive fear or the discourse of fear) from the late 1980s to the mid-1990s.

Second, materials are presented from a case study of news coverage about the death of a young boy in a boot camp. Children play a large role in the discourse of fear. As noted, they are portrayed as both victims and, increasingly, as victimizers. As fear of children becomes more pervasive, a clear sense has emerged that "something must be done," that more drastic measures must be taken. Another major change that has occurred with juveniles is an expanding use of boot camps aiming to instill discipline and respect in youth referred to the court. Often run by for-profit organizations that contract their services to juvenile justice agencies and versions of child-protective services, these organizations emphasize military-type discipline, neatness, respect, as well as physical fitness and punishment. Several children have died while in custody of such camps. The important point for this analysis if that such camps have been opened as a result of fear of children.

I wish to emphasize that children are a critical symbol in the entertainment-oriented fear perspective. "Child-saving" (Best 1990, 1994; Platt 1969) efforts have been around for a long time, and while their activities are relevant for the use of children as icons of fear, they are also different from the incorporation of children and fear into the problem frame. My focus is on what I regard as a relatively new phenomenon: Fear as a perspective or lens for our time.

Let us recap a few key points mentioned previously. Numerous news reports about fear pertain to children. The news media's emphasis on fear with children is consistent with work by Warr (1992) and others on the significance of "third-person" or "altruistic fear"—the concern for those whom you love or are responsible. Specifically, Warr (1992) found that children are the most common object of fear in households. Much of this concern is generated around crime and drugs. For example, in the mid-1990s, crime and violence were regarded by 27 percent of the public as the most important problem facing the country today (Gallup Poll 1995). Except for a brief appearance by "immorality, crime, and juvenile delinquency" in 1965, crime did not reappear among the top public concerns until around 1990, when drug abuse was cited by 18 percent as the second most significant problem. One important contributor to crime's prevalence was the way politicians emphasized crime and drug problems (Roberts and Doob 1990).

Children are at the core of the discourse of fear and represent several of the dimensions discussed in previous chapters, particularly the shifting contours of protection and control. I stated in earlier chapters that a discourse of fear, like all social discourse, is relevant for social control (Staples 1997; van Dijk 1988). I suggest that this is particularly important for everyday social interaction when the discourse involves children (Ariès and Baldick 1962; Best 1990).

Numerous analyses of propaganda have connected the process of fear construction with various political and economic interests, as well as a key political process for constructing state identities (Campbell 1998). Fear defines a cultural space that is shaped with experiences, interpretations, and narratives by storytellers such as journalists, who, uncannily, connect something new(s) with something old. In time, as astute students of propaganda have suggested, today's idiosyncrasy is tomorrow's orthodoxy (Jackall 1994) especially when embraced by common cultural looks. Children play a dual role in terms of innocence and brutality, protection and control. We can justify excess in protecting children, and, increasingly, we can excuse excess in punishing them, particularly—and paradoxically—if extreme sanctions will protect the innocence of children (Best 1990, 1994; Sommerville 1982; Zelizer and Rotman 1985).

I wish to return to an analytical distinction made earlier between parallel and nonparallel use of fear in news reports. Parallel fear refers to the alignment of the coverage with the event and the emotions or concern of the individuals involved. It tends to be localized, momentary, and individually or case oriented. Stated differently, a news topic or event is presented as an occasion or instance of fear. Nonparallel or insidious use of fear refers to general, pervasive, and unfocused use of the word, often in place of another more parallel adjective or adverb. Nonparallel use of fear operates as a perspective, as an evocative framework within which a discourse of fear may be attached connotatively to the topic at hand. In this instance, fear becomes the topic but can be associated with a specific event or activity. Often the topic isn't even an event or a specific act, but sets forth an orientation and a context of meaning for symbolically linking the topic to fear. Parallel use of fear was more common in 1987 than in 1996, with numerous examples of nonparallel fear apparent in 1997–1998. It is when nonparallel use of fear prevails that we may recognize the emergence of a discourse of fear.

The use of the word *fear* in these newspapers between 1987 and 1996 increased in headlines and in the body of reports during this decade (Altheide and Michalowski 1999). This is not simply because there was more news reporting. The use of the word, particularly in headlines, peaked in our sample of newspapers during 1993–1994, followed by a slight decline. Figures 7.1 and 7.2 illustrate the increase in the use of the word *fear* in headlines and news text in three newspapers, the *Arizona Republic* (*AR*), *Los Angeles Times* (*LAT*), and the *New York Times* (*NYT*). Consistent with trends in the use of *fear* by other newspapers in the United States, headlines greatly increased the visibility of fear (Altheide and Michalowski 1999). Comparing the 1987 levels with the high year in 1994 shows the following increases: AR: headlines-123 percent; text-93 percent; LAT: headlines-83 percent; text 27 percent; NYT: headlines 38 percent; text 4 percent.

The focus here, however, is not on the increase per se, but rather its use with

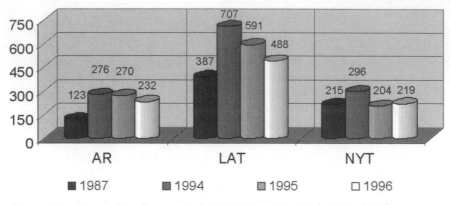

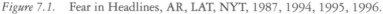

Figure 7.1.   Fear in Headlines, AR, LAT, NYT, 1987, 1994, 1995, 1996.

changing issues and topics over a several-year period. Analysis suggests that
the expansion of fear is due to the emergence of fear as a discourse or perspective for discussing issues and problems. This is particularly true with the way
in which reports about children have come to be more closely associated with
fear. Moreover, when fear appears in headlines, it tends to be associated with
certain topics and issues. Figure 7.3 reports the association of fear in headlines
with a number of social topics (e.g., children, crime, schools, violence) as an
average percentage (1994-1996) of all reports with fear in the headlines for
each newspaper. For example, 28 percent of *Los Angeles Times* (*LAT*) articles
with *fear* in the headlines between 1994 and 1996 featured the word *children*
in the report. The respective figure for crime was 17 percent, and so forth. Figure 7.4 presents a closer look at how reports involving fear with children have

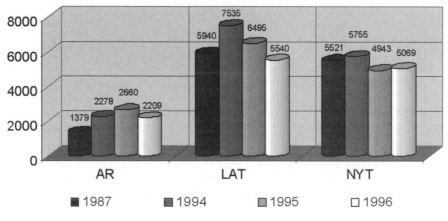

Figure 7.2.   Fear in Text, AR, LAT, NYT, 1987, 1994, 1995, 1996.

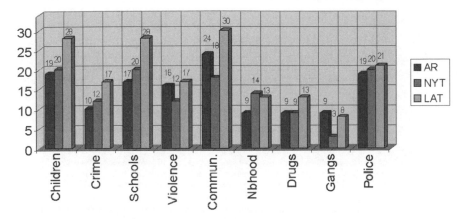

Figure 7.3. Fear in Headlines and Focus on Topic, e.g., Children, as Percent of all Fear Reports, AR, NYT, LAT, (avg. for 1994–96).

changed from 1987 through the respective years of 1994, 1995, and 1996. Each newspaper increased the use of *fear* in headlines and its association with *children* between 1987 and 1994.

Figure 7.5 compares percentages for 1994–1996 with figures for 1987 in order to illustrate change over time, particularly increases in the association of fear with certain topics, e.g., children. Examining the differences between 1987 and the three-year average for 1994 through 1996 shows that while there was some variation between the papers (e.g., the *New York Times* [*NYT*] did not substantially change its fear/gang and fear/violence coverage between 1987 and 1994–1996), coverage of fear and the associated topics tended to increase for most topics, particularly crime, violence, and children. Generally,

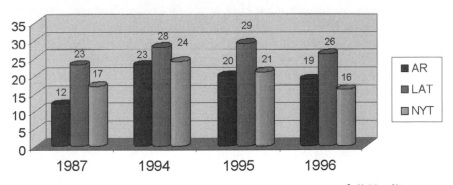

Figure 7.4. Fear in Headlines and Children in Text, as Percent of all Headlines with Fear, AR, LAT, NYT, 1987, 1994, 1995, 1996.

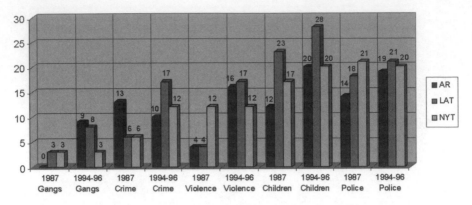

Figure 7.5.   Fear in Headlines and Topics in Text, as Percent of all Headlines with
Fear, AR, LAT, NYT, 1987 and Average of 1994–1996.

however, the newspapers increased their coverage of children during this time
when fear appeared in the headlines—increases of 7 percent in AR, 5 percent
in LAT, and 3 percent in NYT. Moreover, two newspapers increased the association of fear in headlines with crime and violence during the same time period. Analysis of the articles revealed that *children* and several other related
terms are closely associated in newspaper reporting. For example, reports discussing schools and related topics were more likely to begin with headlines
featuring the word *fear.*

A qualitative content analysis was conducted of a sample of articles from
the respective papers in order to examine how fear was being used with children and related topics, such as schools. The articles reflect the concerns with
the safety of children, on the one hand, while stressing that children-as-gang-
members are a major source of problems and danger, on the other hand. However, seldom are both facets of childhood examined in the same report. It was
not uncommon for reports about childhood fears to be related to the youth
world of gang members. Part of my emphasis is to use materials about children and fear to illustrate a shift in the use of fear from experience-as-fear to a
far more general fear-as-experience. The latter is more characteristic of reporting from the problem frame, in which fear is taken for granted as a relevant
context of meaning and reality of everyday life that blends in with children as
victims and perpetrators.

PARALLEL USE OF FEAR IN THE 1980S

The sample newspapers tended to report fear as parallel to specific events
and problems. Major themes included acting out of fear as a kind of justifiable

revenge, rising crime rates, expanding drug use, the impact on specific places for children, the spread of crime to the suburbs, and the impact of drugs and crime on people changing behavior.

For example, an article in the *Arizona Republic* (June 21, 1987) entitled "Self-defense, Yes; Guns, No. Verdict Carries Dual Message in Goetz Trial, Professor Says":

Q: What does the verdict say about society's perception or fear of crime, especially in urban areas?

A: It says a great deal. It says primarily that when people fear that they are about to be mugged, they need not take the risk about whether they are going to be mugged or not. They can shift the costs of ambiguity to the person who has created the confrontation.

New York Times articles between 1985 and 1987 provide themes consistent with the more individual, parallel association. Other themes played to broader concerns about children and drugs, including drugs and drug dealers, fear of violence, fear for young children taking part in illegal activities, fear of retaliation for informing. Especially striking was the emergence of the term "crack plague" and its relationship to fear and crime. Another concern was community, for which a metaphor of war was often used: "The crack trade in southeast Queens has turned middle-class neighborhoods near the Nassau County border into some of New York City's bloodiest drug battlegrounds" (*NYT*, October 19, 1987, sec. A, 1). Similar themes are played out in a half dozen articles analyzed for 1988 through 1990. Fear was often used in reference to coming trends and events.

Other articles reflected the same desperation of an epidemic, and this was not lost on politicians seeking political office. In 1989, one article stated that the two biggest issues in the New York mayoral race were "crime and the crack plague." That same year United Press International (UPI) reported on the visit of William Bennett, President Bush's drug czar, to the New York area. The reporter wrote, "After a day of visiting the worst casualties of the cocaine crack plague, Bennett said a swift, terrible sword was needed to cure the nation's crack problem. 'I saw pregnant addicts, addicted children, babies born with AIDS.'" The crack plague became the cause of all other crimes and evils in New England society, including rising homicide rates, rising street crime, homelessness, the rise of street gangs, the health crisis, the economic situation, and racism.

The discourse of fear and its relevance for children quickly solidified as a police chief in Maine was quoted as saying, "Violent street gangs of young men are symbolic of the crack plague." A New Jersey senator who wanted to introduce stiffer laws for possession or sale of crack was quoted as saying, "We must act now to halt the spread of this crack plague that threatens to turn our children into slaves of cocaine."

Newspaper accounts in the late 1980s continued the trend. There were reports about Long Island residents fearing for children, but the focus was on drugs. Another distinguishing feature is that fear was used mainly in terms of crime, drugs, and crime rates, with a foreboding for the future. The main sources tended to be officials, police, and sometimes residents.

Los Angeles Times articles in the late 1980s also reflected parallel use of fear, with the following main themes: gang activity, violence, and threats; drugs and law enforcement; fears of residents in a housing development; recent news reports about crime and fear; children's fears. While some reports suggested that fear lingers beyond a specific event and can continue to affect children, parents were urged to be aware of it. This theme became even stronger in subsequent years.

For example, three articles dealt with gangs and drugs, the bombing of a police car and how this increased fear, and how parents can help with children's fears, including those promoted by media materials. The use of fear is mostly parallel with specific events, although the notion that children's fears are more general and can even be related to mediated experiences, while not new, does suggest a more general use of the term *fear.*

A specific gang activity is the focus of one article entitled "Sun Valley Specter; Bombing of Squad Car Fans Fears of Street Gang." While it is certainly not the first discussion of gang events in Los Angeles, it illustrates the parallel use of fear derived from a specific event.

> A bomb that caused minor damage to a Los Angeles police car parked outside a Neighborhood Watch meeting in a Sun Valley condominium development may have been planted by a local street gang, police said Wednesday.
>
> Residents of the development said, however, that they are convinced that the bombing Tuesday night was intended to intimidate them for calling the meeting to discuss crime problems in the area. . . .
>
> Robert Birney, one of the police officers at the meeting, said residents had asked to talk with police because of recurring incidents of burglary, loitering and vandalism. . . .
>
> "The bombing of a police car," Birney said, "doesn't make any sense, but these people do a lot of things that don't make any sense."
>
> Clifford Ruff, a spokesman for the Police Department's Community Resources Against Street Hoodlums unit, said *the incidence of gang-related crimes in the area had dropped considerably since 1982. He said it was premature to call the rash of crime at the development evidence of organized gang activity.* (John Nielsen, May 16, 1985, Metro sec., pt. 2, 6, emphasis added)

NONPARALLEL USE OF FEAR IN THE 1990S

In the 1990s, news reports in the sample newspapers tended to stray beyond specific events to more general conditions of fear, including the use of *fear* as an adverb and adjective. Peaking in 1994, this coverage can be characterized as moving to a more *generalized, pervasive, unfocused standpoint* that is characteristic of the discourse of fear, with emphasis on the threats to children. Examining different articles from 1987 and 1994 about children's safety and fears illustrates the shift from a specific concern to a broader, more pervasive statement about fear.

Tracking the emergence of fear as part of suburban reality and such family-oriented activities as buying groceries and attending schools offers opportunities for family spaces to be marketed for their safety potential. Fear, business, planning, and design can coexist, as suggested by an article in the *AR* Business section:

> "Tempe Has Designs on Buildings That Protect People"
> "Crime may not be up, but fear is definitely up," said Salvatore, a partner with Architekton, an architectural firm in Tempe. "If there are design principles that we should follow to assist in getting rid of the fear or making that fear less, it's our task to take those principles and put them into effect." (July 9, 1995)

Other accounts in the *Arizona Republic* in the later years of the study can likewise be characterized as moving to a more *generalized, pervasive, unfocused standpoint*. With this emphasis emerges a discourse of fear as a more general symbolic category and guideline. We may refer to this as an insidious nonparallel use of the word *fear* in replacing adjectives such as *concern* and *worry*. For example, take the article entitled: "Arrowhead Referendum Effort Alive Despite Signature Flap":

> The rezoning case has angered Arrowhead residents who *fear* that a shopping center in their midst would bring crime and congestion; but most neighbors to the east of the site support the rezoning as the best possible solution, given the existing zoning, which is general commercial and multifamily. (July 24, 1995, Glendale Community sec., emphasis added)

NYT articles in the mid-1990s reflect a similar focus on fear as discourse. Particularly noteworthy were such themes as fear of one another; fear of what we can't see or control; and fear creates a domino effect in society.

One *NYT* essay, "Fear Itself; Finding New Reasons to Dread the Unknown" (Tom Weiner, March 26, 1995, Week in Review Desk, sec. 4, 1), used the subway gassings in Tokyo, which had happened one week earlier, to launch into a discussion of fear in popular culture, particularly everyday life. In keeping with a shift in later years to a nonparallel use of fear, more as a condition and feature of social life, this essay drew on various sources, including psychologists and sociologists, in constructing a report about pervasive fear. The dominant message was that there is really so much fearful stuff surrounding us that the world is really fearful, although perhaps not as bad as some would believe. Such reports accompany many other articles about how threatening life is to children and others in our age.

> We are living in toxic times. The boundaries of the body feel as vulnerable as the borders of the country. Invisible, unknowable threats have replaced nuclear bombs as the source of collective fear. . . . The fear is airborne, a toxic cloud—a fear of dying that is fast becoming a fear of living. There's a heart attack hidden in your tuna with mayo, a coronary in that carton of Szechuan chicken. Live smoke-free or die. (*USA Today*, October 1, 1990, 1D)

By the mid-1990s fear for children had become so commonplace in New York popular culture that writers began to use the theme as a basic organizing principle for fiction and drama (Stasio 1995, 27). "Real" news found its way into fiction as reporters and writers dealt with similar themes. The crime columnist for the *New York Times Book Review* suggested that the rise in child danger as a metaphor for recent crime dramas was a trend. Yes, she answered, and this is why:

> There are solid pragmatic reasons why genre authors might be working children into their narratives. By form and definition, the crime novel must have proper victims—characters who are either physically weak or politically defenseless—to enable detectives to perform like proper heroes. Vulnerable on both counts, children make ideal victims. . . . "There's something refreshingly unambiguous about child abuse and murder," Linda Grant notes in "Love Nor Money," which has her San Francisco private eye on the trail of a pedophile. "No danger that you'll end up feeling sorry for the perpetrator or guilty for catching him."

The *LAT* use of fear in the mid-1990s was consistent with what I have already noted about the *AR* and the *NYT*, but with even more of an emphasis on fear as a condition of everyday life, as experience. Often alluding to crime, gangs, drugs, and violence, articles tended to include children as victims in need of more support in addition to their parents, who often lack knowledge and resources to cope with the pervasive fear. Natural disasters and neighborhood problems were more closely linked with the discourse of fear.

LAT articles from 1997–1998 offer themes that are consistent with the other newspapers, but with even more emphasis on crime and fear as a condition of life. Major themes include gang violence, loss of innocent life, threats to children, crime beyond city limits, and technological changes in the look and impact of social life and crime. The latter was apparent in several reports that examined how technology was being used by both drug dealers and the officials dealing with them. Another article examined how drug recipes are available on the Internet. Others looked at tactics for combating youth gangs and drugs and the role of parents in alleviating fears and discouraging drugs and violence. Some articles mentioned how families have fled certain neighborhoods and that there are problems even in rural and outlying areas. A headline proclaims about Palm Springs: "Fear for Children's Future; Violence: Drugs and Gunfire plague neighborhood on city's north side. Yesterday's innocent youth have become today's hoodlums" (*LAT*, April 14, 1997, A3).

In a very rare instance, an ex-convict was used as a source to comment on the bad situation: "I don't understand this new breed," said Daniel Blasingame, who identifies himself as an ex-convict. "The older guys, we don't mess around with these youngsters. They'd just as soon as shoot us as anyone else. There's no respect."

KIDS AS ABUSED

A subset of the topic of children's safety that most clearly illustrates the development of the fear frame over time is coverage of the physical or sexual abuse of children. The change in how this social issue is connected to fear over time consequently changes the meanings in news accounts. For instance, in a 1987 report about a therapy group involving victims of incest, consider how the participants' experience of child abuse is subtly linked to societal danger:

> The girls in the group complained of nightmares, insomnia, anger, feeling fear of sex and repulsion by it, fear of having children, guilt, shame, problems relating to older men and low self-esteem. Not enough research has been done to understand why adults force sex on children, but statistics show that 98 percent of the offenders are men and 80 percent were abused as children, Mayer said." ("Bad Love, Group-Therapy Sessions Help Victims of Incest Overcome Fear, Guilt, Shame," *AR*, January 1, 1987)

The fear and shame experienced by these victims are tacitly linked to the category of adults as offenders. Fear does not leap out at the reader and frame the whole article. The effects of sexual abuse on these victims are reported in a local, individual, and specific manner but are related to the potential danger that adult men pose to young girls. This evocative account is framed as a morality play, with men cast as evil against young, innocent girls. When such an opposition is repeated often enough it becomes credible, plausible, and even natural or inevitable.

Examining the interaction between child abuse and sanctified social arenas in which they take place, such as schools or the community, are important to understanding how the fear frame develops. Reports of this nature challenge the taken-for-granted safety of these social realms, and, over time, these accounts reflect an attempt to attach fear to such social areas in order to mitigate the violation of public sensibility. The following 1987 report contextualizes the issue of sexual abuse in a school setting in a more general fear frame but falls short of exhibiting the characteristics that come to mark the fear frame in later years.

> Tension and fear grew daily as Hester slowly drove his car in front of the young sexual-abuse victim's house. The family feared Hester was armed. So they armed themselves with shotguns and closed off the front of the house. In Hester's case and *many other similar ones,* the government agency failed to make crucial background checks that could have prevented undesirables from invading the lives of numerous Indian children. The 13-year-old was among the first known victims in a wave of recent molestations of Indian pupils by school employees, a toll that since 1981 includes more than 125 boys on reservations in the Southwest. (*Arizona Republic,* "Child Molesters Attracted to Jobs at Indian Schools," October 11, 1987, emphasis added)

With this example, fear as experienced by a young girl and her family is a product of the child molester's (Hester) repeated appearance at her house. The adult male child molester traverses three symbolic boundaries: those of child, school, and home. The problematic nature of reporting on this context might have given rise to the use of *fear* in a different way: "School molestation cases are part of a problem that federal investigators *fear* will grow even larger." Though the fear of incest is not experienced first-hand by the federal investigators, the complexity of the issue contributes to the use of the word in a manner that stylistically parallels and frames this account. The increased frequency of the word *fear* in the later years of this study is partially explained by this type of usage, which does not directly refer to an object that is feared or use fear as a noun, but uses it in a stylistic manner that parallels the fear frame.

A similar account from 1987 shows how the incorporation of fear, again involving notions of school and community, is not yet a taken-for-granted frame: "It happened in Flagstaff on March 12, 1974. Kelly was walking to school alone. It had taken her a long time to fix her hair that morning, and her brothers and sisters left without her. *There was nothing to fear.*" (*Arizona Republic,* "Rapist's Parole Revives Horror of His Vow: I'll Kill Them All," June 14, 1987, emphasis added). Stylistically, by claiming that "there was nothing to fear," this passage evokes a scenario against which the crime account is told. Certain taken-for-granted notions are brought to the fore with this statement, which are then challenged by the account of the sexual assault of this girl. First, the harmonious concept of neighborhood is shattered. Even as it reveals its fragility, this account is a reaffirmation of our desire to believe that neighborhoods should be safe. Second, we must make sense of this crime. In doing so, our interaction with this account reveals the logic that is at work in our perceptions about children, neighborhoods, and schools. Thus, in stating that "there was nothing to fear," the background of daily life must confront the shocking details of this report, which in turn produce fear. Societal constructions of what it means to be a child, a student, a neighborhood member are thrown into jeopardy as the account is related. The attempt in the text to flesh out these notions against a certain contextualization demonstrates a much different approach than what we find in later accounts of this nature. Through the opposition of community, school, children, and neighborhood to accounts of rape, murder, incest, and violence in the *AR,* these contradictions signal a trend in reporting toward engaging fear and a problem frame. It is in this manner that journalistic accounts write themselves into a fear format with the sense-making tool of the problem/fear frame.

CHILDREN AS VICTIMIZERS

Children as gang members and young criminals dominate many of our news reports and popular culture presentations. Fueled by recent school shootings, attention has shifted to efforts to control wayward youth. This includes remanding more juveniles to adult prisons, trying them as adults, and a widespread attack on the juvenile justice system for being too lenient. Part of this rationale involves "net widening," or bringing juveniles to heel earlier than was done previously. The stern "talking to" by patrol officers now often leads to writing field cards, the first step in future "referrals," as well as immediate intervention by sending youngsters to court-ordered counseling sessions.

Kristi Wimmer's (1999) study of the *Arizona Republic*'s coverage of a youth, Nicholas Contreraz, who died in custody of a "boot camp," illustrates how the fear frame dominates "juveniles" and "abused children." At least 18 children have died in such camps as of July, 2001. Nicholas Contreraz, a sixteen-year-old inmate from California, died at the Arizona Boys Ranch on March 2, 1998, from empyema, a massive infection that filled his lungs with more than two quarts of pus. Contreraz's complaints over a several-day period essentially were ignored as he was punished, forced to carry his soiled clothes and to exercise until he died. Wimmer's (1999) analysis of news reports illustrates how culpability was denied even as a few individuals lost their jobs over the tension between the societal fear of the youth and the youth's fear of society's formal agents of social control.

News Sources and Blameshifting

The major news sources defining the situation of children who were injured while in state custody were (1) Arizona Boys Ranch administration, (2) Arizona Boys Ranch residents/witnesses, (3) child welfare agencies, (4) criminal justice organizations, (5) experts, (6) personal, (e.g., family and friends) (7) media representatives, and (8) government agencies. Reports originating with these sources reflected organizational perspectives and language to deal with blame for Contreraz's death. For example, the Arizona Boys Ranch tended to blame the youth, who, they claimed, routinely lied about their health, so these children could never be believed. Child welfare agencies charged with over-seeing the operation of boot camps tended to frame their assertions of blame as abuse by the Arizona Boys Ranch (ABR) staff.

As can be seen upon analysis, news sources presented definitions of the sit-uation that shifted blame to other organizations and individuals through frames, themes, and language. As we saw in Chapter 6, news sources, like in-dividual actors in everyday life, often are faced with resolving contradictions between words and deeds. Social scientists have identified various techniques that social actors employ to accomplish this, including accounts, techniques of neutralization, and disclaimers (Hewitt 1991). In this case, sources shifted their accountability and responsibility for Contreraz's death through the use of accounts that directed blaming language to a different organization or to different members within their own organization. Accounts are language tools that permit actors to correct action that violates an expectation of appropriate behavior (Scott and Lyman 1968). They are social repair devices used to over-come apparent inconsistencies or contradictions, for instance, "Moral people do not kill, but we do support the death penalty." Two major types of accounts are excuses and justifications. Excuses enable the actor to deny that he or she was directly responsible for an inappropriate act (e.g., "Sorry, I bumped into you, but I tripped on the sidewalk"). Justifications are different: The actor ac-cepts responsibility but denies that the act was inappropriate (e.g., "I bumped into you because your fat body was in my way"). Statements about the de-fendants and ABR reflected two types of excuses: scapegoating, which is ex-cusing behavior on the basis of negative traits of others; and appeals to defeasibility, which excuse behavior based upon the misrepresentation of in-formation by others (Scott and Lyman 1968). For example, Bob Thomas, di-rector of ABR, and his staff asserted consistently that youth could not be trusted and that Nicholaus Contreraz was feigning his illness. Thomas argued that these children are really juvenile delinquents who are liars and manipulators:

> "There's only two ways to get out of the Boys Ranch. You can either claim to be beat on, or you can try to commit suicide," and he [Thomas] continued, "they've [residents of ABR] learned to dupe adults with whining and rational-ization. When all else fails, they play for sympathy by claiming sickness, dis-crimination or abuse." (*Arizona Republic,* May 6, 1998)

Making appeals to defeasibilty was an "accounting" technique used by ABR staff members and the ABR nurse in order to blame each other.

> The staff members claim that the nurse incorrectly told them that Contreraz was healthy and could work and exercise, therefore they forced him to work ac-cordingly. Her misinformation led them to believe that he was faking his ill-ness, therefore their behavior should be excused. Nurse Babb uses the same

excuse in her explanations of her behavior. She claims that had she known the amount of diarrhea, vomiting, and other symptoms Contreraz had been experiencing in the dorms, she would have reacted differently. The misrepresentation of information provided to the nurse by the staff members caused her to make a mistake, therefore her actions or inactions should be excused. The blame is shifted between organizations through strong language and graphic descriptions, and enables the sources and the media to define the situation for an audience. (Wimmer 1999, 30)

While the ABR staff was being scrutinized, the child welfare organization—the Arizona Department of Economic Services (DES)—that had responsibility for ABR's general conduct also engaged in skillful blameshifting. Contreraz was sent to the ABR by California social services, which contracted for his stay at the boot camp and, thus, were also implicated in his death. Both the Arizona and California agencies framed their public responses by blaming the ABR's abusive staff and tactics, yet they parted company when California blamed Arizona for improper oversight and for not providing adequate information about ABR's prior referrals for inappropriate conduct:

> While [California] social services blamed Boys Ranch . . . they also concluded that [Arizona] DES continually let the ranch off the hook despite confirmed cases of abuse. . . . AZ DES defends itself by claiming that CA social services should provide AZ DES with more accurate medical records and that DES "[is] glad California is finally beginning to take responsibility for the children they've been sending to our state all these years." (*Arizona Republic*, July 9, 1998)

Director of ABR Bob Thomas, on the other hand, blames the individual staff members:

> When questioned why Contreraz was forced to eat his lunch on the toilet, as had been reported by witnesses, he [Thomas] retorted, "I think, uh, just because he [the supervisor] was short-staffed. I don't think they really meant to be degrading to him. . . . You know, when he got mad, I guess he [Contreraz] would do things like this. And I'm not making excuses for staff, but . . . " (*Arizona Republic*, August 30, 1998)

Then Thomas redirects blame to the California social services people:

> Child Protective Services: Might Contreraz still be alive today if Boys Ranch had properly cared for him?
> Thomas: You could take this a step farther. I mean, you could take Sacramento [County Probation Department]. Should they be charged with failure to protect? I mean, should the mother be charged with failure to protect? Should . . . the probation officer be charged? I mean, we're looking at fault. There's

enough fault to go around for everybody. It was a tragedy, and . . . I'm not trying to negate all responsibility for Boys Ranch . . . (but) what we also found out was, I mean, there was a reason staff, our staff, made drastic mistakes. (*Arizona Republic,* August 30, 1998

The Contreraz death is important because children are not expected to be killed in a correctional boot camp that, after all, has been presented in numerous news reports as helpful and constructive. Seldom is the public given a systematic and thorough look at the living conditions in such facilities. While the popular culture images of adult prisons promote a "tough place" (Surette 1998), juvenile facilities are regarded as different. The assumption seems to be that life is rigorous, yet humane. The evocative accounts of Contreraz's last day illustrate the problem frame at work as Contreraz is cast as a victim of an unfortunate situation, of inattentive individual staff members, but *not* necessarily a fault of an institutional process. As Wimmer notes (1999):

A "hellish day at the Ranch," Contreraz was "fighting back" and was "forced" to work while his "lungs were full of pus" (*Arizona Republic,* March 31, 1998). The language becomes even more evocative as the journalist writes of the "chilling last days" of Contreraz, with the staff described as cruel as they called Contreraz a "baby," "taunted" him, and "told others he [Contreraz] had AIDS" (*Arizona Republic,* April 22, 1998). Words used to describe the treatment of the youths included "yank," "slam," "force," "cruelty," "struggled" and the accounts of witnesses (other Ranch residents) who told reporters what they had seen or experienced:
   "One youth reported that his head was bashed into a wall because he asked to use the toilet. Another, who admitted being disrespectful, said a ranch employee retaliated by 'hitting the bottom of his chin with [a] fist in rabbit-type punches'" (*Arizona Republic,* April 22, 1998). (30)

Another journalist played out the morality play of the problem frame by describing Contreraz's death through the metaphor of Christian/Christ imagery:

Transformed by the merciless magicians at Arizona Boys Ranch from juvenile delinquent to martyr. Four months since Nicholaus Contreraz, 15-year-old petty criminal and troublemaker, was led by his keepers on a modern day Stations of the Cross. . . . He was forced to exercise, ridiculed by staff members for defecating on himself, then made to carry a bucket of his own soiled clothing, to do push-ups over it. . . . The boy collapsed while a staff member told him he deserved an Academy Award. (*Arizona Republic,* July 5, 1998)

Nicholas Contreraz's death is informed by the discourse of fear. No journalist caused the death in a straightforward fashion, although years of context-free reporting on crime, youth, and particularly gangs helped define situations for decisionmakers and citizens that made "drastic measures" like boot camps necessary. But there is still more to it. The problem frame has given us the victim role and children are regarded as likely victims, unless they are also cast as victimizers. Nicholas Contreraz was a victimizer who became a victim in a boot camp.

> These young men are the victimizers that violate the social order by breaking the law, and this society has devised programs like boot camps and juvenile prisons to keep delinquents locked away from innocent individuals they may victimize in the future. The moral panic and fear created by the media and recreated in the minds of the public allow these young men to be put in an environment in which they may become the victim and their caretakers the victimizers. (Wimmer 1999, 59)

There are other accounts of children who are cast as victimizers and then victims. They all share the discourse of fear. Many citizens believe that fear is an effective means of social control. Selcraig's (2000) story about Camp Fear focuses on Gina Score, an overweight eighth-grade girl from a small South Dakota town, who was sent to a boot camp for shoplifting Press-N-Go Fingernails valued at $2.99. This boot camp was one of several started by popular fourth-term governor Bill Janklow, an ex-Marine who campaigned on a commonsense solution to juvenile crime:

> . . . many politicians and frustrated parents have found salvation in the camps' simple goal: to reduce troubled teenagers to their emotional core, back to frightened children, so that their minds will open long enough to imagine a life without drugs, crime, and self-hatred. (Selcraig 2000, 66)

The Camp Fear workers sought to instill discipline in Gina and break her spirit. They succeeded in killing her by demanding that this 224-pound girl complete a 2.6-mile "jog" on a warm, humid day.

> Within a block or two, Gina started lagging behind. As the girls reached each corner of the rectangular route, where they were allowed to rest briefly and drink water, they waited for Gina to catch up. Two youth counselors repeatedly shouted for Gina to keep moving, sometimes interlocking their arms with hers just to keep her going forward down the dusty roads. At roughly 7:45, after the other girls had reached the front gates, Gina staggered and collapsed 500 feet from the finish. Several girls tried to help her up, but staff members, believing one inmate who said Gina had acted this way before at a halfway house, were convinced they had a "behavior problem."
> "Quit faking!" several girls recall a supervisor shouting. "You're embarrassing us." Everyone knew the boot camp credo: Quitting Is Not an Option. When four girls encircled Gina to give her shade, counselors ordered them to back away.
> A staff nurse who checked on Gina at 8:05 said her vital signs were normal

and that she was simply hyperventilating. An hour later, Gina struggled to her feet and began slowly walking back to her cottage. A few hundred feet later, within sight of her air-conditioned cottage, she collapsed again. Her eyes were dilated, her skin pale, her lips purple. She urinated on herself and began frothing at the mouth. Her eyes rolled back in her head. Even when a farmer's manure truck rumbled down the road beside her, Gina didn't budge. The staff still thought she was faking; several girls recall them laughing and telling jokes as Gina lay on the ground. The camp's director came out to assess the situation, but he told the staff to "wait out" Gina, so no one called for an ambulance.

"I was crying," says Christi Battis, a former inmate. "All the girls were crying. . . . How could she be faking it when she was pale blue and wasn't even brushing the flies off her?"

Finally, at 10:47, three hours after Gina collapsed, two physicians happened by and ordered that an ambulance be called. Six minutes later, paramedics were giving Gina oxygen, but on the way to the hospital, her heart stopped. In the emergency room they sent chilled IV fluids through Gina's rigid body and packed her in ice, but a rectal thermometer peaked at 108—the highest it would go. Internally, she had literally begun to cook. With her organs shutting down, repeated attempts to restart her heart were futile. At 12:39 p.m., Gina was declared dead. "It was," said emergency room physician Jerome Howe, "the worst case of heatstroke I've ever seen." (Selcraig 2000, 66)

Gina and Nicholas were killed through a social process begun with the promotion of a discourse of fear that passes through the problem frame as a way to promote entertaining news reports. Victim and victimizer hang on the discourse of fear. Formal agents of social control rely on fear and seek public approval to eradicate the source of these fears, that is, crime and juvenile delinquency. Children are a central part of the symbolic order that promotes the discourse of fear. On the one hand, steps must be taken to protect children, but on the other hand, we must be protected from children.

CONCLUSION

Icons representing timeless myths have been supplemented or replaced by more complex symbol systems that have emerged in an ecology of communication as popular culture. Children and the iconography of fear reside within an ecology of communication that provides evocative answers to referential questions (Ellenius and European Science Foundation 1998). These symbols are provided by the mass media and popular culture, especially those emphasizing the "other" and sources of fear. When external enemies become less symbolically legitimate, the emphasis shifts to the protection and safety of children. This has political consequences for many interest groups, for example, the police and formal agents of social control.

A discourse of fear offers a conceptual elaboration for a process through which numerous messages resonating with themes of fear can be circulated, recast, and institutionally promoted through public policies, media reports, popular culture, and cognitive frameworks. The challenge is to understand how children, who are often presented as innocent victims and who require protection, can also be presented as victimizers from whom society requires protection. Both involve fear but the object of protection is different: in the first case, the state is being asked to protect children from the sources of fear. In the second case, the children are the source of fear and the state is protecting society from them. The two cases come together when children in the state's care are brutalized by the state. Perhaps one way to understand this dynamic comes from Stasio (1995): "Stories of criminal violence allow us to sacrifice the children we love in order to exorcize our fear of losing them. When the genre is really working, both the writing and the reading of such horrors become acts of love."

8

The Lens of Fear

Fear of some kind has always been with us. It's the magnitude and nature of fear that is different today. It seems that fear is everywhere. It is as though fear is attached to many activities and issues, and if it is not attached, it is not far removed from them. Part of the reason is due to the context and times of our lives. Two things that make a big difference are the amount of information we have available as well as the mobility we experience. We are aware of more things happening in the world, we expect more, and so more seems to be possible. We also are more mobile, often spending our adult lives in places different from our childhood. So, our grounding isn't as solid and we do not see as clearly.

It is the way we see that matters. I think that using a metaphor of a lighthouse lens can help us appreciate the role of fear in our everyday lives. The Fresnel lens, developed by Augustine Fresnel in 1822, enabled lighthouse keepers to magnify greatly the focus and power of a candle. This helped ships at sea not only avoid rocky crags, but more importantly, told them where they were in reference to other points of light. Over time, the light and lens became synonymous with lighthouses, and it was this wonderful lens that changed maritime commerce and travel. Most lighthouses were no longer necessary by the 1960s because other technology could provide ships with much better signals about their location and safety. Now associated with another era, most lighthouses, with their Fresnel lenses, are museums that still function, but mainly as demonstrations of the past carried over into the future.

We experience more of our lives through a lens of fear. Concerns, risks, and dangers are magnified and even distorted by this lens. Caution has given way to avoidance. Rarity has been replaced by typicality. And the focus of media attention has taken a toll on our ability to see our way clearly. It is as though the lighthouse keeper and the ship's captain cannot even see one another because of the out-of-control glare coming from a source of light that was once helpful. We must understand this lens in order to help us regain our focus and see more clearly.

Figure 8.1.   The Fresnel Lens.

The discourse of fear originated in religious beliefs and now pervades a secular society. Fear is an orientation to the world. God and organized religion provided salvation from fear in a sacred society. The state and formal social control promise salvation from fear in our secular society. This remarkable shift has major social implications. Fear of God and sin were normal for me as a small boy since my family and I were "believers" in a mythology of damnation and salvation. My world was simple as a child: I was taught to seek salvation for my sins in order to be saved from eternal damnation. God could save me, but then again, if I did not do the right thing, God could also damn me. That was the sacred worldview, where faith was the goal and where commitment and "true belief" were demonstrated to fellow believers on a daily basis, from church service to church service. David Campbell (1998) argues that dangerousness, or the "evangelism of fear," with death as its impetus and salvation as its goal, required concern not only with external issues, but with the self as well:

> The church relied heavily on discourses of danger to establish its authority, discipline its followers, and ward off its enemies. . . . Moreover, it was this

"evangelism of fear," that produced a preoccupation with death. . . . The required familiarity with death demanded of individuals an eternal vigilance against the self. (48–49)

Fear is normal in our time. The major point of this book is that fear has become more pervasive in our lives. I have argued that fear is commonly used in public documents and is becoming part of everyday conversation. And I have suggested a mechanism and process by which this has occurred. This process basically involves the mass media and popular culture in general, and the "discovery" that fear fit rather well with the problem frame, which is a key part of the entertainment format and logic, which, in turn, satisfies commercial demands. Politicians, police, journalists, businesses, and even social scientists have an interest and a stake in fear. Social scientists, for example, monitor it through annual surveys, focusing on indicators of safety and security and examining how people are adjusting their lives. Most of this attention is devoted to fear of crime, but as we saw in previous chapters, fear is not synonymous with crime but rather, travels across topics over a period of time. So what are we to do about fear? What do we know about fear now that we didn't before this and other projects?

A study of fear and popular culture suggests a broader sociology of fear. While such a project is beyond this book, a few key points must be made about the relationship between popular culture and the role and consequences of fear in our lives. This chapter examines the impact of popular culture on our understanding and use of fear. I want to examine how danger, risk, and fear are related, often confused with one another, and to suggest a few implications of these relationships. It is also important to explore connections of fear to critical components such as victims, state power, and social control. I continue with a succinct overview of fear and culture and examine some recent claims about fear. This is followed by a look at the role of fear in social control, the role of news sources and authorities, and some alternatives.

My basic thesis is that fear is contextual and does not exist in a vacuum. The discourse of fear has changed over the last few decades primarily through the work of the mass media and popular culture. Moreover, this culture has pervaded every institutional arrangement in social life. So, a jumping off place for my analysis of how we can avoid negative consequences of the discourse of fear is to simply suggest that popular culture is not just incidental or merely supplementary to other social forces, but, rather, that popular culture has been the key element in promoting the discourse of fear.

Fear is a feature of an ecology of communication that connects information technology to communication formats and social activities and meanings. This requires moving beyond disciplines. Theoretical boundaries are breached when mass media content and forms are part of our everyday lives and contribute to social definitions of self, others, and social issues. I have drawn on work from proponents of symbolic interactionism, structuralism, cultural studies, and poststructuralism who are awash in debates about the origin, nature, and consequences of social interaction, are swimming in mass-mediated symbols, from products to information technology to slogans to political tropes and social issues. Fear is a perspective or an orientation to the world, rather than "fear of something." Fear is one of the few things that Americans share. The discourse of fear is constructed through evocative entertainment formats promoting visual, emotional, and dramatic experience that audience members can identify with, live vicariously, and share. However, it is not just "fear of crime" or a particular thing, but rather a sense or an identity that we are all actual or potential victims held in common by many people. Indeed, studies in other countries (e.g., the United Kingdom) make it very clear that identity, social context, perceptions, and social definitions are very relevant for how safe people feel (Farrall et al. 2000; Van der Wurff, Van Stallduinen, and Stringer 1989). Previous chapters have shown how the object of fear (e.g., crime, drugs, AIDS, children) shifts or travels across topics over time. The sense that something has happened to us, could happen to us, or probably will happen to us connects the present moment with resentments and blame about the past, as well as anxieties about the future.

The most pervasive aspect of this victim perspective is crime. Politicians and state control agencies, working with news media as news sources, have done much to capitalize on this concern and to promote a sense of insecurity and reliance on formal agents of social control—and related businesses—to provide surveillance, protection, revenge, and punishment to protect us, to save us. Even foreign policy and threats of external enemies support fear:

> The constant articulation of danger through foreign policy is thus not a threat to a state's identity or existence: it is its condition of possibility. While the objects of concern change over time, the techniques and exclusions by which those objects are constituted a danger persists. (Campbell 1998, 13)

And,

> The postwar tests of United States foreign policy certainly located the dangers they identified via references to the Soviet Union. But they always acknowledged that the absence of order, the potential for anarchy, and the fear of totalitarian forces or other negative elements that would exploit or foster conditions—whether internal or external—was their initial concern. (Campbell 1998, 30)

It is the fear of the "other" that we anticipate; we see numerous reports about very atypical occurrences, but we see them night after night. News in the problem frame make commonplace what is very rare. Our worst-case scenarios (e.g., murder, kidnapping, terrorist attacks) are always before us. The news and entertainment industry engulfed in entertainment formats see the world this way and reflect it in their productions (Gitlin 1994).

Cultural and political contexts contributed to the emergence of fear as a perspective that pervades everyday life. A massive expansion of electronic media outlets (e.g., cable TV, videotape rentals, the Internet) overlapped historically with unprecedented consumer growth and Gross National Product, the decline of "real" international threats (e.g., the fall of the Soviet Union), and conservative political agendas that used crime and especially drug-related issues to gain political legitimacy (Campbell 1998; Garland 2000). The discourse of fear became a key perspective for selecting, organizing, and presenting materials that were consistent with the entertainment formats of popular culture in a secular society. This perspective enables heterogeneous audiences to share a common explanation of what is wrong with the world and thereby provides a way to fix failed expectations that were inspired by awesome social changes, which fractured public life and communities anchoring selves and identities (Hewitt 1989; Holstein and Gubrium 2000; Jacobs 1969; Oldenburg 1989). Commodification of identities fueled consumption and vicarious participation in popular culture as a substitute for leisure time (Bensman and Vidich 1971; Ewen 1976; Ewen and Ewen 1992; Stein and Vidich 1963). More of our experience came from the mass media as popular culture provided more of the style and substance of everyday life. The entertainment perspective expanded (Jackall and Hirota 1999, 2000) as audiences were transformed into markers. Involvement in the public realm increasingly shifted to mass-mediated information emphasizing fear and crises. The security of life in this world became the dominant orientation and informed social concerns and social situations.

Dramatic entertainment emphasis involves salvation; as a secular society, we are less concerned (notwithstanding increases in church attendance) with spiritual development and justice beyond the grave than we are with lifestyle, occupational success, and consumer rights.

> Danger (death, in its ultimate form) might therefore be thought of as the new god for the modern world of states, not because it is peculiar to our time, but because it replicates the logic of Christendom's evangelism of fear.
>
> Indeed, in a world in which state identity is secured through discourses of danger, some low tactics are employed to serve these high ideals. These tactics are not inherent to the logic of identity, which only requires the definition of difference. But securing an ordered self and an ordered world—particularly when the field upon which this process operates is as extensive as a state—involves defining elements that stand in the way of order as forms of "otherness." . . . In this way, the state project of security replicates the church project of salvation. The state grounds it legitimacy by offering salvation to its followers who, it says, would otherwise be destined to an unredeemed death. (Campbell 1998, 50)

The social context of fear reflects the communication order and the dominant modes of information transfer in a historical period. Fear is involved more in public discourse partly because there is such a massive public discourse that can be centrally guided and directed (but not tightly controlled), including setting agendas with news reports passing through the problem frame and media logic that guides news sources representing certain organizational perspectives. Certainly one key factor that led to the news success of the problem frame was news workers' reliance on formal agents of social control (FASC) as news sources. These sources have become the key agents and definers of social issues. Audience familiarity with the general message—because of numerous previous reports—permits shorthand accounts to resonate with the cold shudder of fear. Every atypical and very rare event is presented "as if" it is but part of a broader sweep of terror.

Fear and victim became linked symbolically through popular culture formats joined in a comprehensive ecology of communication: Technology, communication formats, information, concerns, issues, and choices are joined and overlap. The impact is more pronounced when visual representations dominate. Denzin (1995) has shown how visuals are relevant for individual lives and particularly how social context shapes individuals' behavior, expectations, awareness, and reflexive principles or codes for understanding their place in the "show." "The postmodern mediated self . . . finds its moral solidarity in those narrative tales that circulate in the cinematic culture" (265). Countless news reports, entertainment programs, films, and commercials are the symbolic grounding of everyday life, but there are also movies and other visual images. The media images captured by Denzin are consistent with his overall thesis that the postmodern world is characterized by the cultivation of conspicuous consumption, identified by Hollywood genres stressing money, sex, love and intimacy, crimes of violence, passion and greed, race and its repression. "Gone are the highest ideals of humanity, including freedom, self-respect, open dialogue and honesty" (Denzin 1991, 149).

There can be no fear without actual victims or potential victims. In the postmodern age, victim is a status and representation and not merely a person or someone who has suffered as a result of some personal, social, or physical calamity. Massive and concerted efforts by moral entrepreneurs to have their causes adopted and legitimated as core social issues worthy of attention have led to the wholesale adaptation and refinement of the use of the problem frame to promote victimization. Often couching their causes as battles for justice, moral entrepreneurs seek to promote new social definitions of right and wrong (see Johnson 1995a; Spector and Kitsuse 1977). Victims are entertaining and that is why they abound. They are evocative, bringing forth tears, joy, and vicarious emotional experience. But victim is more: Victim is now a status, a position that is open to all people who live in a symbolic environment marked by the discourse of fear. We are all potential victims, often vying for official recognition and legitimacy. Much has changed since the Church offered salvation to those who shared a worldview that pitted their immortal souls against eternal damnation. Fear of God was produced by the church's road to salvation; the cure, so to speak, showed the punishment that was being avoided. The Enlightenment and rational thought essentially killed the supporting ontology that made the fear of God an everyday reality. Yet, the contribution to our culture and our collective representations remains:

> The problem was that once the "death of God" had been proclaimed, the link between the world, "man," and certitude had been broken . . . an ambiguous situation arose in which there was (and is) a demand for external guarantees inside a culture that has erased the ontological preconditions for them. Modernity is thus an epoch of secret insistence jeopardized by its own legacy of truthfulness and honesty: its bearers demand that every hidden faith be exposed, but faith is necessary to ground the superiority of modern life. (Ashley 1989, 303)

The problem, then, is that we continue to look for salvation but we lack the symbolic means to achieve it.

> However, this ethical impulse cannot be satisfied, particularly when we remind ourselves . . . that the culture of modernity necessitates external guarantees but has erased the ontological preconditions for them. It was this situation, after all, that granted to fear and anger the capacity of securing that which could no longer be reasoned into existence. . . . The evangelism of fear centered on death grounded the church's project of salvation; the evangelism of fear articulated in the anxiety about an unfinished and dangerous world secured the state such that security occupied the position of salvation; now the evangelism of fear enunciated by those hoping to ward off "foreign" intellectual influences works to contain the instability of their representations of the world. (Campbell 1998, 193)

So, we have known for some time that fear is circularly (or reflexively) joined to the "other," a role played by the Devil (Antichrist, etc.) for more than two thousand years. Fear was part of the process of protecting us and affording us salvation. This fear was realized in everyday-life terms as people tried to "be good" in order to avoid damnation, as well as punishing those who violated the sacred rules. (Not keeping the Commandments, for example, also implied that any among the elect who knew about such violations would take steps to prevent their breach, including punishment.) There were, of course, many unintended consequences of this ontology, including the inquisition, the Salem witch trials, and, according to Weber (1954, 1958), the rise of capitalism.

It is apparent then that the origins of a sociology of fear preceded the modern state and crime control efforts. Thus, while it is certainly correct, in my

view, that conservative political agendas have benefited from joining fear and
victim with crime control agendas, the issue is much bigger, particularly the
relationship between fear and everyday-life culture. Crime control efforts contributed to the most recent visual image and identification of the extension of
the victim role to citizens. However, this has all been communicated through
news reports that have been developed, constituted, produced, packaged, presented, and then reacted to through the evocative problem frame discussed
throughout this book. For example, Garland (2000) notes that crime control
was a strategy that included the development and linkage of individuals to
victim:

> The new imperative is that victims must be protected, their voices heard,
> their memory honoured, their anger expressed, their fears addressed. . . . A po-
> litical logic has been established wherein being "for" victims automatically
> means being tough on offenders. A zero-sum policy game is assumed wherein
> the offender's gain is the victim's loss.
> The symbolic figure of the victim has taken on a life of its own, and plays a
> role in political debate and policy argument that is quite detached from the
> claims of the organized victims' movement, or the aggregated opinions of sur-
> veyed victims. . . . This is a new and significant fact of contemporary cul-
> ture. . . . But what is sufficiently acknowledged is the degree to which the figure
> of the victim has come to have the status of a "representative individual" in con-
> temporary society. . . . Whoever speaks on behalf of victims speaks on behalf of
> us all. . . . Outrage and anger are the culture's antidotes to fear and anxiety, and
> the open expression of these emotions is part of the consolation and therapy it
> offers. (351–352)

These concerns lead to a broader formulation of fear that takes into account
social and cultural context and the ways in which these are communicated and
shared. An ecology of communication is relevant for connecting fear and victim. Both are embedded in evocative visual and dramatic entertainment formats that provide the symbolic direction, meanings and media for shared
language, perspective, and topics. Other work has shown that fear and victim
are informed by perceived membership (Altheide et al. 2001). Crime and
threats to the public order—and therefore all good citizens—are part of the
focus of fear, but as noted throughout this book, the topics change over time.
What they all have in common is pointing to the "other," the outsider, the
nonmember, the alien. However, Schwalbe et al. (2000) have shown that "othering" is part of a social process whereby a dominant group defines into existence an inferior group. This requires the establishment and "group sense" of
symbolic boundaries of membership. These boundaries occur through institutional processes that are grounded in everyday situations and encounters, including language, discourse, accounts, and conversation. Knowledge and skill
at using "what everyone like us knows" involves formal and informal social-

ization so that members acquire the coinage of cultural capital with which they can purchase acceptance, allegiance, and belonging. Part of this language involves the discourse of fear.

> Discourse is more than talk and writing; it is a way of talking and writing. To regulate discourse is to impose a set of formal or informal rules about what can be said, how it can be said, and who can say what to whom. . . . Inasmuch as language is the principal means by which we express, manage, and conjure emotions, to regulate discourse is to regulate emotion. The ultimate consequence is a regulation of action. . . .
>
> When a form of discourse is established as standard practice, it becomes a tool for reproducing inequality, because it can serve not only to regulate thought and emotion, but also to identify Others and thus to maintain boundaries as well. (Schwalbe et al. 2000, 433–434)

It is not fear of crime, then, that is most critical. It is what this fear can expand to, what it can become. As sociologist Bernard Beck (n.d.) notes, we are becoming "armored." Social life changes when more people live behind walls, hire guards, drive armored vehicles (e.g., sport utility vehicles), wear "armored" clothing (such as the No Fear brand and "big-soled shoes"), carry mace and handguns, and take martial arts classes. The problem is that these activities reaffirm and help produce a sense of disorder that our actions perpetuate. We then rely more on formal agents of social control (FASC) to save us by policing them, the "others," who have challenged our faith.

ADJUSTING THE LENS OF FEAR

The Fresnel lens operated by providing magnified light from many small refracting lenses onto a main bull's-eye that shone through the night. It was part of an ecology of communication in its day. Its structure played with light, within the limits of nineteenth-century technology, to produce an incredibly intense light that could be seen for many miles. But as a mere light, it could only mark land or dangerous rocks. Its real contribution as a navigation device occurred when each lighthouse was assigned its own distinctive signature of blinks and flashes that let mariners know precisely where they were along the coast and what to look for as the journey continued. As noted earlier, this innovation contributed to modern shipping and commerce.

Shedding some light on fear can help us avoid dangerous encounters. I have argued that the discourse of fear is akin to a constant light or perspective and orientation that are prevalent throughout our culture. The specific topics change through which fear shines or is reflected. And like the Fresnel lens, one topic addresses the others and is carried over, producing a much stronger reflection than would be otherwise expected. Thus, for example, the concern with drugs took on added significance in the face of previous reports about crime. The fear involved with drugs was quickly added to that of children, both in terms of protecting children from drugs, as well as protecting us from children who use and sell drugs.

Constructing the discourse of fear is a major accomplishment of the mass media and marks a significant change in the role of the mass media as a social institution. The mass media and popular culture do not merely report on events or issues. We do not merely obtain information from the mass media. Rather, a media logic and expansive communication formats have moved beyond the technology into the foundations of our daily lives. Virtually everyone is an audience member of some form of popular culture today. It is part of products, events, and the operation of our most basic social institutions, including education, business, religion, sports, and politics (Altheide and Snow 1991).

Aaron Doyle (2001) provides one of the most comprehensive studies of the role of media logic in guiding organizational decision making, particularly in criminal justice agencies. This project qualifies as a critical experiment to test competing ideas about the nature and impact of mass media formats and content on organizational cultures and action. This is a solid sociological study of the role of the mass media in social life. The work is theoretically driven by three distinctive, albeit complementary, perspectives on the mass media's relevance for social change, social action, and social institutions. The three approaches are labeled "medium theory," "media logic," and "institutional perspective." The writing is excellent as the author moves from abstract concepts to elaborate on specific courses of action that should follow if the various perspectives are correct. In this way, empirical opportunities are opened to investigate the most innovative theoretical approaches offered in the last two decades for making sense of the mass media's impact on social life.

It is the overall comparative research design that is most creative in this project. It is an ambitious approach to triangulation. Rather than use one set of data, the author examines four case studies: (1) an entertainment show—*Cops*—that has come to define an expanding genre; (2) the expanding role of surveillance cameras and home video use by criminal justice (CJ) agencies; (3) how the media and CJ agencies covered, reflected, and evaluated Vancouver's Stanley Cup Riot; and (4) Greenpeace's use of media. Doyle used several different methods to collect data, including ethnography, interviewing, content analysis, and secondary materials. Data consisted of field notes, interview transcripts, numerous print and electronic media transcripts, and descriptions including analysis of visuals.

This triangulated design permits analysis to extend across several venues of possible media impact, such as the police themselves or the activists themselves. While there are, of course, other realms of media impact not fully investigated in this study, for example, the role of the mass audience, several important dimensions are covered, which permit careful analysis of various dimensions of media influences.

The resulting analysis and compelling literature review offer empirical evaluation of significant work about the role of the mass media. The basic conclusion is that the media logic perspective predicts what various institutional actors do, but these actions are also influenced by institutional workers, who are the major news sources on whom media workers depend. The communication logic and bureaucratic struggles for control and defining the situation are very much related and in a fundamental sense are reflexive and help constitute each other. In this sense, an ecology of communication is articulated whereby information technology, mass media logic and formats, and institutional conduct are joined interactively and over time as human actors take into account the perspectives, approaches, and rules by which other players in this scenario of public attention and newsworthiness operate.

A very helpful appendix concerns how this study contributes to not only the massive literature on mass media and social change, but also what it contributes to significant debates in criminology and social control. Mass media reports and perspectives are shown to be significant for ongoing issues about the relative significance of spectacles or surveillance as social control. Moreover, the message is stressed and empirically demonstrated that any significant theoretical work on criminology and social control must attend to the relationships of media logic and bureaucratic authorities in defining social situations and conducting social interventions, social change, and social control. An implication of Doyle's work is that spectacle and surveillance are joined in a media age in which popular culture and entertainment formats inform fashion, prayer, prison, and politics. Spectacle and surveillance are connected through the police, who are both stars and producers of entertainment-oriented media programs and news reports, but who are also the main architects of law and order ideology. We watch and are reminded of crime, danger, and, more broadly, the pervasive "meta logic" of fear that is resonated through media logic. "In particular, as policing and broadcast television came together, spectacle becomes bound up with surveillance" (Doyle 2001, 288). Thus, Doyle observes, audience members are implicated in their own control.

One implication of the work by Doyle and others (e.g., Marx 1988; Staples 1997; Best 1995; Burke 1966; de Certeau 1984; Couch 1984; Edelman 1988; Ericson and Haggerty 1997; Ericson, Baranek, and Chan 1991; Gamson 1998; Hall 1997) who have shown that the mass media, social control, and surveillance are connected is that common perspectives and communication styles are involved. They are coproducers, and if the images that they are promoting are inaccurate and individually or socially destructive, then they are involved in mass-mediated terrorism, which was defined earlier as "the purposeful act or threat of violence to create fear and/or compliant behavior in a victim and or audience of the act or threat" (Lopez and Stohl 1984).

Sheriff Joe Arpaio in Phoenix, Arizona, routinely operates as a media-justice figure and is a prime example of one who engages in mass-mediated terrorism. During his tenure as sheriff, there have been several lawsuits brought against the county for misconduct and brutality, including a successful several-million-dollar settlement for the bludgeoning death by jail guards of inmate Scott Norwood. Well known for "publicity stunts" (e.g., the use of chain gangs) to attract attention and promote a repressive penal policy which has gained him widespread voter popularity, Arpaio has instituted a tent city, where inmates swelter in the Arizona sun. More recently, he began Jailcam on the Internet, with which various parts of the inmate booking process can be seen (e.g., prebooking, booking, intake, holding), including partial views of women's toilet facilities that have been touted on several Internet pornography sites. After the cyber "visitor" is greeted with the message, "First live web cam from inside a working jail," they are then given this warning:

> This is a real life transmission of the Maricopa County Sheriff's Office Madison Street Jail. Instances of violence or sexually inappropriate behavior by detainees during the booking process may occur. Viewer discretion is advised. This is a jail not a simulation. The persons in this transmission are either employees of Maricopa County Sheriff's Office, other police agencies in Maricopa County or arrestees. Under the United States and Arizona Constitution a person is innocent until proven guilty in a court of law.

Arpaio's regime exemplifies the media-criminal justice relationship as well as "othering" (Schwalbe et al. 2000) and the degradation of inmates, many of whom remain in jail because they cannot afford bail. He works closely with the local news media that carry his self-promotional materials. The presumed innocence of the accused is made a mere technicality as news media are given ample information and access to many cases. An example occurred in Phoenix, Arizona, during May and June 2001 when Jefferson Davis McGee, age 30, was arrested by the Maricopa County Sheriff's Department as a suspect in the homicide of a young girl. McGee was picked up during a "sheriff's canvas" of the area on the basis of an outstanding "theft charge" (i.e., shoplifting), although some items believed to be leads were taken from the van in which he lived. His bail was $2,500, but he did not have the requisite 10 percent required (or $250). Individuals accused of child-related crimes, particularly sexual ones, typically are placed in protective custody. McGee was not. According to one news report:

> Officials said McGee was the first of several people held as "investigative leads" in Byrd's murder, but never labeled as official suspects. And while criminal defendants arrested on child molestation charges are routinely placed in protective "administrative segregation," McGee never fell into that category be-

cause he was booked only on a warrant relating to a failure to appear in court on a shoplifting charge.

McGee would have been held away from the jail's general population if he had requested it, according to Sheriff's Office spokesman Dave Trombi.

"Generally, inmates who fear for their safety will ask to be placed in administrative segregation," he said. "Mr. McGee did not ask for it. He did not feel he was in danger". (*Arizona Republic,* June 2, 2001, B1)

McGee was held with the general population in the Madison Street Jail. While technically he was in jail because of the theft charge, he was arrested because he was a potential suspect in the homicide. This information was made available and several of the TV stations referred to him by name, adding that detectives regarded him as a "good lead." Inmates, who tend to be quite moralistic and oppressive in their views of child batterers, heard these reports. A group of twelve people beat McGee so badly that his spleen had to be removed. Arpaio stated, "I don't think we did anything wrong. . . . He wasn't put in jail as a sex offender. He was in as a shoplifter. I can't control the news media" (*Arizona Republic,* June 7, 2001, B10). Another suspect was arrested several days later.

RISK, DANGER, AND FEAR

Risk, danger, and fear are wrapped up in the discourse of fear because of the ways in which they have been used. It can be useful to separate them. As Beck (1992), Ericson and Haggerty (1997), Adam, Beck, and Van Loon (2000) have noted, our risk society is a feature of people having more information about risks and then acting on this information by either seeking more information, avoiding activities, or demanding protection. Much of this has occurred through the expanded use of evocative communication formats that present the world through the problem frame. As noted earlier, fear is a key element of creating the risk society, organized around communication oriented to policing, control, and prevention of risks (Ericson and Haggerty 1997; Staples 1997). A constitutive feature of this emerging order is a blanket reminder of fear. "Fear ends up proving itself, as new risk communication and management systems proliferate" (Ericson and Haggerty 1997, 6).

Risk was part of a social ecology that involved changing legal foundations about property and capital investment. What is distinctive about risk in this context is that it required public legitimization that more was at stake than merely an individual's health or fortune. There emerged the sense that the collective good was to be served by this. This notion would become more important in later years with the emergence of the victim, as noted previously.

> Risk implies a kind of active as well as passive solidarity among the individuals composing a population: no one may appeal to a good driving record to escape the constraints of the group. All must recognize their constitutive weakness or, better, recognize that by their very existence they are a risk to others. Each individual must bend to the imperatives of group solidarity.
>
> The moment a population is identified as a risk, everything within it tends to become—necessarily becomes—just that. Risk has an allusive, insidious potential existence that renders it simultaneously present and absent, doubtful and suspicious. Assumed to be everywhere, it founds a politics of prevention. The term prevention does not indicate simply a practice based on the maxim than an ounce of prevention is worth a pound of cure, but also the assumption that if prevention is necessary it is because danger exists—it exists in a virtual state before being actualized in an offense, injury, or accident. This entails the further assumption that the responsible institutions are guilty if they do not detect the presence, or actuality, of a danger even before it is realized. (Ewald 1993, 221–222)

The discourse of fear has been created because of an expansive entertainment-oriented media logic, particularly the use of the problem frame that promotes risk and danger as fear. The discourse of fear tends to focus on a relatively small number of these, but as I have noted throughout this book, it is the perspective or orientation of the discourse of fear that is significant. Nevertheless, in terms of ordinary language use, risk, danger, and fear are quite different. Figure 8.1 suggests some of the ways in which these terms differ. We are all subjected to many potential risks (e.g., food and drink, transportation, recreation, asteroids, random shootings). Risks and danger signify an awareness of potential harm, and they are often associated with specific acts or objects. Many of these risks are not included in our discourse of fear, and, indeed, there are many cultural jokes about government agencies trying to protect us from certain maladies. Most people perceive very few of these potential risks as dangerous, but nevertheless do take precautions (e.g., wearing seatbelts, safety glasses, holding on to the sides of a ladder as we climb).

Fear is much different. It is an emotion. It is a general orientation that harm is imminent and that steps should be taken to avoid the source of fear or to attack the object of fear.

> Fear is a fundamentally different psychological experience than perceived risk. While risk entails a cognitive judgment, fear is far more emotive in character. Fear activates a series of complex bodily changes alerting the actor to the possibility of danger. (Ferraro 1995, 95)

Fear involves blame and attacking the source of fear. Popular culture and especially news reports confuse risk, danger, and fear. One way this is done is through the continued space of victimization. Fear produces victims and re-

Figure 8.2.   Danger, Risk, Fear and the Mass Media.

inforces the notion that everyone is actually or potentially a victim. The emotional reaction of fear is desired. The main goal, after all, is to attract audiences in order to sell advertising time (or space) to commercial sponsors. Crime news has been a staple of this kind of reporting for several decades. Regularly scheduled newscasts can be easily filled by selecting readily available police reports about shootings, kidnappings, or violent assaults. Seldom is context and understanding included in the report, but rather, the sense of urgency, suffering, victimization, and threat to all is, which is often followed with precautions for viewers to keep their doors and windows locked.

The major impact of the discourse of fear is to promote a sense of disorder and a belief that things are out of control. Figure 8.3, adapted from Ferraro (1995), suggests that fear reproduces itself, or becomes a self-fulfilling prophecy. Social life can become more hostile when social actors define their situations as fearful and engage in speech communities through the discourse of fear. And people come to share an identity as competent "fear realists" as family members, friends, neighbors, and colleagues socially construct their effective environments with fear. Behavior becomes constrained, community activism may focus more on "block watch" programs and quasi-vigilantism, and we continue to avoid downtowns and many parts of our social world because of "what everyone knows."

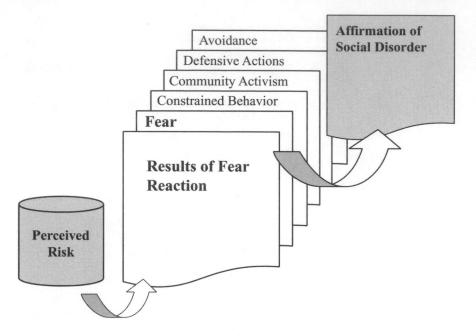

Figure 8.3.   Fear Reactions. (Partly adapted from Ferraro 1995)

DEALING WITH FEAR

It is possible to take more control of our social environment. But much of this action begins not with cleaning up the streets as much as with focusing on our symbolic environment, understanding how our meaning machines are operating, and trying to provide some options. A responsible news media will take action to move away from fear-oriented infotainment. Recent changes (since 1997) in select journalistic organizations are encouraging as stations like KVUE in Austin, Texas, began following a different protocol for presenting crime stories. This station's news management examined how crime news was being covered and agreed essentially with several decades of social science research that much of the coverage was sensational, dramatic, and had no social value whatsoever. Accordingly, they set forth five rules of thumb for evaluating potential crime news:

1. Does action need to be taken?
2. Is there an immediate threat to safety?
3. Is there a threat to children?

4. Does the crime have significant community impact?

5. Does the story lend itself to a crime-prevention effort?

Many in the industry as well as newspaper writers criticized KVUE for not presenting "all the news." The strongest claim was that their ratings would fall and that people would switch channels to the traditional blood and guts leading local TV newscasts across the country. To KVUE's credit—and perhaps their relief—the ratings have held and their new brand of TV journalism has become more popular, at least to the extent that other stations across the country are talking about change.

Social scientists can also do more to reduce the sense of victimization. One way, of course, is to understand the role of the mass media in what we see, hear, and feel. Relatedly, we can try to follow Joel Best's (2001) advice and put issues in more of a historical and cultural perspective, acknowledging the tremendous progress and gains that have been made in many endeavors of social life, including health, human and civil rights, gender and youth rights, as well as economic and environmental awareness and improvements. Ironically, it seems that social progress is seldom acknowledged and, indeed, may even contribute to a sense that things are worse than they used to be. Progress, Best suggests, has led to heightened expectations about perfection and the focus on the relatively more numerous smaller problems that are seemingly endless and without quick fixes, and this in turn leads to a sense of disillusionment. Social scientists can attempt to provide better information to journalists and encourage them to discuss context, present different perspectives and voices on issues, and, above all, avoid the confines of the problem frame.

Part of the difficulty is that the problem frame has been so successful, the formulae are readily available, and producers and consumers share and prefer the evocative and visual media formats. With the growing number of media outlets, some modest familiarity with "what the news guys want," and a less critical and more fragmented audience, the situation is ripe for moral entrepreneurs to promote their causes of deserving victims. Fear, after all, is a perspective that is learned from others. Except for exceptional and pathological instances, we become what our salient "others" model and affirm for us. When speech communities and broad social lenses provide perspectives that celebrate fear—and its many victims—we should not be surprised that people embrace fear, enjoy it, and even play with being a victim.

VICTIM IDENTITY, OR FUN WITH FEAR

The connections between fear and victim can also be seen in the way that news reports cover audience members who accept the victim identity.

In August [1999] a mother in Mesa, Arizona, claimed that she was sexually assaulted last week in her child's school's restroom during "Meet Your Teacher" day, as some 500 parents were visiting their children's teachers. Upon leaving a doorless restroom that opens onto the school's courtyard, she claimed that a "man with cigarette breath, dirty fingernails and long, messy hair had placed a sharp object to her neck, knocked her unconscious and assaulted her." It was later established that she had wounded herself and cut up her clothing in order to get some attention, particularly from her husband. As the woman spent two days in a hospital, school officials, police, and parents acted as though it were all true, and "safety was on the minds of everyone." A school spokesperson agreed with the Mesa police that the schools are "safe places for students, teachers and parents." Despite the hoax, security procedures that emerged remained in place, including identification badges. (*Arizona Republic,* August 18, 1999, A1)

Fun and games look different in a mediated society. On the one hand, we continue to enjoy life in conventional and traditional play and games. On the other hand, more of our lives, identities, and concerns are informed by popular culture as we participate as audience members. Of course, popular culture producers do not merely reflect the broader culture, but rather, they draw on some aspects of everyday experience and then mold this into familiar entertainment formats that are known and vicariously experienced by audience members.

My general argument is that we need to reconsider fun in a mass-mediated world. A partial beginning to this ambitious endeavor might be to suggest that fun be viewed as a social ecology involving context and relationships with a media environment, select social institutions (e.g., occupations, media), friends, and family. I am not focusing merely on media information, but rather on a more encompassing mediated experience, one that becomes a frame of reference shared by others (as audience members) as well as organized claims makers.

Audiences often play with fear and victimization in the context of news reports and popular culture. Following the insights of Greg Stone (1970) and some of his students, *play* is conceived here as a "collective representation: it represents the arrangement of the society and historical era in which it is carried on" (545). For our purposes this means that play is contextual, usually linked to other activities and concerns, including socialization and social control. Stone argues that play helps selves imbue social worlds with significance. For one thing, we encounter roles and identities, often fantastic ones. "Fantastic drama often serves to maintain and keep viable the past of the society— its myths, legends, villains, and heroes. This is also true of the items of the technology of child's play" (549). But our attention here is on adults' play, and I suggest that mass media involvement is a central feature of how adults play, particularly since entertainment is a critical feature of everyday living outside the workplace. The following comments are intended to illustrate the place of fear in news reports, particularly how certain role performances of victim have become so institutionalized that they are quite acceptable, credible, and therefore useful for certain dramatic enactments. I argue that media portrayals of not just danger, but more broadly, fear—and especially fear of crime—provide opportunities for (1) audiences who play with the repetitive reports as dramatic enactments of fear and dread in our lives, and (2) individual actors who seek roles that are accepted as legitimate "attention-getters" in order to accomplish favorable identities vis-à-vis particular audience members, such as the woman described at the beginning of this section.

A key role that is part of audience play involves victim and victimization (Altheide et al. 2001). Popular culture plays to victim in several morality plays featuring good versus evil and strong versus weak. Played out in entertaining news reports, reality TV shows, crime dramas, and TV documentaries as well as more graphic programs (i.e., with more explicit violence), it is the world of predators and prey, criminals and citizens, violent men against women, and, increasingly, adults against children. Stories tend to be told from the perspective (voice) of the victim or criminal justice agents; seldom do we hear or see the accused outside of a prescribed role, for example, in handcuffs.

A salient part of the play of fear involves cultural oppositions that are often repeated and eventually become taken for granted and implicit. These include good–evil, innocence–evil, men–women, adults–children, majority–minority, and more recently, school–community. The opening example is not the only one in which false reports of violence are claimed. A news report about a case in Tucson follows:

"Shock and Anger as Teacher Admits Shooting Herself"
"Please help me. I've been shot." A teacher's frantic phone call to a police dispatcher on Monday set in motion a massive manhunt at an Arizona school, and brought a sharp reminder that fear in US classrooms is still very much alive, nearly a year after the Columbine High School massacre.
A very different version of events emerged yesterday, however. Prosecutors were seeking to have the teacher, Kathy Morris, admitted to a mental institution after she confessed that she had in fact shot herself, and there was no mystery attacker.
Morris, 35, described as a popular science teacher and choir leader with 13 years in the classroom, had told police she had been singled out and shot by a shaven-headed young Hispanic man. Her story led investigators to interrogate a 12-year-old Hispanic pupil whom she had singled out as a possible culprit in a string of threatening letters.
The episode had all the ingredients of other cases of school violence—with a heavily armed SWAT team sweeping the school, counselors descending in force to reassure children, and a flood of cards, flowers and messages of support going to the hospital where Morris was being treated for the wound to her shoulder.

Fear rapidly turned to anger, however, after powder burns on Morris' clothes indicated that she was shot at point blank range—not from 6 ft away, as she alleged. A search of her hospital room turned up a .38 calibre revolver, hidden in her handbag under a false bottom of cardboard secured by Velcro.

Morris is now claiming that she shot herself to highlight a lack of security at her school, but "obviously, we're dealing with irrational thinking and irrational behaviour here," said a police spokesman, Deanna Coultas.

The teacher also sent herself the death threats, made from letters cut from magazines, investigators said. The incident prompted public apologies to Hispanic pupils, who account for about half of students at La Cima Middle School, in a region that is a gateway to the United States' border with Mexico and is heavily Mexican-American.

"We're very sorry, Hispanics," said a banner strung on a school fence.

As the full story emerged, some students ripped up the sympathy cards they had left for Morris.

"All morning we were working with faculty and with students and parents to develop empathy, support and concern for this teacher who had been victimised in a very tragic way, as we knew it at the time," said principal Phil Woodall. "And then at noontime it takes a 180." (*Scottsman,* April 13, 2000, 12)

The oppositions that become part of the discourse of fear can be illustrated in another way as well. With repetition, the connections between fear, children, schools, and suspected assailants who fit stereotypes are easy to accept even when they are false. Katheryn Russell's (1998) study of sixty-seven publicized racially tinged hoaxes between 1987 and 1996 illustrates how storytellers frame their accounts in social identities that are legitimated by numerous reports and stereotypes of marginalized groups, such as racial minorities. For example, in 1990 a George Washington University student reported that another student had been raped by two black men with "particularly bad body odor," in order to "highlight the problems of safety for women."

In spring 1999, two Mesa, Arizona, fifth-grade girls, playing a game of Truth or Dare, told a detailed story about a knife-toting transient who grabbed them as they were leaving an elementary school. They fought off the man, who, they said, "chewed his nails," and escaped to a neighbor's house. For a day, police and neighbors patrolled the neighborhood questioning various people, only to have the girls admit that the story was made up.

That many people would accept and, indeed, enact scenarios of strangers—usually poor, crazy, unkempt, and minority—assaulting children and others at schools is not too surprising in view of the numerous news reports that are repeated following any incident. When people pretend that they have been assaulted, abducted, or in some way harmed by strangers, they are acting out a morality play that has become part of a widely shared discourse of fear. The scenario, cast of characters, even detailed descriptions resound through popular culture as audiences become participants in constructing the social reality that constrains them. News formats providing familiar information can, as Cerulo (1998) argues, have considerable social impact:

> When it comes to violence, media stories may unintentionally form public images of right and wrong. . . . Story-tellers must consider the very real possibility that the routine formatting of violent accounts may be constructing social opinion rather than reflecting it. Thus, the role of story sequencing in violent accounts must enter discussions of media responsibility. (141)

Formal agents of social control often provide security measures fitting their definitions of the problem; these security measures that emerge during a particular event soon become institutionalized and taken for granted as part of the social fabric of life (Altheide 1995).

CONCLUSION

At the start of this book I discussed my childhood fear of God and how a community of believers tried to save my soul through fear. I also mentioned Judy, the gun-toting woman in low-crime Scottsdale, who was convinced that packing a firearm would save her. Neither Judy nor I had a clue about the social processes operating then, but I do now. Fear accumulates and is deposited over a wide social terrain. Like agates formed forty million years ago in the interstices of cooling magma and transported by rivers to oceans and then beaches ever since, fear retains its essential elements. The chemistry of agates can be uncovered through analysis, although most people who find them don't really care about that; agates are merely pretty rocks, which, when polished, assume a gemlike character separating them from other earthen surfaces. The origin of a specific fear can also be uncovered in specific instances, but most people do not care about where it began; one fear merely gets strewn with others on the beaches of our experiences and social encounters.

Social fears are related to personal fears in complex ways. Unraveling the relationships for specific fears is an avowedly psychoanalytical task that has been largely neglected, thus opening up another opportunity for social researchers. For example, fear of crime may be connected to certain compulsive behaviors, paranoia, and so forth (for example, locking doors, double-checking windows, avoiding strangers), but these are now sanctioned by public officials as reasonable prudent, responsible, and even intelligent activities.

We are the sum of our emotions, including our loves minus our fears. As fears accumulate, the love portion will decrease unless we take steps to increase this. Such action is necessary if we are to avoid deficit being, a condition that befalls more individuals. These circumstances are known by various terms and behaviors, including anomie, alienation, paranoia, and residing in gated communities. I am suggesting that we can also know them as play, as an emerging form by which individuals participate through media logic in an increasingly mass-mediated society.

The discourse of fear has major implications for social justice and especially our standards of justice. Fear destroys justice. A just society can never come from fear. Every oppressive society—particularly in the modern era—has been consumed with fear of the "other" and has justified the extreme horrific and often genocidal actions that have been taken as necessary to deal with the evil other. Part of the fear industry promotes fear by offering solutions that attack the objects of fear. Promises of safety, restitution, and so forth are exchanged for justice. Criminal justice agency officials, politicians, and the numerous social scientists that engage in research and activities involving victim advocacy, for example, often are promoting narrow, self-serving agendas that destroy freedom and promote vengeance and social control. (Gerber 2001)

Awareness of the mediated nature of fear and victim can assist serious students of justice to understand the broad contexts and social processes that must be considered if we wish to develop a reflexive theory of justice that is not simply procedural or punitive, but that attends to the pragmatic dimensions of social acts that makes justice personal (Johnson 1995a). Who gets to define the situations that govern us all? Who sets the speech communities by which we acquire and display identities? And by what criteria is social conduct evaluated as competent and sensible? Words are powerful when they become symbolic frames that direct discursive practices. In an era in which information is packaged and manufactured, when popular culture is driven by entertainment formats, and when agents work to transform risks into fear with state-sponsored solutions, the social and the cultural become one. Fear is constructed and it is real. The entertainment-inspired frame is embodied in the emotions and justice of everyday life. Osborne (1995) refers to this as "mediachosis":

> A state of consciousness characterised by unconscious acceptance of electronically transmitted modes of perception and thought. A state of being in which cynicism, mistrust and paranoia predominate and in which the media, rather than other human institutions, provide acquired cultural perceptions. (37)

Fear is a key element of the effective environment because it is a major feature of the entertainment format of popular culture in our postjournalism era. Far more is involved than the insights by Gerbner and Gross (1976) about media contributions to perceptions of a "scary world." My focus is not merely with media content or with some public perceptions, although we draw on them in this analysis. My concern is with identifying a discourse that is pervasive and provides a framework for viewing others and issues alike, for clothing risks and potential danger with a jacket of fear, with one size fits all. I have addressed how the cloth is tailored, by whom, and with what implications. I have also suggested that fear is a larger part of our symbolic landscape at a time when the social terrain is comparatively routine, predictable, and safe. The public increasingly turns to formal agents of social control to solve the problem by more force and more prisons. Nearly six million Americans are in jail or prison, on probation or parole. That is more than the combined population of Montana, North and South Dakota, Wyoming, and Idaho. Likewise, formal surveillance pervades our culture through various testing mechanisms and visual scrutiny—fifteen million Americans were tested for drugs during 1995–1996. One can see the surveillance and voyeurism on Jailcam. As William G. Staples (1997) observes, "Today's culture of surveillance, I would argue, is being built on a foundation of seduction, desire, fear and salvation" (130). Danger surely lurks in occasional missteps and periodic acts of terror. But danger does not produce a shared environment of fear; we can deal with danger, we can be educated about it, take steps to avoid it or minimize its impact. Danger is not enigmatic. Fear is. Danger does not define an expanding array of news reports. Fear does. Danger can be dealt with one event at a time. Fear cannot. We must return to a sense of proportion, of selected potential dangers. Only by identifying and discussing the processual features of fear as a communicated meaning can we gain a perspective on contemporary life. This book is one attempt to help.

References

Adam, Barbara, Ulrich Beck, and Joost Van Loon, eds. 2000. *The Risk Society and Beyond.* Thousand Oaks, Calif.: Sage.

Ailes, Roger, and Jon Kraushar. 1988. *You Are the Message: Secrets of the Master Communicators.* Homewood, Ill.: Dow Jones-Irwin.

Altheide, David L. 1976. *Creating Reality: How TV News Distorts Events.* Beverly Hills, Calif.: Sage.

———. 1985. *Media Power.* Beverly Hills, Calif.: Sage.

———. 1994. An Ecology of Communication: Toward a Mapping of the Effective Environment. *Sociological Quarterly* 35: 645–683.

———. 1995. *An Ecology of Communication: Cultural Formats of Control.* Hawthorne, N.Y.: Aldine de Gruyter.

———. 1996. *Qualitative Media Analysis.* Newbury Park, Calif.: Sage.

———. 1997. The News Media, The Problem Frame, and the Production of Fear. *Sociological Quarterly* 38: 646–668.

———. 2000. Identity and the Definition of the Situation in a Mass-Mediated Context. *Symbolic Interaction* 23: 1–28.

Altheide, David L., Barbara Gray, Roy Janisch, Lindsey Korbin, Ray Maratea, Debra Neill, Joseph Reaves, and Felicia Van Deman. 2001. "News Constructions of Fear and Victim: An Exploration Through Triangulated Qualitative Document Analysis." *Qualitative Inquiry* 7.

Altheide, David L., and John M. Johnson. 1980. *Bureaucratic Propaganda.* Boston: Allyn & Bacon.

Altheide, David L., and R. Sam Michalowski. 1999. Fear in the News: A Discourse of Control. *Sociological Quarterly* 40: 475–503.

Altheide, David L., and Robert P. Snow. 1979. *Media Logic.* Beverly Hills, Calif.: Sage.

———. 1991. *Media Worlds in the Postjournalism Era.* Hawthorne, N.Y.: Aldine de Gruyter.

Ariès, Philippe, and Robert Baldick. 1962. *Centuries of Childhood: A Social History of Family Life.* New York: Knopf.

Ashley, Richard K. 1989. Living on Border Lines: Man, Poststructuralism, and War. In *International/Intertextual Relations: Postmodern Readings of World Politics,* edited by James and Michael J. Shapiro Der Derian. Lexington, Mass.: Lexington Books.

Atkinson, Paul, and David Silverman. 1997. Kundera's Immortality: The Interview Society and the Invention of the Self. *Qualitative Inquiry* 3: 304–325.

Bailey, Frankie, and Donna Hale. 1998. *Popular Culture, Crime, and Justice.* Belmont, Calif.: West/Wadsworth.

Beck, Ulrich. 1992. *Risk Society: Towards a New Modernity.* Newbury Park, Calif.: Sage.

Beckett, Katherine. 1996. "Culture and the Politics of Signification: The Case of Child Sexual Abuse." *Social Problems* 43: 57–76.

Beniger, James R. 1986. *The Control Revolution: Technological and Economic Origins of the Information Society.* Cambridge, Mass.: Harvard University Press.

Bennett, W. Lance. 1988. *News: The Politics of Illusion.* New York: Longman.

Bensman, Joseph, and Robert Lilienfeld. 1973. *Craft and Consciousness: Occupational Technique and the Development of World Images.* New York: John Wiley & Sons.

Bensman, Joseph, and Arthur J. Vidich. 1971. *The New American Society: The Revolution of the Middle Class.* Chicago: Quadrangle Books.

Berg, Bruce L. 1989. *Qualitative Research Methods for the Social Sciences.* Boston, Mass.: Allyn & Bacon.

Berger, Peter L., and Thomas Luckmann. 1967. *The Social Construction of Reality: A Treatise in the Sociology of Knowledge.* New York: Doubleday.

Best, Joel. 1990. *Threatened Children: Rhetoric and Concern about Child-Victims.* Chicago: University of Chicago Press.

———. 1994. *Troubling Children: Studies of Children and Social Problems.* Hawthorne, N.Y.: Aldine de Gruyter.

———. 1999. *Random Violence: How We Talk about New Crimes and New Victims.* Berkeley: University of California Press.

———. 2001. Social Progress and Social Problems: Toward a Sociology of Gloom. *Sociological Quarterly* 42: 1–12.

———, ed. 1995. *Images of Issues.* Hawthorne, N.Y.: Aldine de Gruyter.

Best, Joel, and Gefald Horiuchi. 1985. The Razor Blade in the Apple: The Social Construction of Urban Legends. *Social Problems* 35: 488–499.

Black, George. 1991. Rolodex Army Wages a Nintendo War: TV's Deskbound Generals Tune Out on the Crucial Issues—Morality, Economics, Values. *Los Angeles Times,* January 27. Opinion sec., 7.

Blumer, Herbert. 1962. Society as Symbolic Interaction. Pp. 179–192 in *Human Behavior and Social Processes,* edited by A. M. Rose. Boston, Mass.: Houghton Mifflin.

———. 1969. *Symbolic Interactionism: Perspective and Method.* Englewood Cliffs, N.J.: Prentice Hall.

Bourdieu, Pierre. 1977. Cultural Reproduction and Social Reproduction. Pp. 487–511 in *Power and Ideology in Education,* edited by Jerome Karabel and A. H. Halsey. London: Oxford University Press.

Brady, John Joseph. 1976. *The Craft of Interviewing.* Cincinnati: Writer's Digest.

Brissett, Dennis, and Charles Edgley. 1990. *Life as Theater: A Dramaturgical Sourcebook.* Hawthorne, N.Y.: Aldine de Gruyter.

Brooks, David. 1999. Brian Lamb's America: In Praise of C-Span, Our National Historian. *The Weekly Standard,* November 8, 21–25.

Burke, Kenneth. 1966. *Language as Symbolic Action: Essays on Life, Literature, and Method.* Berkeley: University of California Press.

———. 1969. *A Rhetoric of Motives.* Berkeley: University of California Press.

Campbell, David. 1998. *Writing Security: United States Foreign Policy and the Politics of Identity.* Minneapolis: University of Minnesota Press.

Cantril, Hadley, H. G. Wells, Howard Koch, Hazel Gaudet, and Herta Herzog. 1940. The Invasion from Mars: *A Study in the Psychology of Panic.* Princeton, N.J.: Princeton University Press.

Carey, James. 1989. *Communication as Culture: Essays on the Media and Society.* Boston, Mass.: Unwin Hyman.

Cerulo, Karen A. 1998. *Deciphering Violence: The Cognitive Structure of Right and Wrong.* New York: Routledge.

Cerulo, Karen, M. M. Ruane, and M. Chayko. 1992. Technological Ties that Bind: Media Generated Primary Groups. *Communication Research* 19: 109–129.

Chermak, Steven. 1995. *Victims in the News: Crime and the American News Media.* Boulder, Colo.: Westview Press.

Chiricos, Ted, Sarah Eschholz, and Marc Gertz. 1997. Crime, News and Fear of Crime: Toward an Identification of Audience Effects. *Social Problems* 44: 342–357.

Chiricos, Ted, Kathy Padgett, and Marc Gertz. 2000. Fear, TV News, and the Reality of Crime. *Criminology* 38: 755–785.

Cicourel, Aaron Victor. 1964. *Method and Measurement in Sociology.* New York: Free Press of Glencoe.

———. 1974. *Cognitive Sociology: Language and Meaning in Social Interaction.* New York: Free Press.

Close, Ellis. 2001. "A Brownout in Los Angeles." *Newsweek* June 18,: 32.

Clover, Carol J. 1992. *Men, Women and Chain Saws: Gender in the Modern Horror Film.* Princeton, N.J.: Princeton University Press.

Comstock, George. 1980. *Television in America.* Beverly Hills, Calif.: Sage.

Cooley, Charles Horton. 1922. *Human Nature and the Social Order.* New York: Charles Scribner's Sons.

Couch, Carl J. 1984. *Constructing Civilizations.* Greenwich, Conn.: JAI Press.

Couch, Carl J. 1995. Oh, What Webs Those Phantoms Spin (SSSI Distinguished Lecture, 1994). *Symbolic Interaction* 18: 229–245.

Couch, Carl J., David R. Maines, and Shing-Ling Chen. 1996. *Information Technologies and Social Orders.* Hawthorne, N.Y.: Aldine de Gruyter.

Crane, Diana. 1992. *The Production of Culture.* Newbury Park, Calif.: Sage.

Crichton, Michael. 1999. *Timeline.* New York: Alfred A. Knopf.

Deaver, Michael. 1988. Sound-Bite Campaigning: TV Made Us Do It. *Washington Post,* Oct. 30: C7.

de Certeau, Michel. 1984. *The Practice of Everyday Life.* Berkeley: University of California Press.

DeFleur, Melvin L., and Sandra Ball-Rokeach. 1982. *Theories of Mass Communication.* New York: Longman.

Denzin, Norman K. 1991. *Images of Postmodern Society: Social Theory and Contemporary Cinema.* Newbury Park: Sage.

————. 1995. *The Cinematic Society: The Voyeur's Gaze.* Thousand Oaks, Calif.: Sage.

Denzin, Norman K., and Yvonna S. Lincoln, eds. 1994. *Handbook of Qualitative Methodology.* Newbury Park, Calif.: Sage.

Desmond, Robert William. 1978. *The Information Process: World News Reporting to the Twentieth Century.* Iowa City: University of Iowa Press.

Devji, Mantosh Singh. 1996. Resurrect Dead Soul of America. *Arizona Republic,* November 10, H3.

Douglas, Jack D. 1970. *Understanding Everyday Life: Toward the Reconstruction of Sociological Knowledge.* Chicago: Aldine Publishing Co.

Doyle, Aaron. 2001. How Television Influences Social Institutions: The Case of Policing and Criminal Justice. In *Sociology,* Department of Sociology. Vancouver: University of British Columbia.

Eason, David L. 1986. On Journalistic Authority: The Janet Cooke Scandal. *Critical Studies in Mass Communication* 3: 429–447.

Eco, Umberto. 1979. *The Role of the Reader: Explorations in the Semiotics of Texts.* Bloomington: Indiana University Press.

Edelman, Murray J. 1971. *Politics as Symbolic Action: Mass Arousal and Quiescence.* Chicago: Markham Publishing Co.

————. 1985. *The Symbolic Uses of Politics.* Urbana: University of Illinois Press.

————. 1988. *Constructing the Political Spectacle.* Chicago: University of Chicago Press.

Ellenius, Allan, and European Science Foundation. 1998. *Iconography, Propaganda, and Legitimation.* New York: Oxford University Press.

Epstein, Edward J. 1973. *News from Nowhere.* New York: Random House.

Ericson, Richard V. 1993. "Is Anyone Responsible? How Television Frames Political Issues" (Book Review). *The American Journal of Sociology* 98: 1459–1463.

Ericson, Richard V., ed. 1995. *Crime and the Media.* Brookfield, Vt.: Dartmouth University Press.

Ericson, Richard V., and Kevin D. Haggerty. 1997. *Policing the Risk Society.* Toronto: University of Toronto Press.

Ericson, Richard V., Patricia M. Baranek, and Janet B. L. Chan. 1987. *Visual-*

izing Deviance: A Study of News Organization. Toronto: University of Toronto Press.

————. 1989. *Negotiating Control: A Study of News Sources.* Toronto: University of Toronto Press.

————. 1991. *Representing Order: Crime, Law and Justice in the News Media.* Toronto: University of Toronto Press.

Ewald, Francois. 1993. Two Infinities of Risk. Pp. 221–228 in *The Politics of Everyday Fear,* edited by Brian Massumi. Minneapolis: University of Minnesota Press.

Ewen, Stuart. 1976. *Captains of Consciousness: Advertising and the Social Roots of the Consumer Culture.* New York: McGraw-Hill.

Ewen, Stuart, and Elizabeth Ewen. 1992. *Channels of Desire: Mass Images and the Shaping of American Consciousness.* Minneapolis: University of Minnesota Press.

Farrall, Stephen, Jon Bannister, Jason Ditton, and Elizabeth Gilchrist. 2000. Social Psychology and the Fear of Crime. *British Journal of Criminology* 40: 399–413.

Ferraro, Kenneth F. 1995. *Fear of Crime: Interpreting Victimization Risk.* Albany: State University of New York Press.

Ferrell, Jeff, and Clinton R. Sanders. 1995. *Cultural Criminology.* Boston, Mass.: Northeastern University Press.

Fishman, Mark. 1980. *Manufacturing the News.* Austin: University of Texas Press.

Fishman, Mark, and Gray Cavender. 1998. *Entertaining Crime: Television Reality Programs.* Hawthorne, N.Y.: Aldine de Gruyter.

Fiske, John. 1987. *Television Culture.* New York: Methuen.

Fowler, Roger. 1991. *Language in the News: Discourse and Ideology in the British Press.* New York: Routledge.

Friend, Tad. 2001. "Dead Air: Don Hewitt and TV's News-Magazine Menace." *The New Yorker* May 7, 2001: 90–92.

Fritz, Noah, and David L. Altheide. 1987. The Mass Media and the Social Construction of the Missing Children Problem. *Sociological Quarterly* 28: 473–492.

Furedi, Frank. 1997. *Culture of Fear: Risk-Taking and the Morality of Low Expectation/Frank Furedi.* London: Cassell.

Gamson, Joshua. 1998. *Freaks Talk Back: Tabloid Talk Shows and Sexual Nonconformity.* Chicago: University of Chicago Press.

Garland, David. 2000. The Culture of High Crime Societies: Some Preconditions of Recent "Law and Order" Policies. *British Journal of Criminology* 40: 347–375.

Gerber, Rudolph J. 2001. "On Dispensing Justice." *Arizona Law Review* 43(1) Spring: 135–172.

Gerbner, George, L. Gross, M. Morgan, N. Signorelli, and M. Jackson-Beeck. 1978. "Cultural Indicators: Violence Profile No. 9." *Journal of Communication.* 28: 176–207.

Gerbner, George, and Nancy Signorielli. 1988. *Violence and terror in the mass media.* Paris: Unesco.

Gerbner, George, and Lawrence Gross. 1976. The Scary World of TV's Heavy Viewer. *Psychology Today,* 9 (11) 41–45.

Gitlin, Todd. 1980. *The Whole World Is Watching.* Berkeley: University of California Press.

———. 1994. *Inside Prime Time.* London: Routledge.

Glaser, Barney G., and Anselm L. Strauss. 1967. *Discovery of grounded theory: strategies for qualitative research.* Chicago: Aldine Pub. Co.

Glassner, Barry. 1999. *The Culture of Fear: Why Americans Are Afraid of the Wrong Things.* New York: Basic Books.

Goffman, Erving. 1959. *The Presentation of Self in Everyday Life.* Garden City, N.Y.: Doubleday.

Goodykoontz, Bill. 2000. Candidates and Comedy: Who's Winner? *Arizona Republic,* April 2: E1.

Graber, Doris S. 1984. *Processing the News: How People Tame the Information Tide.* New York: Longman.

Grimshaw, Allen Day, and Peter J. Burke. 1994. *What's Going on Here?: Complementary Studies of Professional Talk.* Norwood, N.J.: Ablex.

Grodin, Debra, and Thomas R. Lindlof. 1996. *Constructing the Self in a Mediated World.* Thousand Oaks, Calif.: Sage.

Grossberg, Lawrence, Ellen Wartella, and D. Charles Whitney. 1998. *Mediamaking: Mass Media in a Popular Culture.* Thousand Oaks, Calif.: Sage.

Gunter, Barry. 1987. *Television and the Fear of Crime.* London: John Libbey. London: John Libbey.

Gusfield, Joseph R. 1989. Constructing the Ownership of Social Problems: Fun and Profit in the Welfare State. *Social Problems* 36: 431–441.

Hall, Peter M. 1997. Meta-Power, Social Organization, and the Shaping of Social Action. *Symbolic Interaction* 20: 397–418.

Hall, Stuart. 1977. Culture, Media, and the Ideological Effect. Pp. 315–348 in *Mass Communication and Society,* edited by M. Gurevitch, J. Wollacott, and J. Curran. London: Edward Arnold.

Heath, Linda, and Kevin Gilbert. 1996. Mass Media and Fear of Crime. *American Behavioral Scientist* 39: 379–386.

Hertog, James K., and David P. Fan. 1995. The Impact of Press Coverage on Social Beliefs: The Case of HIV Transmission. *Communication Research* 22: 545–577.

Hewitt, John P. 1989. *Dilemmas of the American Self.* Philadelphia: Temple University Press.

———. 1991. *Self and Society: A Symbolic Interactionist Social Psychology.* Needham Heights, Mass.: Allyn & Bacon.

Hillman, M., J. Adams, and J. Whiteleg. 1990. *One False Move . . . A Study of Children's Independent Mobility.* London: PSI Publishing.

Hirsch, Paul. 1980. "The 'Scary World' of the Non-Viewer and Other Anomalies: A Reanalysis of Gerbner et al. Findings, Part 1." *Communication.*

Holstein, James A., and Jaber F. Gubrium. 1995. *The Active Interview.* Thousand Oaks, Calif.: Sage.

———. 2000. *The Self We Live By: Narrative Identity in a Postmodern World.* New York: Oxford University Press.

Iyengar, Shanto. 1991. *Is Anyone Responsible? How Television Frames Political Issues.* Chicago: University of Chicago Press.

Iyengar, Shanto, and Donald M. Kinder. 1987. *News that Matters.* Chicago: University of Chicago Press.

Jackall, Robert, ed. 1994. *Propaganda.* New York: New York University Press.

Jackall, Robert, and Janice M. Hirota. 1999. *Experts with Symbols: Advertising, Public Relations, and the Ethics of Advocacy.* Chicago: University of Chicago.

———. 2000. *Image Makers: Advertising, Public Relations, and the Ethos of Advocacy.* Chicago: University of Chicago Press.

Jacobs, James. B., and Jessica S. Henry. 1996. The Social Construction of a Hate Crime Epidemic. *Journal of Criminal Law and Criminology* 86: 366–391.

Jacobs, J. B. and K. A. Potter. 1997. Hate Crimes: A Critical Perspective. *Crime and Justice* 22: 1–50.

Jacobs, Jane. 1969. *The Death and Life of Great American Cities.* New York: Modern Library.

Jenkins, Philip. 1998. *Moral Panic: Changing Concepts of the Child Molester in Modern America.* New Haven, Conn.: Yale University Press.

Jenness, Valerie. 1995. Hate Crimes in the United States: The Transformation of Injured Persons into Victims and the Extension of Victim Status to Multiple Constituencies. Pp. 213–237 in *Images of Issues,* edited by Joel Best. Hawthorne, N.Y.: Aldine de Gruyter.

Johnson, John M. 1995a. Horror Stories and the Construction of Child Abuse. Pp. 17–31 in *Images of Issues,* edited by Joel Best. Hawthorne, N.Y.: Aldine de Gruyter.

———. 1995b. In Dispraise of Justice. *Symbolic Interaction* 18: 191–205.

Katz, Jack. 1987. What Makes Crime "News"? *Media, Culture and Society* 9: 47–75.

Kellner, Douglas. 1995. *Media Culture: Cultural Studies, Identity and Politics between the Modern and Postmodern.* New York: Routledge.

Kidd-Hewitt, David, and Richard Osborne. 1995. *Crime and the Media: The Post-Modern Spectacle.* London: Pluto Press.

Kwok, Abraham, Pamela Manson, and Susan Leonard. 1993. Execution Spotlight Dimming: Foes Fear Issue Also Will Fade. *Arizona Republic,* April 15: B1.

Lopez, George A., and Michael Stohl. 1984. *The State as Terrorist: The Dynamics of Governmental Violence and Repression.* Westport, Conn.: Greenwood Press.

Lowry, Brian. 1998. Brave New World for Iraq Coverage; Television: There Are Now Three All-News Cable Channels, Creating a Difficult Environment for Network News Operations. *Los Angeles Times,* December 17: Calendar sec., F1.

Lyman, Stanford M. 1997. The Drama in the Routine: A Prolegomenon to a Praxiological Sociology. Pp. 286–294 in *Postmodernism and a Sociology of the Absurd.* Fayetteville: University of Arkansas Press.

MacKuen, M. and S. L. Coombs. 1981. *More than News: Media Power in Public Affairs.* Beverly Hills, CA: Sage.

Maines, David R., and Carl J. Couch. 1988. *Communication and Social Structure.* Springfield, Ill.: C.C. Thomas.

Manning, Peter K. 1987. *Semiotics and Fieldwork.* Newbury Park, Calif.: Sage.

———. 1998. Media Loops. Pp. 25–39 in *Popular Culture, Crime, and Justice,* edited by Frankie Bailey and Donna C. Hale. Belmont, Calif.: West/Wadsworth.

Manning, Peter K., and Betsy Cullum-Swan. 1994. Narrative, Content and Semiotic Analysis. Pp. 463–478 in *Handbook of Qualitative Research,* edited by Norman K. Denzin and Yvonna S. Lincoln. Newbury Park, Calif.: Sage.

Marcus, George E. 1997. *Cultural Producers in Perilous States: Editing Events, Documenting Change.* Chicago: University of Chicago Press.

Margolis, Howard. 1996. *Dealing with Risk: Why the Public and the Experts Disagree on Environmental Issues.* Chicago: University of Chicago Press.

Martin, Dick. 1977. *The Executive's Guide to Handling a Press Interview.* New York: Pilot Books.

Marx, Gary T. 1988. *Undercover: Police Surveillance in America.* Berkeley: University of California Press.

Massumi, Brian. 1993. *The Politics of Everyday Fear.* Minneapolis: University of Minnesota Press.

McDonald, James H. 1994. Te(k)nowledge: Technology, Education, and the New Student Subject. *Science as Culture* 4: 537–564.

McLuhan, Marshall. 1960. *Explorations in Communication.* Boston, Mass.: Beacon Press.

McLuhan, Marshall, and Quentin Fiore. 1967. *The Medium Is the Massage.* New York: Bantam Books.

Mead, George Herbert, and Charles W. Morris. 1962. *Mind, Self, and Society from the Standpoint of a Social Behaviorist.* Chicago: University of Chicago Press.

Meyrowitz, Joshua. 1985. *No Sense of Place.* New York: Oxford University Press.

Mills, C. Wright. 1959. *The Sociological Imagination.* New York: Grove Press.

Montini, E. J. 1999. Scamming a Great Generation. *Arizona Republic,* January 17: B1.

Naphy, William G., and Penny Roberts. 1997. *Fear in Early Modern Society.* Manchester, N.Y.: Manchester University Press.

Oldenburg, Ray. 1989. *The Great Good Place: Cafés, Coffee Shops, Community Centers, Beauty Parlors, General Stores, Bars, Hangouts, and How They Get You through the Day.* New York: Paragon House.

Osborne, Richard. 1995. Crime and the Media: From Media Studies to Post-Modernism. Pp. 25–48 in *Crime and the Media: The Post-Modern Spectacle,* edited by David Kidd-Hewitt and Richard Osborne. London: Pluto Press.

Perinbanayagam, R. S. 1991. *Discursive acts.* New York: Aldine de Gruyter.

Pfuhl, Erdwin H., and Stuart Henry. 1993. *The Deviance Process.* Hawthorne, N.Y.: Aldine de Gruyter.

Platt, Anthony M. 1969. *The Child Savers: The Invention of Delinquency.* Chicago: University of Chicago Press.

Powell, Michael. 1999. How to Bomb in Selling a War. *Washington Post,* May 17:CO1.

Rau, Robin Ann. 1993. The Role of Sources in News Coverage of the Don Harding Execution. P. 42 in *School of Justice Studies.* Tempe: Arizona State University.

Roberts, Julian, and A. Doob. 1990. News Media Influence on Public Views on Sentencing. *Law and Human Behavior* 14: 451–468.

Russell, Katheryn K. 1998. *The Color of Crime: Racial Hoaxes, White Fear, Black Protectionism, Police Harassment, and Other Macroaggressions.* New York: New York University Press.

Sasson, Theodore. 1995. *Crime Talk: How Citizens Construct a Social Problem.* Hawthorne, N.Y.: Aldine de Gruyter.

Schlesinger, Philip, Peter G. Murdock, and Phillip Elliott. 1983. *Televising "Terrorism": Political Violence in Popular Culture.* London: Comedia.

Schorr, Daniel. 1993. The Theodore H. White Lecture. The Joan Shorenstein Barone Center.

Schutz, Alfred. 1967. *The Phenomenology of the Social World.* Evanston, Ill.: Northwestern University Press.

Schwalbe, Michael, Sandra Godwin, Daphne Holden, Douglas Schrock, Shealy Thompson, and Michele Wolkomir. 2000. Generic Processes in the Reproduction of Inequality: An Interactionist Analysis. *Social Forces* 79: 419–452.

Scott, Marvin, and Stanford M. Lyman. 1968. Accounts. *American Sociological Review* 33: 46–62.

Selcraig, Bruce. 2000. Camp Fear. *Mother Jones.* November/December ; 66–71.

Shapiro, Michael. 1996. The Lives We Would Like to Set Right: Why Journalistic Outrage Is Not the Best Approach to the Child Welfare Story. *Columbia Journalism Review,* November/December:45–48.

Sharp, Barbara Ann. 1999. Sanctioning Female Sex Offenders, a Media Analysis. P. 105 in *School of Justice Studies.* Tempe: Arizona State University.

Shaw, David. 1994. Living Scared, Why Do the Media Make Life Seem So Risky? P. A1 in *Los Angeles Times,* September 11. Republished in *Arizona Republic,* April 28, 1996.

Simmel, Georg, and Kurt H. Wolff. 1964. *The Sociology of Georg Simmel.* New York: Free Press of Glencoe.

Snow, Robert P. 1983. *Creating Media Culture.* Beverly Hills, Calif.: Sage.

Sommerville, C. John. 1982. *The Rise and Fall of Childhood.* Beverly Hills, Calif.: Sage.

Soothill, Keith, and Sylvia Walby. 1991. *Sex Crime in the News.* New York: Routledge.

Sparks, Richard. 1992. *Television and the Drama of Crime: Moral Tales and the Place of Crime in Public Life.* Milton Keynes, UK: Open University Press.

Spector, Malcolm, and John I. Kitsuse. 1977. *Constructing Social Problems.* Menlo Park, Calif.: Cummings Publishing Co.

Staples, William G. 1997. *The Culture of Surveillance: Discipline and Social Control in the United States.* New York: St. Martin's Press.

Stasio, Marilyn. 1995. Crimes against Children: The Trend in Mysteries. *New York Times,* Book Review sec., 27.

Stein, Maurice Robert, and Arthur J. Vidich. 1963. *Sociology on Trial.* Englewood Cliffs, N.J.: Prentice Hall.

Stone, Gregory. 1970. The Play of Little Children. Pp. 545–553 in *Social Psychology through Symbolic Interaction,* edited by Gregory P. Stone and Harvey F. Farberman. Waltham, Mass.: Ginn-Blaisdell.

———. 1992. Appearance and the Self. Pp. 86–118 in *Human Behavior and Social Processes,* edited by A. M. Rose. Boston, Mass.: Houghton Mifflin.

Surette, Ray. 1998. *Media, Crime and Criminal Justice: Images and Realities.* Belmont, Calif.: West/Wadsworth.

Taschler-Pollacek, Heidrun and Helmut Lukesch. 1990. "Fear of Victimization as a Consequence of Television Viewing? A Study of Older Women"; "Viktimisierungsangst als Folge des Fernsehkonsums? Eine Studie an alteren Frauen". *Publizistik.* 35: 443–453.

Terkel, Studs. 1974. *Working.* New York: Encyclopedia Americana/CBS News Audio Resource Library.

Topping, Seymour. 1998. The Military and the Media Suspend Hostilities: Latebreaking Foreign Policy. *Columbia Journalism Review,* 58.

Tuchman, Gaye. 1978. *Making News.* New York: Free Press.

Tufano, Enrico Celestino. 1998. Hate in the News. P. 72 in *School of Justice Studies.* Tempe: Arizona State University.

Unsworth, Barry. 1995. *Morality Play.* London: Hamish Hamilton.

Van der Wurff, A.dri, Leendert Van Stallduinen, and Peter Stringer. 1989. Fear of Crime in Residential Environments: Testing a Social Psychological Model. *Journal of Social Psychology* 129: 141–160.

van Dijk, Teun A. 1988. *News as Discourse*. Hillsdale, N.J.: L. Erlbaum Associates.

Vogel, Steven. 1998. Military Trains a Special Corps of Public Relations Troops: 3,500 Journalists a Year are Schooled at Brand-New Center at Fort Meade. *Milwaukee Journal Sentinel*. October 25: 6.

Waller, Paul. 1991. "The Politics of Child Abuse." *Society* 28: 6–13.

Waller, Willard. 1961. *The Sociology of Teaching*. New York: John Wiley & Sons.

Warr, Mark. 1990. Dangerous Situations: Social Context and Fear of Victimization. *Social Forces* 68: 891–907.

———. 1983. "Fear of Victimization: A Look at the Proximate Causes." *Social Forces* 61: 1033–1043.

———. 1992. Altruistic Fear of Victimization in Households. *Social Science Quarterly* 73: 723–736.

Weber, Max. 1954. *Max Weber on Law in Economy and Society; Edited with Introd. and Annotations by Max Rheinstein*. New York: Simon and Schuster.

———. 1958. *The Protestant Ethic and the Spirit of Capitalism*. New York: Scribner.

Weiler, M., and W. B. Pearce. 1992. *Reagan and Public Discourse in America*. Tuscaloosa, AL: University of Alabama Press.

Weingartner, Rudolph H. 1962. *Experience and Culture: The Philosophy of Georg Simmel*. Middletown, Conn.: Wesleyan University Press.

Westfeldt, Wallace, and Tom Wicker. 1998. *Indictment: The News Media and the Criminal Justice System*. Nashville, Tenn.: First Amendment Center.

Willis, William James, and Albert Adelowo Okunade. 1997. *Reporting on Risks: The Practice and Ethics of Health and Safety Communication*. Westport, Conn.: Praeger.

Wimmer, Kristi. 1999. Blameshifting in News Reports about the Death of a Child. In *School of Justice Studies*. Tempe: Arizona State University.

Wuthnow, Robert., ed. 1992. *Vocabularies of Public Life: Empirical Essays in Symbolic Structure*. New York: Routledge.

Zelizer, Viviana, and A. Rotman. 1985. *Pricing the Priceless Child: The Changing Social Value of Children*. New York: Basic Books.

Zerubavel, Eviatar. 1997. *Social Mindscapes: An Invitation to Cognitive Sociology*. Cambridge, Mass.: Harvard University Press.

Zhondang, P., and G. Kosicki. 1993. Framing Analysis: An Approach to News Discourse. *Political Communication* 10: 55–69.

Zillman, D. Wakshlag, J. 1987. "Fear of Victimization and the Appeal of Crime Drama," in *Selective Exposure to Communication.*, edited by D. Zillman and J. Bryant. Hillsdale, NJ: Elrbaum.

Zurcher, Louis A. 1977. *The Mutable Self: A Self-Concept for Social Change*. Beverly Hills, Calif.: Sage.

Index